Lesbian and Gay Fostering and Adoption

of related interest

The Dynamics of Adoption
Edited by Amal Treacher and Ilan Katz
ISBN 1 85302 782 0

Permanent Family Placement for Children of Minority Ethnic Origin
June Thoburn, Liz Norford and Stephen Parvez Rashid
ISBN 1 85302 875 4

Issues in Foster Care
Policy, Practice and Research
Edited by Greg Kelly and Robbie Gilligan
ISBN 1 85302 465 1

First Steps in Parenting the Child Who Hurts
Tiddlers and Toddlers
Second Edition
Caroline Archer
Adoption UK
ISBN 1 85302 801 0

Next Steps in Parenting the Child Who Hurts
Tykes and Teens
Caroline Archer
Adoption UK
ISBN 1 85302 802 9

The Adoption Experience
Families Who Give Children a Second Chance
Ann Morris
Adoption UK
Published in association with The Daily Telegraph
ISBN 1 85302 783 9

Child Adoption
A Guidebook for Adoptive Parents and their Advisers
R.A.C. Hoksbergen
ISBN 1 85302 415 5

Lesbian and Gay Fostering and Adoption

Extraordinary Yet Ordinary

Edited by
Stephen Hicks and Janet McDermott

Foreword by
Pat Verity and Gerri McAndrew

Jessica Kingsley Publishers
London and Philadelphia

First published in the United Kingdom in 1999 by
Jessica Kingsley Publishers
116 Pentonville Road
London N1 9JB, UK
and
400 Market Street, Suite 400
Philadelphia, PA 19106, USA

www.jkp.com

Copyright © 1999 Jessica Kingsley Publishers

Second impression 2000
Third impression 2002
Printed digitally since 2005

Library of Congress Cataloging in Publication Data
A CIP catalog record for this book is available from the Library of Congress

British Library Cataloguing in Publication Data
Lesbian and gay fostering and adoption: extraordinary yet ordinary
1.Gay adoption 2.Gay parents
I. Hicks, Stephen II. McDermott, Janet
362.7'33'08664

ISBN-13 978 1 85302 600 3
ISBN-10: 1 85302 600 X

2/08

Contents

Acknowledgements 7

Foreword by Pat Verity and Gerri McAndrew 9

Introduction 11

The Stories

'Arranged Parenting': Nita and Clare's story 17

'Heavy-Duty Kids?': Simon's story 29

'A Mechaiyah – A Complete Joy...': Kate's story 37

'Staying Power': Emma and Louise's story 47

'Out of Step': Paul and Richard's story 54

'The Eye of the Storm...': Barbara's story 62

'..."No one Ever Learned Us"...': Dfiza and
Anne's story 68

'Caring Across the Spectrum': Mark and Paul's story 74

'Single Black Lesbian': Olivette's story 80

'The Impossible Dream': Sarah and Christine's story 86

'Things Might Look A Little Cloudy Now, But...': 97
John and Rob's story

'A Family, Not Pretend But Real!': Jean and 106
Trixie's story

'Matched': Kath's story   115

'A Great Asset': Mike and Brian's story   121

'You May Have to Count to Ten, No Twenty,   129
Sometimes...': Sandra's story

'A Special Mothers' Day Card': Elizabeth   137
and Mary's story

'No Regrets': Shula's story   142

Editorial Essay   147

Appendix: Useful Organisations   199

References   201

About the Editors   205

Acknowledgements

We would like to thank members of the Lesbian and Gay Foster and Adoptive Parents Network (LAGFAPN) and the Positive Parenting Campaign for suggesting this book, and particularly those members who were responsible for overseeing the project: Markie Barratt, who also conducted interviews and commented on the manuscript; Andrew Cobley, who conducted interviews, wrote up stories and acted as a reader of the manuscript; Jennie Lazenby, who conducted interviews and provided us with transcripts and comments; Maggie Murdoch; Maggie Walker; and Jolyon Denton-Williams, who conducted interviews and wrote up stories. They provided us with invaluable help, advice and hard work, without which the book would not have been possible.

We are grateful to others who read and commented on the manuscript for us: Seni Seneviratne, Julia Sohrab, Pat Verity and Madeleine Walton. Our thanks also go to Paul Tyrer for working on one of the stories, to Tarzan Almas for advice and to Everton Earle for his helpful research. We are especially grateful to Julia, Madeleine and Paul for their advice and constant support throughout the project. Pat Verity and Gerri McAndrew of the National Foster Care Association provided us with an excellent foreword. Our thanks also go to Tara (aged 11) for the cover illustration.

Foreword

It takes courage to apply to foster or adopt children knowing that your life is about to be scrutinised. If you are a lesbian or a gay man, single or in a partnership, that courage has to be greater. This book contains the stories of lesbians and gay men who have taken this step knowing that they will face prejudice and will need to be 'out' to a range of people. Many have done this whilst knowing from their work experiences how difficult it is going to be. Their over-riding wish has been to give children a good experience of care.

This book is a timely addition to a much-neglected aspect of foster care and adoption practice. Many people have built their knowledge on the press reports that have surrounded the placement of children with lesbians or gay men. These reports have tended to heighten fear and reinforce a link between paedophilia and homosexuality in the minds of the general public. Rarely has there been any informed discussion of gay and lesbian parenting or child caring. This book therefore is welcome in putting forward the views of the people who are generally on the receiving end of ill-informed and hurtful publicity. It does this without blame, with understanding and in a way that simply says 'this is how it is for us'.

The book contains a wide variety of fostering and adoption experiences, from shared care and emergency placements through to permanent fostering and adoption. It includes contributions from black and white lesbians and gay men. The experiences, as told, are as the adults perceived them. Critics might say they are one-sided, but they raise one's awareness. What is striking is the reasonableness of the people involved in spite of the blatant prejudices some describe. The children placed range in age from birth to young adults, some with disabilities. As with many of the children who are looked after, a number would be described as having 'challenging behaviour'.

The experiences of the carers demonstrate a wide level of skills amongst social workers undertaking carer assessments, and a lack of focus from some on what is needed in order to ensure that a young person's needs are matched by their carer's skills.

A significant number of the contributors describe how they were turned down without any discussion about what they could offer children as soon as social workers knew they were lesbian or gay, even though they were approved as carers. Their feelings of frustration, anger and sadness can only be imagined when they see the same children advertised time and time again – often over a year later – and realise that siblings have been split when they had wanted to care for them all.

Many of the issues experienced in relation to the children are the same as for other carers – for example, acceptance by the wider family, behaviour, working with previous carers or moving children either home or on to other families. But few of the lesbian and gay carers did not experience homophobia once their sexuality was known. Even carers who had not been out at the time of their assessment and were already established foster carers offering a well-used, good service found that, once they decided to be open about their sexuality, the attitudes of some social workers changed. But children seemed to be able to handle their parents' or carers' sexuality in a much more straight-forward, pragmatic way, although some carers were concerned to ensure that children were not bullied. Most carers were able to find ways of alerting schools to potential problems and found them co-operative.

The book ends with an excellent essay that pulls out the issues using examples from the case studies and relates these to available research. The over-riding impression left by the book is that here is an under-used resource for children and young people. Few of the carers in the book looked after young people who were gay or lesbian. They are providing care for a wide range of children and young people very successfully. It is a humbling experience to read the accounts of people who have gone through so much prejudice throughout their lives and yet are willing to expose themselves still further because they know that they can provide good care to children.

If, as a society, it is children that are our main concern, we must consider how we can provide them with the best carers. Local authorities need to ensure that the systems that they operate do not prejudice the coming forward of, or use of, a range of people who have the skills to meet the needs of a wide range of children.

Pat Verity (Policy and Services Manager) and Gerri McAndrew (Executive Director),
National Foster Care Association.

Introduction

This book is a collection of personal accounts by lesbians and gay men who have fostered or adopted children. Its publication coincides with the tenth anniversary of the only other major text to deal with this topic in Britain: *Fostering and Adoption by Lesbians and Gay Men* edited by Jane Skeates and Dorian Jabri in 1988. A lot has changed in those ten years, not least the law affecting child care, and there are now greater numbers of openly lesbian and gay foster or adoptive carers. However, many other things remain the same, most dishearteningly the stereotypical and discriminatory views of lesbian and gay families highlighted by Skeates and Jabri which figured in recent debates concerning the adoption law review and the approval of gay carers by some local authorities. Whilst the Skeates & Jabri study involved eight interviews with lesbians and gay men (three male couples, two female couples, a single man and two single women), this book, in contrast, tells the stories of seventeen different households – twenty-seven adults caring for forty children or young people in all. Thus, ten years on, the lesbian and gay community has far more experience of people who have actually been approved to foster or adopt children, and are doing so, and these are the stories we wanted to be told.

The lesbians and gay men involved in this project are all members of national support networks, including the Northern and the London support groups of the Lesbian and Gay Foster and Adoptive Parents Network (LAGFAPN) set up in 1988. We were also helped by members of the Positive Parenting Campaign in Manchester, a group concerned with lesbian and gay parenting issues set up in 1990. These groups came together to form an editorial collective to oversee the project and the book is a direct response to the feeling that we ought to produce something which tells some of the stories of lesbian and gay fostering and adoption, whether they be stories of success, triumph, struggle or even some failures and disappointments.

There have been some positive changes in the field of fostering and adoption by lesbians and gay men in recent years. All of the contributors to this volume have been successfully assessed and approved by local authorities to care for children and, even though many of these accounts do portray lengthy and disheartening struggles, it is now the case that some social services departments are willing to assess lesbians and gay men on their merits. This is a very different picture from the one in which lesbians and gay men either had to hide their sexuality if they applied to care for children or were rejected outright on the basis of their sexuality alone. Good practice with lesbian and gay carer applicants has been slowly developing in some local authorities.

There is also more evidence available now about children who live with lesbian or gay carers/parents. There are accounts by children themselves (Evans 1995; Rafkin 1990; Saffron 1996; Wakeling and Bradstock 1995) and there is also important research evidence about the effects of growing up in a lesbian or gay family.[1] All of these studies point to the absence of negative developmental consequences for such children (Bailey *et al.* 1995; Harne and Rights of Women 1997; Tasker and Golombok 1997).

In fact, lesbian and gay parenting has been around, in its many different forms, for years but has only emerged recently as an issue of great social importance (Ali 1996; Benkov 1994; Martin 1993; Wakeling and Bradstock 1995). This seems to be to do with the fact that lesbians and gay men who have children are now far more open about their sexuality and 'coming out' as a lesbian or gay parent has taken on a new political significance. This is also the case with regard to lesbian and gay fostering and adoption. Whereas in the past lesbians and gay men were far more likely either to keep their sexuality hidden from social workers or to view fostering and adoption as closed to them, now they are likely to come out as openly lesbian or gay at the start of the assessment process. This was the case for most of, though not all, the contributors to this volume.

The fact that not all lesbian and gay carer applicants are able to come out, however, points to ongoing discrimination that still exists within both social work and the wider society (Brown 1998). The story is not wholly a positive one. Many still regard lesbians and gay men as 'unnatural' parents and believe that they should be actively barred from caring for children. Lesbian and gay parents have become an easy target for new right family groups, especially in Britain and North America, and with regard to fostering and adoption specifically, there have been ongoing legislative debates about the appropriateness of lesbian and gay carers.

---

[1] Although research on the children of gay men is more limited, there is a new study of gay fathers/carers being carried out by Fiona Tasker in the Department of Psychology at Birkbeck College, London.

Why This Book?

One of the main reasons for compiling the book was the lack of material dealing with lesbian and gay fostering and adoption specifically. While most literature concerning foster and adoptive care tends to ignore or marginalise issues of sexuality, books about lesbian and gay parenting rarely devote much space to fostering and adoption. Applying to be considered as a foster or adoptive carer, and being subsequently assessed by social workers, is a very different process indeed from having birth children either from former heterosexual relationships or by insemination and co-parenting arrangements.

We therefore wanted to produce a record of the experiences of some lesbians and gay men who have been successfully approved to care for children, and are doing just that. These are stories rarely heard, and this is partly to do with wanting to protect the children and their whereabouts from exposure to the press. Thus the book is a chance for lesbians and gay men to tell their accounts on their own terms. These are our lives, our stories, extraordinary yet ordinary, unusual yet everyday, sometimes funny, sometimes sad, but mostly a triumph against all odds.

The LAGFAPN support groups are often contacted by the media, or by people wanting to research aspects of lesbian and gay fostering and adoption, with requests to speak publicly about their experiences. This is a dilemma for most of the contributors in this volume. While none of them is ashamed of their sexuality or that they are caring for children – in fact, far from it! – most are keen to protect themselves and their children from the glare of unwanted and unsympathetic publicity. Having your house targeted and your family attacked by people who find out that you are lesbian or gay foster or adoptive parents is a very real risk and, sometimes, a disturbing reality. One gay male couple who had wanted to contribute to this book had to withdraw their story at the last minute because of their experiences of being 'exposed' in national newspapers. They've also had to move house in the past because they were targeted by neighbours and others in their community. Another couple in the book, Mike and Brian, talk about hurtful publicity in their own case.

The stories were written over a period of about a year from summer 1996 to mid-1997. They were produced in a number of different ways. Some people chose to write their own account, while others preferred to be interviewed. Some interviewed each other, while some spoke to one of the editors. Sometimes the stories just flowed naturally as people had so much that they wanted to say, while for others the process involved a more painstaking series of drafts, revisions and discussions. Most of the stories have been anonymised to protect the identities of the adults and the children. As editors, we've tried to maintain some consistency in the way that the stories are presented but we also wanted to retain differences in personal styles. We've also been keen to ensure that the book is representative of who lesbian and gay foster and adoptive parents are, so you will find accounts here by gay men and lesbians, single people and couples, and a number of black[2] contributors. The stories deal with adoption and fostering in its many forms – long-term, short-term, task-centred, emergency and respite care. The book does not include accounts by children because we feel that this is another project, another book.

The stories appear in no particular order and are followed by an editorial essay, bibliography and list of resources. The editorial essay, as well as providing an overview of some of the issues of research and policy relating to lesbians and gay men as foster and adoptive parents, also pulls out the main themes that arise from the stories in this volume. We wanted to do this because we think that there are a number of important themes which recur throughout the book and that these do have some significance for those interested in lesbian and gay fostering and adoption, whether they be other lesbians and gay men who might be thinking about applying or social workers, educators, trainers, policy makers and those who work in child care organisations.

We suggest that readers might like to leave the editorial essay until after they have read the stories. Our essay refers to individual contributors when we pull out themes, so readers might like to acquaint themselves with the stories first before going on to read about what we think are the important recurring issues.

This book is about the process of being assessed as potential carers, sometimes painful, sometimes enjoyable, and of eventually caring for a child, or children, with all the joys, dramas, sorrows, happiness, arguments, fun, and love that this brings. We don't think that the contributors regard themselves as 'special' people – in fact, they probably see themselves as quite ordinary – but these *are* special stories because they show a great determination to succeed, frequent courage and, most of all, the will to make real changes to the lives of children who have been disadvantaged or abused in many different ways.

Research has revealed the creativity of lesbians and gay men in redefining 'the family' and forging new kinship patterns (Weston 1991). This book represents a part of this process and embodies the transformation of a society based on the traditional biological family to one made up of a multiplicity of 'family' forms. These are real families, not 'pretended' ones as they are called in Section 28 of the 1988 Local Government Act, it's just that they are made in different ways.

2   In this book we use the term 'black' to refer to non-white people of all nationalities whose heritage is Asian or African and to refer to the indigenous peoples of the Americas and Australasia.

The Stories

'Arranged Parenting'
Nita and Clare's Story

Nita and Clare are a lesbian couple in their mid-thirties who have adopted a ten-year-old Asian girl called Lubna. Nita is Asian and Clare is white. They were out to their adoption agency and the adoption was recently completed with an adoption order in Nita's name and a joint residence order giving them both parental responsibility for Lubna. Their story is told through a series of remembered conversations.

'What do you think about children?'

'Very nice.'

'No, you know what I mean. What do you think about having children?'

Nita turned over and snuggled her head into the hollow of Clare's shoulder. She let go the lingering threads of a dream and concentrated on the question. 'You mean giving birth?'

'Not necessarily, just being a mother, however we might do it.'

'I'd love to have children, but I'm not bothered about having my own', Nita responded slowly. She had always assumed in a sweeping unspecific way that she would have children, but once she had come out as a lesbian the prospect seemed to become less likely, life was so busy and she kept thinking she was still young, there would be time enough later.

'I wouldn't want to give birth!' Clare was emphatic. 'All that pain and blood, doesn't bear thinking about, and anyway, the world's already over-populated. What is it they say? One child from the developed world uses ten times the food and energy and money that a child from the developing world uses?'

'Yes, and there are plenty of children already born that need a home, look at all the children in care, especially black children', Nita continued eagerly. 'Have you seen those posters on the bus stops on High Street? They're advertising for adopters and foster parents. I was thinking, we'd make good parents, wouldn't we? We could offer love and security.'

'Too right!' Clare responded, and they were quiet for a while trying to imagine being parents and thinking of everything they had brought each other: warmth, love, laughter, a passion for India, a love of Scotland.

'You know Saira and Linda did it, didn't they?' Nita interrupted the silence. 'They had Sonia placed with them as soon as they were approved. It was incredibly fast.'

'But they weren't out, were they? I don't want to lie – I'm not ashamed of my sexuality, and it's no basis on which to start a family.'

'Anyway, we're useless at lying. We'd just get ourselves in a pickle', Nita agreed. 'Look, we're middle-class with loads of childcare experience, loads of support from our familes, we're both teachers. We've got everything going for us. Someone has to be brave enough to be out, so why not us? If someone had done it before us, the door might be open already.'

Nita and Clare didn't tell a lot of people to begin with, just those who they knew would be the core of their support network, like Nita's parents, who live nearby, and close friends, some of whom had children they were closely involved with. Everyone was very supportive, some were concerned that they might be disappointed or face a lot of obstacles and prejudice. Some were not sure whether to take it seriously at first.

Clare phoned her mother one Sunday afternoon. 'Hello, it's me, Clare. How are you, Mummy?'

'Fine. Your brother's just been round cutting the grass. It's like a jungle out there. He says they're all well. How are things with you and Nita?'

Clare decided to plunge in. 'Oh, fine. In fact, we're thinking of applying to adopt.'

'What? A child?' asked Hilda in disbelief.

'Well, not a humpbacked whale', Clare responded curtly.

'That's a big thing to do. What do you want to complicate your lives for? I thought you were both so happy?'

'We are and we want to adopt.' Clare was starting to feel frustrated by her mother's response.

'Well, I must say I don't think they'll let you', Hilda cautioned.

'We'll have to convince them, won't we?' Clare breathed deeply. I'm not going to get angry, she told herself.

'But you haven't got a garden. You'll have to move, won't you?'

'I think not having a garden will be the least of our problems', Clare laughed. 'Anyway, we've got a backyard. The thing is, they want adoptive parents to reflect a wide range of families, not just rich people with big houses and big gardens.'

'You know, Maureen adopted and then she and Clive got divorced and now Enid looks after the children more than Maureen. They're always with their grandma. It's not right, is it?' Hilda mused conversationally.

Clare counted to ten in her head. 'Well, anyway, we're applying to adopt. They'll be Asian or Asian mixed-race children to match Nita and me.'

'Why does that matter?' Hilda argued. 'Children are children whatever their colour.'

'It's important for the child to feel part of the family where she's placed and Nita's Indian and I'm white'. Race always was a sticky issue for Hilda, thought Clare.

'But Nita was born here', Hilda asserted.

'So? She's still Indian.'

'Mmm. Well, lovely to hear from you Clare. I'll have to go, it's choir practice in a minute. Love to Nita. 'Bye.'

''Bye', said Clare as the phone went dead.

Their first move was to ring the local authority adoption agency anonymously and ask what their policy was on approving lesbians and gay men for adoption. The reply was firm. The authority operated an equal opportunities policy and all potential adopters would be considered on their merits as potential parents. Armed with this knowledge, but aware of the emptiness of much equal opportunities rhetoric, Nita and Clare knew they still had to pick the moment to disclose their sexuality very carefully.

'So, what's all this I hear about you wanting to adopt?' Alia said curiously.

'The grapevine works fast. Yes, I'm on the waiting list to be assessed', Nita smiled.

'Have you told them you're a lesbian?'

'Not yet, but we're going to', responded Clare.

'What? Are you mad? If you do, they'll never give you a child, especially not an Asian child.'

'But we'd make good parents', Nita protested.

'No one's denying that, but be realistic. This isn't a political act, you know.'

'No it isn't, but someone has to be honest and make a case for lesbian parenting', Clare argued.

'So, you two are going to take on the council, are you?' Alia smiled.

'If we have to, but it's not about that, not yet anyway. It's about us wanting to adopt. We've loads of skills. We're offering them two fully participating parents with lots of childcare experience, which is more than they'll get with most heterosexual couples. The only possible reason they could turn us down is on discriminatory grounds. If they do, then it'll be clear cut', Clare explained.

'Remember, no one has ever tried to adopt being out here, so we don't know what they'll say', Nita joined in. 'Those lesbians who have adopted have been economical with the truth, to say the least.'

'Apart from Sue, and she was turned down', Alia reminded them.

'That was ten years ago and we don't know the facts of the case. It might not have been about her sexuality', said Clare.

'If you really wanted to be parents, you'd lie', Alia asserted.

'Oh yes, and spend our lives wondering who's going to tell on us? It's dishonest. I'm not prepared to pretend that Clare's just a good friend or a childminder', Nita insisted decisively.

Nita approached the agency initially as a single adopter and was sent on a preparation course for single black adopters, which had a safe, positive atmosphere. After the course she told them she wanted to go ahead with the assessment and asked for Marcia to be her social worker, first because she was the only black worker and, second, because Marcia had lesbian friends. The first assessment visit was one of the most difficult moments in the process as Nita had to explain that she wasn't single and that her partner was a woman. Marcia was a little stunned but digested the new situation quickly and was happy to take on a joint assessment.

The assessment was long and intensive but Nita and Clare felt lucky to have Marcia as their social worker. She was honest, straightforward and very enthusiastic about the combination of skills and experience she felt they had to offer as adopters. However, she was fairly new to adoption and the department as a whole was nervous about taking a lesbian couple to panel. There were occasions when decisions about how the application should be processed were changed. For instance, originally the referees were two women friends, one of whom was a single parent. The other was in a heterosexual relationship and had a child but her partner was not involved in providing the reference. They were later asked to supply a third reference from a heterosexual couple with children, interviewed together, which they duly did. There were also delays in going to panel while the panel received extra equal opportunities training addressing the issue of sexual orientation and the department waited for a member who was known to be homophobic to leave. Marcia left Nita and Clare to fill in the assessment form on their own and then used the answers as a basis for discussion and as the main body of the completed Form F. She was amazed at the reams written and was satisfied with most of it as it stood. There were a few points on which they had lengthy discussion, the most thorny being the male role models in their lives and whether or not they would adopt a boy.

'I want to ask you about what you've said about disabled children. I know you've ticked all these categories but I think you need to really think about what you're prepared to take on. There's no reason why you should take a child with any disability at all. You've got as much right as any other couple to have a perfectly normal healthy child, a baby even. You mustn't think you have to accept anything you don't want to.'

'It's all right,' Nita smiled, 'we're actually fine about some kinds of disability. We've got lots of experience of children with learning difficulties at work, and we really feel okay about the things we've ticked.'

'Well, I'm just saying I see you with an ordinary healthy little baby or toddler in a few months time and that's what I think you should hold out for', Marcia insisted defiantly. 'Now, I know we've talked about this before but I think we need to return to the issue of you saying you'll only take girls and not boys.'

'We don't feel confident about parenting a boy', Nita explained.

'Is it that you don't like boys?' Marcia suggested, playing devil's advocate.

'No, it's not that. We have more boys in our lives than girls at the moment. Najma's got two sons, Shaheen's got three sons and Ruth's got a son, and we look after them all. It's just that we know about growing up as a girl but not as a boy. Other lesbians feel confident bringing up boys but it's not for us', Clare asserted.

'I'm sorry to push you on this but I know it will be an issue with the panel. If you were offered a sibling group with a boy, would you take them?'

'No', replied Clare.

'Would you consider them then?', Marcia re-phrased quickly.

'No', Nita repeated, thinking this was getting farcical. 'It's not that we don't like boys, but we don't want to spend all our energy on them when there are lots of girls out there who need us and who we'd be much better at bringing up.'

'The thing about boys is, you either bring them up to be sensitive and caring – which means they end up only relating to women while men beat shit out of them – or you bring them up to be "lads" – which means football, aggression and everything we don't have to put up with in our lives at present', Clare explained starkly.

'I'm sorry to labour this point but I really do think it could be the difference between getting you through panel and not', Marcia insisted. 'If you were offered a sibling group with two girls and a baby boy, would you consider them – just consider?'

Wearily, Clare looked at Nita. 'I don't think so.'

'Okay,' Marcia persevered, 'what about if you had two girls placed with you, you went to court and they were adopted and then, a year or two later, the birth mother had another child, a baby boy, the girls' brother, and he was to be placed for adoption. Would you consider taking him?'

Nita and Clare looked at each other again, doubtfully, and then Nita said: 'Yes, I suppose we'd consider that.'

'That's good', Marcia smiled with relief. 'I can work with that at panel. I can say you would consider a boy, given the right circumstances, but you'd prefer a girl or girls. Sex preference is not unusual in adoption.'

A year after the first contact with the agency, Nita and Clare were approved to adopt up to three children aged seven and under. They were the first 'out' lesbian couple to be approved by the local authority. They held a spontaneous party for friends and family but, in the midst of the celebrations, they knew it was only the first step. Some people were still saying they would never be successful in having a child placed with them.

They began scouring the adoption publications for Asian and mixed-race Asian girls under eight. Marcia brought possibilities from time to time and they rang up social workers themselves. As with many black and mixed-race adopters, they were referred to the British Agencies for Adoption and Fostering (BAAF), who offer a computerised system for linking children with particular needs with suitable families across the country. Because the Asian communities in their area are small and close-knit, it was not appropriate for them to be considered for children from within their local community.

'Hello, I'm ringing about Rukhsana and Noreen who are advertised in BE MY PARENT. BAAF gave me your number. I've been ringing all week to speak to someone.'

'Yes, sorry about that, we're very busy. You know we're looking for an Asian or Asian mixed-race couple for these sisters, don't you?'

'Yes, I'm Asian and my partner's white. Also the area we live in is very multi-racial and has a big Asian community.'

'Good. These girls have had a lot of moves and their behaviour can be challenging. They're in separate foster homes at the moment but meet regularly, and we want to place them together. We're looking for energetic parents who can dedicate a lot of time and energy to them. Would you like to tell me a bit about yourselves?'

'Well, we've certainly got time and energy. I work part-time and my partner is currently working full-time, but she wants to go part-time if we adopt children under five so that we can take equal responsibility for looking after them.'

'Sorry, did you say "she"?'

'Yes, my partner's a woman.'

'I see. We have had quite a lot of enquiries about these girls, some of which look like strong possibilities for linking, but I'll take your details in case the possibilities we're currently pursuing fall through. We'll get back to you if need be. Now, can you spell your name for me...'

Rukhsana was subsequently placed on her own and they are still looking for a family for Noreen, even though Nita and Clare could have offered them a home together. As the couple offer no specific religion and as Nita is not fluent in an Asian language, there were many occasions where they were told they were ruled out because an agency was looking for a particular religious and linguistic background for a child. They also ruled out some children suggested to them because the children were older than they had been looking for or they were not sure the racial match was appropriate.

They enquired about another Asian sibling group who were in three separate white foster homes. They were visited by two social workers, who postponed the visit twice before being directed to attend by a line manager and were visibly uncomfortable throughout their stay – in one case to the extent of not even taking her coat off or having anything to eat or drink, despite the two-hour journey to get there. Nita and Clare were eventually turned down by that authority's panel on the advice of their legal department, who said that as lesbianism is not an accepted lifestyle in the Hindu faith, it could be argued under the Children Act that their 'chosen way of life' meant that they could not provide a suitable environment for the upbringing of these children. This was despite the fact that they had been told the children had a multi-faith background and were not being brought up in any particular religion. This interpretation of Hinduism was also challenged by a Hindu social worker from Nita and Clare's authority. The couple took out an official complaint and some recommendations for future practice were made. The report on the complaint investigation acknowledged that Nita and Clare had demonstrated that they could meet the cultural and linguistic needs of the children, yet found that the authority had acted within the spirit and letter of the Children Act and the panel decision could not be reversed. These, and some other children they enquired about, are still not placed even though Nita and Clare were offering a secure and loving home.

As the months passed, Nita and Clare began to feel that they would never be seriously considered for a child they felt was right for them and they began to lose heart. The helplessness and the not knowing were strange. They had always seen themselves as being in control of their lives and now someone else was choosing for them. The matchmakers were weighing carefully Clare's sprawling Essex family, Nita's Indian heritage and her family's migration from India, their friends, childhoods, work, holidays in Scotland and, inevitably, their sexuality. They had to be optimists, had to believe that someone would be wise enough and experienced enough to arrange a suitable match now that they had committed themselves to 'arranged' parenthood.

'I don't know why you're putting yourselves through all this. What's wrong with the turkey baster?' Sandra, a lesbian friend, admonished one day.

'Lots. What's going to happen to all these kids with anonymous donors as dads?' replied Clare.

'They don't need dads', responded Sandra.

'No, you're right, they don't. But everyone needs to know their roots. What did Bob Marley say? "Trees without roots can't grow". Especially black kids', Nita explained. 'Look at how long it took me to sort out my identity, and I had it all there in my home.'

'Well, you could have gone for a known donor', Sandra argued.

'And how easy do you think it would be to find an Asian donor?' Nita countered.' And what would we be looking for? An Indian donor? A Hindu? A Muslim? Because, you realise, I'd have to have the baby, unless I wanted to be the only black person in a white household. And then what about when the baby's born? Is it realistic or right not to involve the man in the child's life? And do we want to artificially involve a man in our life like that?'

'But it's taking so long. It would have been quicker to get pregnant', Sandra protested.

'Well, I've no burning desire to reproduce. I don't even know if I'm fertile. The thought of having a Jackson and recreating the genes of my parents fills me with dread. My family are bonkers', Clare intervened, laughing.

'It's not for us', Nita concluded emphatically. 'Anyway, the bottom line is we don't want to give birth, we want to adopt. We always talked about parenting in terms of adoption. It's a positive choice for us.'

Eighteen months after approval they finally saw Lubna's details in an adoption magazine. She was eight, older than the age at which they had generally been looking, but everything about her leapt out as being a perfect match – her interests, her experiences, even down to her birth mother being from the same city in India as Nita's father. They were just about to go to India on holiday so they didn't do anything immediately. But Lubna's social worker had seen a letter about them that their social worker had sent round a number of local authorities. On their return they found that Lubna's social worker had already contacted their social worker and wanted to visit them with a homefinder and a friend of Lubna's family who was supporting the adoption. Nita and Clare were very nervous, but as soon as the visitors arrived they knew this was going to be very different from their previous experience of a visit by children's social workers. Everyone was relaxed and positive and by the end of the visit it was apparent that the social workers wanted to proceed to the matching panel.

Two months later, Nita and Clare were matched with Lubna. She had been with the same black foster parent, Thelma, for nearly four years, which could have been very difficult, but Thelma was wonderful and totally supported Lubna in feeling good about the move. Nita and Clare were terrified of meeting Lubna because they had been warned that she was not positive about adoption, but they had made a video and a book about themselves which she saw beforehand. She knew from the beginning that they were lesbians and she knew about lesbians from the soap operas on television. By the time she met them it seemed as if she had already decided she liked them. From then on it was a dream come true, everything they could have hoped for and more. It was love at first sight. She bonded with them immediately and was starting to pack her things up to take to her new home at the end of the first week. The introductions spanned a hectic two-and-a-half weeks, at the end of which she moved in and they all started their life together, just over two years from the day Nita and Clare had been approved to adopt.

Nita and Clare have always been joint parents and Lubna has always been adamant that they should be treated equally, both coming to school for concerts and parents' evenings and all three doing everything together as far as possible. The school Lubna goes to, just around the corner, has a very mixed intake with children from many different black communities, other children who are fostered and adopted, children in single parent families, children living in extended families and other children from lesbian households. Lubna is assertive about fending off what she regards as nosey enquiries but she has also not found herself particularly unusual in a very cosmopolitan inner-city environment. She has grown in confidence in defending the family and insisted on attending Gay Pride this year. On their return, she could be heard lecturing her friends on the meanings of key words such as 'heterosexual' and 'homosexual' and testing them on their understanding!

It took eighteen months from placement to reach the final adoption hearing due to legal complications specific to Lubna's case, but the case was finally heard in the High Court. The application was for an adoption order in Nita's name and a joint residence order giving both Nita and Clare parental responsibility for Lubna. This is very important because it gives Lubna the security of knowing that both Nita and Clare are equally responsible for her and committed to caring for her together.

'Good morning Lubna. I'm your barrister, Angus Mackenzie.'

'He sounds like Nigel from *The Archers*', whispered Lubna.

'Can I speak with these ladies for a moment?' He took them aside. 'Well, it's sixty-forty in our favour. This judge is new – reward for serving on some government quango – but he can be picky, he may want to make something of the… errr…', he shuffled uncomfortably, '…the same sex thing.'

'Ladies, he called you ladies!' Lubna giggled as he moved away to speak to the court usher.

After a nerve-wracking two-hour wait, the barrister, official solicitor and guardian *ad litem* all went into the court. Nita and Clare smiled at the judge through the court room's glass doors, hoping he'd see they were human beings. Then they were called into court, leaving Lubna happily playing pontoon with their social worker.

Everyone was smiling as they entered the court. Angus spoke: 'My lord, Nita and Clare have been in a stable relationship for the last seven years. They have provided Lubna with a secure and loving home. You will have seen from all the reports, my lord, that Lubna is flourishing.'

The judge responded enthusiastically: 'These reports are some of the best I have seen and the court is thankful for all the hard work that has gone into them. Be assured they are read and much appreciated.'

The social workers beamed at the compliments being bestowed upon them. As the words droned on, Nita and Clare realised the enormity of the moment. This man was God. He could make or break their dreams.

Angus concluded: 'Therefore, my lord, I move that the adoption order be granted in the name of Nita and a joint residence order be granted in the names of Nita and Clare.'

'Absolutely,' replied the judge, 'And I'd like to meet the child – the most pleasurable part of my duties – if you would bring her to my chambers.'

Nita and Clare hugged as everyone congratulated them. Then Clare leapt up and ran out of the court. Lubna was still happily playing cards with Sue.

'It's all done, we're adopted!' cried Clare. 'The judge wants to meet you.' Lubna frowned mistrustfully but she was reassured that it was just a formality. In his chambers, Lubna played with the judge's wig produced specially from a black tin box.

'She seems an absolute delight!' the judge enthused.

'She is!' Nita and Clare chorused.

Postscript: December 1997

When Lubna was placed she was adamant that she did not want any siblings, but, two years later and after the adoption had been to court, she changed her mind. She was ten by then and decided she wanted a much younger sister. We began looking again and soon saw Neelam's details in an adoption newsletter. She was described as a ten-month-old mixed-race Asian baby with a moderate hearing loss and they were looking for a family with at least one Asian parent and possibly other children. She had been in care with a white foster family since she was a few days old.

Once again we were preparing to go on holiday to India! Two social workers from the authority where she was living visited us a fortnight before we went away. They had been considering another couple but, after the visit, they were very keen on us and said they would wait for us to get back from India. Once we got back, everything happened very quickly. We were re-assessed as a family to take a second child and Lubna was interviewed separately, which she enjoyed. Our local panel approved us to take a second child and the panel in the city where Neelam was in care matched us with her without any problems. When she finally moved in she was sixteen months old and she settled incredibly well. She's an absolute joy and she and Lubna have great fun together. Clare is now on adoption leave and in the future we will both work part-time in order to share being at home to look after Neelam. Clare will be the named adopter when it goes to court and we will apply for a joint residence order directing that she live with both of us, as we did with Lubna. We've already started thinking about a younger sister for Neelam!

'Heavy-duty Kids...?'
Simon's Story

Simon is a white, 30-year-old, single gay carer who has provided both emergency and, more recently, community foster care. He lives in Yorkshire and is a Learner Support Worker for disabled students at a local college. As an emergency carer, Simon took fifteen different placements on a short-term basis but he now cares for two young men, Peter aged 15 and Ian aged 14, longer term. He also looks after Andrew, an 18-year-old young man with learning disabilities, on a privately negotiated respite care basis.

I was twenty-five when I decided that I wanted to foster and was working as a residential social worker in homes for children aged eight to sixteen years. I'd been doing that for about five years and was becoming increasingly frustrated by the work. I felt that the kids with the most problems, the ones that were the hardest work, were getting picked on by staff and other children and I could see their lives twisting in a downward spiral, just getting worse and worse. I decided that I could do more positive work with children like that on my own at home. I felt I would be able to do more good and I wanted to work with the harder kids. I thought that young people like that would find it easier in a family environment, which I felt I could give them. In the children's homes they had no consistency and their daily routine seemed to be dominated by being worried about which members of staff were on shift. I thought that they ought to be doing normal things like wondering what was for tea and being kids again.

I'd also been looking after Andrew for about two years before I applied to foster. Andrew comes to me on a privately agreed respite care arrangement and I've cared for him for about seven years now. He came to me when he was 12 years old and I was 22, initially for every evening after school, weekends and holidays, which is actually a lot more than usual respite arrangements. He is learning disabled, has severe brain damage and is hyperactive. His Mum just couldn't cope on her own. I even used to take him back to his Mum's in the evenings and put him to bed. He seemed to have become a lot calmer and could do small jobs if I asked him, like making a cup of coffee, so we tried him coming just for weekends, but he's getting worse again and it looks like we might go back to the old arrangement. That's because at home he doesn't get enough attention and is not encouraged to mix with other people, which I think is really important. I think Andrew understands that I'm gay because he is able to tell the difference between people who are just friends and those who are more than friends. I've tried to explain it to him and I think he has a basic knowledge of what's going on, but he doesn't really care as long as he is getting enough attention.

I decided to go ahead with applying to foster when I saw an advert from my local authority in the local press. The advert had their equal opportunities statement attached to it, which they don't usually do, and so I thought I would apply. I definitely wanted to foster because I felt the most need was for people to look after older children and that's what I wanted to do. Adoption was concerned with younger children and that didn't interest me. Also, I saw fostering as more of a job since I knew that I wanted to work with the more demanding young people.

I rang my local council and said I was interested. They sent me an information pack and invited me along to a big open evening. There were about 150 people there, all couples or single women. I was the only single man there! That made me think that they wouldn't take my application seriously so I went and asked one of the social workers whether they'd consider a single man. She said it didn't make any difference and that I should fill in the application form. I didn't say I was gay at that stage as it didn't feel the right time to tell them.

I sent in the application and then a male social worker came to see me at home. He was supposed to stay half an hour but stayed for two and I wondered if he kept waiting for me to come out! I didn't say anything at that stage though. Apparently, this social worker had thought I might be gay anyway because some of the postcards I had on my walls were homoerotic, but he didn't say anything to me. The social workers raised the issue about my postcards much later, but I'd already removed them by that stage as I'd realised they weren't happy with them and they weren't appropriate if children were going to be about. Actually, I think the postcards were fairly innocent. Some were pictures of famous women, some showed two men together – one was a man doing up another's tie. Nothing pornographic! But I'd taken them down anyway, so they were happy.

Then I went to the foster carers' preparation group course. It was about six weekends spread over six months. It was all straight couples and me! Of the ten households there, only three of us got through. We looked at children's difficult behaviour, how we viewed our houses and what we used the different rooms for, how we would work with social services, what we would cover in the home study and the issue of children making allegations. The men also looked at how we would deal with a child displaying sexually inappropriate behaviour. I found the course quite hard because I had no one at home to discuss it all with, so I got little feedback on my ideas and thoughts. I was very conscious that we were being judged too and felt that it was important to get our points across.

We didn't do anything about lesbian and gay issues, but after about the fourth session I decided I had to come out to one of the social workers. I knew that both of the course leaders were lesbians so that made it a bit easier, but I really felt I had to choose my moment carefully and went to speak to one of them separately. I was thinking: 'Right, this is it...they might reject me, but at least I'll have tried and been honest.' The social worker said that it didn't make any difference and that they'd probably guessed anyway!

The next stage was the home study part of the assessment. A lesbian social worker did this, which was unusual because normally the same worker that did the initial home visit would do the home study, but they wanted a gay worker to do it because they felt she might handle it better. Although I knew she was a lesbian, she didn't tell me so until I had been approved. And I don't really think having a gay worker made the assessment any better. My current linkworker is heterosexual and she is far better at tackling the issues and being an advocate for gay carers.

We did cover sexuality in the assessment because I was asked about previous partners and what I would do if I were to start a new relationship since I was single at the time. We talked about my growing up gay and coming out and she also asked how I would cope with either gay or straight kids. I got the feeling they thought I'd be offended at the idea of caring for young straight men or that I would be too embarrassed to handle it, whereas I said that I'd just get on with it. I've never had any gay kids but I said that if I did, I'd probably have worried more about what they were up to, having gone through that myself and seeing how damaging some bits of the gay scene can be! We also talked about how I would need some gay-specific support as a carer, but they never came up with anything. They also asked me what women would come to my house and what female influences there would be on the children. I explained about that and pointed out that most of my friends are women.

I think the social workers were worried about whether I would get through the fostering panel or not. They told me I ought to explore other avenues, and other authorities, in case I was turned down. There were two rotating panels at that time and they deliberately took me to the more 'liberal' one. My approval went through fine and, to the social workers' amazement, there were no extra questions to be answered. Nevertheless, it took two months before I was told I was approved. This was because they were supposed to find some gay-specific support group for me, which they never did. I was approved for two boys aged nought to eighteen years. I hadn't bothered to specify an age range. I was also approved for one 'special needs' boy aged eight to eighteen years. It was their decision to specify boys but I was happy with that because I didn't feel it appropriate for me to care for young women.

In my first two years of approval I was an emergency carer, which means children staying for anything up to 28 days, although they often stayed longer. In all, I had fifteen placements in that time. My first was an 'easy' placement to ease me into fostering – two brothers aged seven and twelve who came to me while their mum was in hospital and ended up staying three months. That was a nice placement to start with. The boys weren't relating well to their mum, they never helped her at home, and they'd experienced physical violence. I got them doing housework and when they went home that carried on! That family has no social work involvement now, which is good.

I've normally taken adolescent boys, usually between 12 and 14, from children's homes that couldn't cope with them. So I did end up doing what I set out to do, taking what my linkworker calls 'heavy-duty kids'. Only about two of the young men came from birth families to me. All of them were moved on into new long-term placements or went back to their original placements. I did take one younger one, William, who was seven. He used to run around the house squeaking! His home life was very unsettled and, apparently, I was a calming influence on him and he used to squeak with joy! School and his social worker were really pleased with the work I did with William and his mum even phoned me from prison to say thanks.

I was never really out to any of the emergency placements. The fostering and adoption unit suggested it might not be wise since all of the placements were so short-term, but I maintained that I wouldn't lie if asked. It never came up though. One or two of the birth families have made grumblings about it in meetings but I've always been surrounded by social workers. Ian's mum even now says things like 'that poof who looks after my son' but that's actually more about her resentment that he's in my foster care. Ian is a respite placement, as he attends a residential school, and I actually have far more contact with him than his mother does and I think she is angry about that. She tries to undermine the placement by saying nasty things about me to Ian but he seems to cope with it by separating bits of his life into little boxes.

After my two years of emergency caring I decided I wanted to change to do community foster care, which means the children can stay for anything up to two years initially and longer if approved by the matching panel. There were a number of reasons why I wanted to change. Ian had been placed with me short-term and I wanted to offer him a long-term home and he wanted to stay. Also, I felt that the emergency care was too limited because the children were always moved on just as I'd achieved some change. They sometimes came back to me but their behaviour was back to square one again. So I wanted to do longer-term work with the young people.

I had an allegation made against me by one young man, which really showed me how vulnerable I was to that kind of thing. Ian, John and this other lad, Stephen, were all placed with me at the time and Stephen was being moved on to another placement. Basically, he didn't want to leave and was jealous that Ian was staying with me so he made an allegation to get at me I think. He told another foster parent that I had touched him on the leg. This was reported to social services, who then removed all the children from my care. I know they had to investigate it but it was handled really badly. A social worker just phoned me up and said they had to remove the kids. They turned up early evening. Ian and John barricaded themselves in their bedrooms and were shouting verbal abuse at the social workers from the windows. It was like war. It took three hours to get them out of the house. I think it really blew it for Ian because he was moved from me, not allowed back for a year and now they've placed him back with me again. At the time I just gave in to the social workers' way of thinking and went along with it, but I think now that I should have been more forceful and said what a good job I'd been doing for Ian.

The allegation was fully investigated, they even interviewed all the children I'd ever cared for, and they decided it was unfounded. I didn't want to make a big fuss about vindicating myself because I didn't want to put Stephen through any more hassle despite what he'd done. I knew I hadn't done anything to him and that was enough for me. We had reviews about the whole thing and my request to become a community foster carer was recommended by the social workers. The investigation took about three months and I was supported by social services. My linkworker kept in contact, even phoning me at weekends, and a manager left me her contact number if I needed to talk.

The social workers reassessed me to be a community foster carer and changed my age range to between three and eighteen years for special needs children and eight to fourteen years for others. I sometimes feel they've put me in the bracket of 'gay carer' having 'special needs children'. I don't see it like that but I think they do. I've had two community placements which are ongoing, Peter and now Ian, who has come back to me. Peter came in summer last year, so he's been here just over a year and the plan is for him to stay until he's eighteen. Peter actually asked to come to me because he'd been before on a two-week respite from another placement. He doesn't have any contact with birth family except for occasional birthday cards, so he came from a children's home. He has mainly behavioural problems and gets into loads of trouble which he lies about. At one time he was getting into trouble for stealing women's underwear from shops. My response was to get him some as he obviously wanted it. The stealing has stopped since. I was quite matter-of-fact about it really and talked to him about it, and the social workers thought I'd handled that pretty well. I bought him some books on growing up and becoming a teenager and we talked about that too.

Peter knows I'm gay because I've told him. Gay and lesbian issues were on television a lot because there was a gay character in *Eastenders* and a lesbian wedding in *Friends*, so we were talking about that. He said he didn't know any gay people and so I said that you couldn't always tell who was gay and explained that I was. He took it fine. I think he had guessed anyway. He certainly wasn't embarrassed or upset by it. I told him it was up to him whether he wanted to tell others and that I would respect his decision on that. I don't know if he has told anyone else but he does talk to me about it. Someone at school had called him a 'poof' because he'd been riding on a bike with another lad and he asked me whether that meant he was gay. He does worry about people calling me names because he knows that Ian's mum is homophobic towards me.

Ian has been placed back with me now, but on a respite basis as he attends a residential school. He was removed from my care for about a year and had three placements in that time. My linkworker suggested to me that I consider whether I'd be prepared to have him back. Initially I was unsure as I'd just wanted to put all the stuff about the allegation behind me, so I had to think about it as it felt like a very serious decision. Eventually I said yes, so he's now back here until they find him a full-time family. I don't know whether they've got me in mind for that because they know I'd take him!

I was approved as a single carer and that's still how I'm registered. For most of the time that I've been a foster carer I have been single and, in some ways, that's far easier because you don't have to deal with a partner's feelings about the kids or their behaviour. But being single also means you don't get so much support or feedback. I tend to get my support from other foster carers. As an emergency carer I used to attend the support meetings and the coffee mornings, some of which were at my house. I told that group I was gay and they were okay about it as they'd all got to know me. As a community foster carer I haven't been to a support meeting yet but I'm going to my first one soon. I don't know if I'll tell them I'm gay but I certainly won't tell them at my first meeting. My other source of support has been the LAGFAPN lesbian and gay carers group in the North. The discussions are more relevant to my own experience, even if the group is mainly lesbians.

Recently I have started a relationship with a man who is disabled. Initially the boys were jealous and didn't want to accept him but they're coming around now. I had to tell social services about my partner and so I told my linkworker as soon as the relationship began. In fact, I was worried about allowing him in the house until the social workers had done police checks. Basically that was just because I wanted to be really careful about it all and tell them what was happening. I told the childrens' social workers too, so that they could tell me if the boys raised any problems. My linkworker said I was being over-cautious about it all and that single women carers don't usually tell them about partners unless someone moves in, but I just wanted it all out in the open.

Being in a relationship makes fostering different. I have to be careful about what I say about the boys to my partner as I think if I told him everything about them and what they've done, he'd freak. For example, I didn't think I had to tell my partner about Peter and the women's underwear but then my partner found some of it so I had to explain it all. I've also had to explain that when I am fed up with the boys I'll let off steam by calling them names, but not in front of them! I do it in private, so they won't hear, but my partner was shocked to hear me cursing them one day. But you have to get your frustrations out and I'd never say it to their faces. That's the same for any parent.

I think fostering has prevented me having relationships in the past. One time I was seeing someone and one lad I was looking after got hold of this man's phone number and made a sexually abusive phone call to him. It was awful and had to be looked into and the lad was moved. That incident put paid to that relationship very quickly! Some gay men run a mile when they hear that you are a foster carer. I usually tell people I meet, in the pub or whatever, but gay men are just not used to having kids around. Some are very self-orientated, just wanting to be out on the scene and in the clubs, and they're just not used to having to put the needs of two little people first. Also, I don't get to go out as much and it's hard to make plans very far in advance. If I do meet someone, I've got to go through all that stuff about explaining why the children are so demanding and why their behaviour can be so difficult sometimes, and that's a lot to expect a partner to take on board.

The other side of the coin is not being able to tell everyone that I'm gay because I've got the boys. Some people's prejudices are such that they don't think gay men should care for children, even if they say they're not prejudiced about homosexuality. I remember a gay comedian, who used to be a school teacher, saying to his audience: 'If you don't laugh at my jokes, I'm going to go back to teaching your children!' That joke is actually about the idea that 'gays are okay but they shouldn't be around children'. Some people also still have the attitude that all gay men are child abusers or they think that I haven't got the 'correct lifestyle' to bring up young heterosexual men. But they don't think it works the other way around! Also, there's this idea that men don't care for children anyway or if they do, they're 'odd'. I only know one other gay man who is fostering.

If I had to sum it up, I'd say the worst bits are the sometimes horrendous behaviour of the children I've cared for – drugs, self-harm, smashing up the house. They can be like a tornado ripping through the house destroying everything, or they 'want such-and-such and they want it now'! Fostering can feel like it's taken over your whole life at times and you can feel like you've given so much of yourself that there's nothing left. That's really hard to explain to a partner if they want to see you but you're just completely wiped out. Dealing with difficult behaviour can be the hardest thing, especially when one of the boys kicks off in the middle of the street and everyone else is watching. You can see it on their faces thinking: 'Well he's not brought his kids up right!'

I don't really know why I do it. Sometimes I really do wonder why. But when Peter asks for a hug, that makes a huge difference because he's never hugged anyone before. Or when a child is surprised to find that I really do care about him, or when he manages to achieve something that people thought he'd never do, it's definitely worth it! If I'm a 'role model' for the boys at all, it's that they see a man doing all the housework – and that they have to do some too – and also that I try to explain things the way they are, to be straight-talking and not cover things up, being open even when they are not. Because it doesn't always go both ways. Fostering can be a very selfless task where the kids take and take with very little give. But that doesn't mean I wouldn't still do it! I don't just see it as a job because it's too hard, I could get a much easier job! And sometimes it's really 'in your face', but it's a challenge. You have to be so many things – mother, father, saint, sinner, counsellor, cleaner, cook – and I wouldn't have it any other way!

'A Mechaiyah – A Complete Joy…'
Kate's Story

Kate is 39 years old and is a white Jewish woman who lives with her white partner, Poppy. Poppy has been a director of a small national charity and now works for a television company. Kate worked in community care services and now works with ex-offenders and crime prevention, having had a brief interlude where she ran her own chocolate company. They have provided respite care for Joshua since he was five years old. He stays at weekends. They live in London in a flat with a garden. Joshua is now 16.

I suppose I opted for the middle course of part-time parenting. My partner, Poppy, and I hadn't decided at that stage in our lives and in our relationship whether we were going to have our own kids, but I wanted to provide respite care for a disabled child. I was working in community care services at that time. Very pragmatically, I had a spare bedroom and no close involvement with children so I thought it would be a matching up of various facets of my life. The decision to apply to do respite care was as boring as that really.

It was ten years ago that I applied. At that time I had a mix of lesbian and gay friends and straight friends. Most people thought it was a good, worthy and kind thing to do – fostering a disabled child – like it was 'selfless' of me, which of course wasn't the motivation at all. I was certainly satisfying my own needs of wanting to be involved with a child.

We still hadn't ruled out having our own kids but I made a decision, with Poppy's agreement, to provide respite care for a child. Over the course of the years we decided not to have our own kids, for all sorts of reasons – partly because we find part-time parenting really suits us, it meets all our nurturing needs – although the garden meets the rest of Poppy's – and also because we get on and enjoy the rest of our lives as total free spirits. I'd envisaged respite care being ongoing so I didn't think it was something we'd do just for six months or a year. I knew it would be a matter of years. Part-time parenting suited us because we both had full-time jobs at the time and respite care fitted in very neatly around our work. So when we didn't have Joshua, we were able to sustain our normal boring lifestyles.

I applied by just ringing my local social services. I probably wouldn't have bothered if I had lived in a right-wing borough but I'd seen an article in *Capital Gay* magazine which said that a nearby local authority was recruiting lesbian and gay foster parents so I thought maybe there was a good chance that my own authority would consider me. Also, I knew it was a 'right-on' borough. My local council didn't have a respite care scheme though, which is quite unusual. Most sensible boroughs do have respite care schemes and I wanted to provide respite care and knew it was only possible for a child with a disability. In a sense, they made an exception and organised it through fostering so that I could care for a disabled child.

I came out to the social workers almost at the very start of the assessment process, probably in the first meeting. Partly, this is because I can never remember being a lesbian is something you are not supposed to just tell everyone! It always just comes out. There are very few sentences in my life which don't include the word 'Poppy'. It all just comes out but, also, I thought that if there was going to be any hassle, I'd get it out of the way now and then if the social workers said they didn't want any 'dykes', that would be the end of it. But it was never an issue for them. Poppy wasn't living with me at the time of the assessment so it was just me that was assessed as the carer. I am approved as a respite carer and Poppy as the carer's partner.

Having Joshua come and stay certainly changed our weekends! Particularly in the early days, we had to totally tailor things around him. When he first came he was five years old. He was very sweet and very gorgeous, a spindly little thing. He was incredibly limited, said very little and what he did say was repetitive. He was very slow and what he talked about was Michael Jackson and 'zombies', but not in a particularly entertaining way! He'd mainly say: 'Where do the zombies come from?' and we'd have to say: 'They come out of the graves'. He didn't like being read to, or playing a game, or any activity, so it was very difficult entertaining him within the house. He refused to walk so it was quite difficult getting him out of the house. He could walk because he didn't have a physical disability, just a learning disability, but he wouldn't walk! Poppy and I spent many hours luring him from one lamp-post or car to the next, or to the next motor bike, trying to just get him down the road and to the underground station so we could get out of the house. Our weekends revolved around Joshua and they went quite slowly because he was very difficult to occupy.

We wanted the respite care to be a positive relationship between us, Joshua and Mary, his mother. Each bit had to work because it can't work if there is substantial tension. Mary, I think, didn't really know any lesbians or gay men, but she does now and what we agreed with the social worker was that I would meet Mary and Joshua so that they would have some sense of me. This was so Mary would see that I am just a normal person and then the terrible news that I was a lesbian would be broken to her a week or so later! She was rather surprised to hear I was a lesbian and she had to think about whether it was okay. You know, I think she was a bit daunted and a bit worried but decided to go with it. Her social worker had reassured her that it would all be okay and she, I think, very bravely and generously didn't let the average person's misconceptions about lesbians and gays get in the way. I think it was very good that she was prepared to put her anxieties or preconceived ideas to one side, especially as she was so protective of Joshua, and just trust us to get on with it.

Since then, as we have got to know each other, it has been fine and it has just ceased to be an issue and she has been terribly relaxed about the whole thing. Indeed, she appeared with us on the *Out on Tuesday* film,[1] which was extremely generous of her and was very 'out' of her – partly, I think, not so much for her and her kid being looked after by two lesbians but more because we were foster parents and the potential stigma of her child being fostered. I think that was much more of an issue for Mary, rather than the lesbian thing, so it was very very good of her, but she wanted to do it as a way of thanking us for what we've done. So there is give and take. We very rarely do things with Mary as our relationship is mainly with Joshua. It is only in the last few years that we have ever done anything with her other than have a little chat when I pick Joshua up from her house. More recently, over the last few years, occasionally, we will go out for a meal together. When I was running my business, Mary came and helped me with my chocolate packaging and she was a star.

We were told very little about Joshua before he came to us other than that he had a learning disability. He was described as 'hyperactive', which is absolutely ludicrous as he was the least hyperactive child I have ever met! He was practically inert with passivity and inactivity, so that was a bit strange. We were expecting a wizzy little thing, zooming about the place, when, in fact, he was just totally static, so that was surprising. Otherwise, I didn't really have any expectations at all about what he would be like so it was just a miracle he turned out to be such a lovely, sweet, good natured, funny child. It's sort of like a fairy story isn't it? Possibly, if I'd thought he was going to be very clever, I'd have been very disappointed because he is not very clever, but he is really gorgeous.

---

1   See Parmar (1989) in bibliography.

Only right at the beginning did we have any active input from the social workers. The first social worker we had after Joshua was with us was called Janet and was really good and really nice and really supportive. She came and talked about feelings and parenting and so on and was amazingly useful as it was all slightly daunting in the early days. Otherwise, it is now quite rare for us to see a social worker from one year to the next.

The classic incident was when one social worker came to see us on a Friday afternoon and Joshua was being particularly boring and going on and on about Michael Jackson! I just thought: 'Well, it is up to the social worker if he wants to say anything or react more interactively with Joshua', but our social worker didn't interact because he fell asleep! Joshua was excelling himself with dullness but I still think it was a bit rum for the social worker to fall asleep!

The saddest situation was an evening when Joshua must have been about six and he just cried all evening. It was terrible. In the early days he would say, fairly continuously, most of the weekend, 'I want to go home. When am I going home? When am I going home?' I think I accepted that, on balance, he didn't want to be here but I'm afraid it was partly just too bad because Mary had to have a break. It's just like if a kid doesn't want to be at school. I'm afraid there just comes a stage where it is just too bad, as long as one is doing one's best and being kind and all the rest of it. So it was part of that whole sort of syndrome of Joshua feeling sad and wanting to be at home, but it just reached a crescendo for him. He was just beside himself and inconsolable. Poppy was carrying him around most of the evening just trying to get him to stop crying. It was awful. It was very very traumatic and then I said to Poppy, who was carrying Joshua at the time: 'Maybe we should ring Mary?' Poppy was very annoyed with me because he had just more or less calmed down and stopped crying and then he just absolutely erupted and Poppy thought it was extremely foolish of me. We didn't ring Mary and we got over that evening and there has never been anything like it since. That really was a memorable evening. So sad, it was awful, poor little thing.

Over the last few years I've had increasing contact with Joshua's school as we have challenged his 'statement'. Children with special educational needs are formally assessed and given a statement of how such needs are to be met within the education system. Challenging the statement has been a whole long drawn-out process. We've tried to get it put into Joshua's statement that he should have a thinking skills programme. There has been a schlepped-out fight with them and it ended up going to a special educational needs tribunal, which is like a sort of court. The head of the education service's legal department was there with a barrister and so on. It was all very grim. We were well supported by a wonderful, very expert woman from a specialist charity, but we lost.

So, we have had a lot of contact with the school and have maintained a very good relationship throughout all this. The headteacher, who I really like and respect, managed to maintain a really good relationship even though I was in dispute, not so much with the school but with the authority. I am now a governor of the special school, which goes from ages five to sixteen, so Joshua has been there as long as we have had him. Also, I am starting up their parent-staff association so I am increasingly involved with the school. As far as I am aware, they have been totally relaxed about us being lesbians.

I think the issue of Joshua having two lots of parents is the only thing that is complicated for the school and that they are not particularly good about. They often forget to send me stuff that they are sending to his Mum. It is really important for me to get all the information from school about how Joshua is doing. On the other hand, until recently, and in some ways much more importantly, Joshua came to us via the school bus. He was dropped off by the school bus and it always varied because it would be every two or every three weeks, so sometimes I'd pick him up myself rather than the bus and so on. Over nine years of dropping Joshua off on a different bus than the one he normally goes home on, they never ever got it wrong! He was always on the right bus, which was an absolute organisational miracle. It was very careful of them to have always managed that. Sometimes I rang the day before, sometimes two minutes before he was due to step on the bus, and they always managed to get it right because it would have been very very traumatic for Joshua going off on his home bus with no one being there.

Joshua has William Syndrome, a feature of which is obsessional interest in some things – like Michael Jackson and zombies. He has become interested in other things now, notably Motorcross, which is like motorbike scrambling, and we have photos of him doing it. That is really great because it is a bit more age-appropriate and it is a change after relentless Michael Jackson and also it is a real skill. He has managed to teach himself to ride a push-bike, which is incredible for a young person with major co-ordination problems, balance problems and spatial awareness problems. His favourite favourite thing, which drives me demented but I do do it, is to go to 'Forbidden Planet' in New Oxford Street and look at the covers of videos, and to look at the covers of totally inappropriate horror-type magazines. He just loves it. It makes him very very happy and it is very very boring for me and also I don't really approve of it, you know, because I think it is all too ghastly and it is a very hot claustrophobic place. This is where my true altruism comes in. This is me being something like a saint, quite frankly, by taking him to see these bloody magazines!

He went through a phase, I think he was about nine or ten, of when people came round he would give this great long speech about how he has got difficulties, 'I've got learning difficulties', and he would go on about that quite a lot and pour out his heart a bit about that. Very recently we've told him what his mum told him, that he has got William Syndrome. We've been involved with the William Syndrome group and he has met other kids with William Syndrome. I don't think he understands what it means. I don't know if he has really connected it with his difficulties.

Joshua is very different nowadays as, some ten years on, he is a fairly energetic and independent 16-year-old, so he is much more able to do his own thing. There will be hours where he is doing his own thing in the lounge and I will probably be working in the study so my lifestyle at weekends isn't so different now. In the last year he has made some progress with reading and has been able to recognise individual words, but not enough to be able to read fully. He is not resourceful and has never really been able to play by himself – creative play – and as he can't read, it makes home-based activities quite challenging. What he does love doing is watching videos so it is this whole dilemma about TV and kids and how much time to let a child watch TV! At the end of the day I think: 'Well, I'm afraid I've got to get on with my life', which tends to run to a lot of work at weekends. If that's the only way I can manage to have Joshua, by him watching what is probably too many videos, then, on balance, it is a fairly small price to pay because the rest of the weekend is more active for him.

Perhaps the hardest thing is just how slow the changes have been. Just until recently, when he had a bit of a spurt, you know, his development has been painfully slow. And although I, in particular, working in learning disabilities services, should be able to take that in my stride, I do still find it enormously frustrating. He still doesn't know the difference between left and right and until recently has had almost no reading skills. He finds thinking things through very very difficult and he can't think too hard or too fast or too much or about things which are too complicated.

On the other hand, he is a total joy. You know, he is unbelievable. I know it sounds biased, it sounds Jewish. I am his mum, or his foster mum, but he is quite exceptional. He is just so good natured. He has been coming for ten years and I think just once he was in a slightly bad mood! You know it is just bizarre and he is great and he is just sweet and friendly and funny and good company. He is just a pleasure, *a mechaiyah* as we say in Yiddish, a complete joy. Our friends also enjoy being with Joshua and most of them are very very good at being able to pitch the conversation right, which is quite an art in terms of both using language that Joshua can understand, not making it too complicated, and also being prepared to stick with quite limited topics. Also, they don't patronise him. If he goes on and on and on, they will say so.

Poppy and I were in a relationship for two years before Joshua came and have been in a relationship for ten years since. The vast bulk of the time Poppy and I have been together we have had Joshua. He is very much a bond for us as there is not that much that Poppy and I do together. Sounds terrible doesn't it! We do leisure things together but other than that we don't have many shared responsibilities or activities so Joshua is very bonding in that respect. Although, I must say, Joshua is my responsibility when he comes for the weekends and I make all the arrangements and do everything with Joshua. If I can't for some reason, Poppy will look after him, but I am definitely the primary carer. Joshua has brought a lot of joy into our lives, which is nice, and had a major impact on our day-to-day language and humour. I think we don't realise how so many of the words and phrases we use are little in-jokes and 'Joshua-nonsenses'.

Having Joshua had a much bigger impact on our relationship with our friends than it has had on our own relationship. Almost all of our friends have children. Looking after Joshua gives us an understanding of what it is like having children, which I don't think we'd have had really before, so it gives Poppy and me a point of contact with our friends.

I think, ten years on, Joshua has finally twigged what is going on between Poppy and I. We, rightly or wrongly, have always been conservative about the whole sort of lesbian bit and I don't think even now we've ever used the word 'lesbian' in relation to ourselves in front of Joshua. Although from day one Poppy and I have always been physically affectionate with each other, nothing sexual but certainly physically affectionate, we have never gone on about the fact that we are lesbians. However, from day one we have made it very very clear that we love each other and we care about each other. Obviously we sleep in the same bed together, but I think that because Joshua has a learning disability he is very slow to catch on.

As recently as about a year or two ago, even though it has always been very clear that we love each other and all that, he said to Poppy something about 'when she gets married or when she finds a husband'. It was really surprising. I think Joshua has been confused because Poppy is still very close to her ex-boyfriend and we tell Joshua this. Like, sometimes on a Friday night, Joshua will be over here with me and Poppy will be going out to see her ex-boyfriend for a meal or whatever and we always say to Joshua: 'Poppy's out with her ex-boyfriend.' I think that has just really confused him and made him think that Poppy is just biding her time waiting for 'Mr Right' to turn up! I told Joshua that Poppy hasn't got a boyfriend any more but she has got a girlfriend and I'm Poppy's girlfriend. Joshua went: 'Oh ho ho, two girls' and just by my spelling it out to Joshua it was a great revelation, as if he hadn't noticed for the last six or seven years that Poppy and I hold hands, kiss, and go to bed together. I think he has finally twigged because at school they are doing stuff on personal relationships and sexuality and the feedback I get from the teachers is that he is fairly relaxed about all this. In fact, he has said to them: 'My foster mums are lesbians'. So someone has obviously told him.

I thought I was fairly okay about Joshua and sex, until he had his first kiss. Basically, I completely over-reacted and cried! He was 12 or 13 at the time but I just completely flipped and I got it into my head that this was it and it would be the end of all our lives as we used to know it. I just very very seriously over-reacted and was terrible with Joshua, really deplorable. I thought I was liberal and relaxed but I just went into 'Victoria Gillick mode' telling him that kissing wasn't wrong and it wasn't that he was bad but that I was very very upset and he shouldn't have done it in public and that was very bad! It suddenly made me think of Joshua as a vulnerable teenager. I had images of teenage spots, pregnancy and Aids zooming round my head in a hysterical way. I rang Poppy and I was saying: 'Something terrible has happened. He has kissed a girl!' Poppy obviously thought I had gone completely nuts and she calmed me down and talked to Joshua and apologised for my mad behaviour! When I finally calmed down I did apologise to Joshua a lot and said it was very bad of me to have over-reacted. It was quite a revelation how badly I handled it so now I just don't talk to him about sex, which is dreadful. His mum and school do talk to him about it. Poppy would also, and probably in a very calm and sensible way.

We have never let Joshua see us without any clothes on in case it gets misinterpreted by social services or someone else, so we have just always played safe because it is just safer. I don't believe in that as parenting, since it's not generally a good way to behave, but if he was living with us permanently, I'd think it might be different. I was very worried in the early days because his communication was so poor, but I was just nervous about social services and lesbians. Not that they were at all twitchy, but I was just very worried about him verbally misconstruing or misrepresenting something. The nearest we got was when I had some people round from the Labour Party one day and Joshua said something about us sleeping together, which sounded like me, Poppy and Joshua all sleeping in the same bed. It was exactly the sort of thing which just came out. I don't know whether it was just a muddle in his head or just a muddle on his tongue but that is the only time and he has certainly never done it intentionally to hurt us.

Class has been quite a substantial issue because Poppy and I are extremely middle-class and both have well-paid jobs. Mary is Irish working-class and on the dole. Joshua has managed to handle the differences in income and lifestyle between his home and here extremely well. We have tried to be careful and sensitive about balancing the need to give Joshua incentives to stay here without being flashy and spoiling him – in particular, not setting up anything that makes things more difficult for Mary when he is at home. I think that for years we were quite worried that Mary would think we were pathologically mean! Particularly in the early days, we used to give really tiny birthday and Christmas presents, so anything that went home would be very small. Also, the class thing has been very very apparent during this whole statementing process because I think it has been a bit of a mystery to Mary, a bit of a nightmare. Everything, from the language used to the whole fact has been fairly confrontational and I think it has been a rather horrible undermining process for her because I think she has been quite left out of it or quite daunted by it. And that has been something we have had to weigh up at each stage, about whether it's worth it in terms of what we are trying to achieve for Joshua. That's been quite difficult but I am afraid we have stuck with it, although we have finally dropped the statementing battle, much to Mary's relief and ours in fact. So, yes, class has been an issue.

I'm Jewish and some bits of that just totally mystify Joshua. We are Kosher here so we don't have pig or shell-fish in the house. It gets terribly complicated because we are also vegetarian in the house, but we do let him have chicken take-aways because they are broadly Kosher. At least they are not pig or shell-fish, but he can't have pork so that whole bit is a bit confusing for Joshua. We go to my parents place quite often on a Friday night where they do more religious-type stuff. We have prayers with the meal and he wears a *yarmulka* (head covering) and all that sort of business. So he has had some contact with Jewish rituals, which I hope he likes. It is good to have contact with another culture.

For the last few years Joshua has come to us every other weekend. However, it's varied over the years. Originally it was a weekend a month, Friday to Monday, and then it was every other weekend, Friday to Monday. Now it's every other weekend, alternating one day and two days. What is likely to change is how frequently he comes and also whose decision it is. This is a key concept of Joshua's, quite rightly, as he always wants to know whose decision it is. Normally, about things like whether he can have a Chinese meal or an Indian meal, he says: 'Whose decision is it?' He is quite right to pin us down to whose decision it is and, therefore, when he is an adult, we have said to Mary that we think it would be appropriate for Joshua to decide when he comes and I think things will change a lot then. He will sometimes come over just for the afternoon or just to go out for a bit or move in for a week or whatever. It will be much more flexible, it will be much more variable, I would imagine, than it is now. The relationship will change and I think we feel it should change from being a respite care arrangement, fundamentally to give Mary a break, to be more about Joshua's relationship with us, so that it is much more in his control.

I think it is a pity more people don't part-time parent. I think it is just really great and it is still very unusual as a choice of parenting, which I think is a shame because it has been fabulous for us and I think it has been very beneficial and good for Joshua. He couldn't be at home all the time because Mary just couldn't cope as a single parent. It's made a total difference in my life. It has been brilliant and he is a source of much joy. He met our need to parent absolutely perfectly and fitted in really well with our lifestyles. I think we were among the pioneers in terms of lesbians and gay men fostering but I was always very cautious about things that could be misconstrued either by Joshua verbally or by anyone else. For example, I would make sure there were no dresses in the fancy dress. I am afraid we even didn't have dolls and maybe just kept things very safely stereotypical so nothing could be construed about us brainwashing Joshua or trying to change his sexuality or just being deviant with him!

Poppy and I are such a sort of devoted, boringly loving couple! I mean we get on most incredibly well. This is very dull but we almost never argue and it is just always sweetness and light. For Joshua to experience that sort of stability, and see such a positive happy stable relationship, I should think is really nice for him. We really hope he will find a life partner and settle down and all that stuff. I suppose it is nice for him to see a positive lesbian couple and all that. The whole thing with Joshua being so lovely, and the relationship with Mary, has all worked so very well. Yes, we are like the Waltons, the lesbian Waltons! It is just so gorgeous but it just has been like that. Amazing.

Postscript: August 1997

Joshua is now 16, has left school and is in a special class in a mainstream college. Kate says: 'He has grown from the sweet child he was to a sweet young man and the relationship is much more on his terms and equal now, rather than respite care. My mother has since died and Joshua often talks about how sad that is and how he misses her.'

'Staying Power'
Emma and Louise's Story

Emma and Louise are a white lesbian couple. They have been together for over 16 years and currently live in Manchester. Emma is 49 and Louise 35 and they have two foster children, a son aged eight and a daughter who is almost seven. The children have been with them for just over two years. Emma has worked in psychiatry, for Women's Aid, and, since being in Manchester, has worked with survivors of sexual violence. She has recently given up work to give more time to the care of their children and she helps out at their school on a voluntary basis. Louise is a manager for a bank and is also a parent governor of the children's school. Emma has written their story.

Louise and I got together in early 1981. At that time I was 33 and Lou was not quite 19. I started thinking about children almost straight away because, for the first time in my life, I felt that I'd met someone with whom I wanted to settle down. As Lou was so much younger, however, it was not practical to do anything about it and so I put my feelings about children on the back burner for the next five years. During this time we moved to West Yorkshire and life was feeling fairly settled.

Once we had decided to pursue the possibility of children, our first thought was that I should attempt to get pregnant. We approached a local BPAS (British Pregnancy Advisory Service), who were very positive about inseminating lesbians but were concerned about my weight. They claimed that fat women didn't get pregnant and, even if I did, the doctor was concerned about the strain on my heart and was not sure he could take the risk. We challenged him to show from tests that I was not fit and, after a further year of seeing specialists, BPAS agreed to inseminate me for nine months. Part of the BPAS process had involved seeing a counsellor and she had recommended that we also consider adoption. It had never before occurred to us that this could be an option for us.

Whilst I was undergoing tests to prove my health, we also advertised for sperm donors in a local paper. This provided some very weird responses, but one, however, appeared reasonable and so Lou arranged to phone him a couple of times a month and go and collect his donations. She would drive along the motorway with the jar stuffed inside her bra to keep it warm whilst I waited for her at home! All attempts at insemination failed, including those by BPAS, and, although I had only been trying for a year, we were finding it very stressful and decided to give up.

During this period, however, we had made our first approaches for adoption. I phoned our local authority, who arranged to send a social worker out to see us. She arrived, a middle-aged woman in twin-set and pearls who stayed for twenty minutes then later sent a letter confirming that they had no children suitable nor were they ever likely to have any children suitable for placing with us. The letter gave no reasons why so we appealed to the Director of Social Services, who simply reiterated the statement in the original letter.

We next tried two other local authorities, one in a northern city and the other in another large town nearby. The latter said they had sufficient carers to meet their needs and the other that although they were prepared to consider a lesbian couple, they were not prepared to travel the sixteen miles to do the assessment.

Next we tried a children's voluntary organisation in another city. The woman there was really supportive, saying she didn't think there would be a problem as they were always trying to encourage people to adopt. On our next visit, however, she had found out that her organisation had no policy for approving lesbians or gays but she was keen to get one introduced. With this aim in mind, she hunted out research that had been carried out on lesbian parenting so that she could present this to the next national committee meeting in London. However, this, together with our case, continued to be placed on the bottom of their agenda and the committee always ran out of time before getting to it.

It felt like the whole thing was becoming our mission. We were getting more and more determined not to be defeated. We contacted BAAF (British Agencies for Adoption and Fostering), who sent us information about the *Be My Parent* newsletter. We were given details of where to go to look through the newsletter. If there were any children we were interested in, we had to contact the agencies quoted. This involved going to the house of a heterosexual couple who appeared to be quite religious. They would lock us in their front room while we looked through the newsletter and we would knock on the door when we wanted to be let out. Although this was a very awkward and strange situation to find ourselves in, we were becoming very used to exposing ourselves in our quest to become parents. It was also exciting to see pictures of actual children needing homes and made the whole thing seem more possible again.

We went to see the book a few times and sent for additional information and videos on several children. We came close on only one occasion, with a particular girl in Yorkshire. The social workers were fairly positive and felt that it wouldn't be too far to travel to assess us but they had another couple interested who were already approved. Some social workers were openly hostile when they found out that I was a lesbian, saying things like: 'We don't place children with just anyone'.

Before embarking on our quest we had never been made to feel as much like second-class citizens as we were now being treated. We exposed ourselves to the worst insults and bigotry we had ever encountered. No one had any qualms about telling us that we were unfit or unsuitable or had no right to think we might be suitable. We were stuck in the situation of not being able to express an interest in particular children without having been approved and not being able to persuade anyone to approve us.

In 1988 we moved to Nottinghamshire and it was around this time that BPAS agreed to start my inseminations. This meant that twice a month I had to travel to my appointments. Again, after nine months of inseminations I did not manage to become pregnant and, although my GP was prepared to make a case for BPAS to continue, I'd had enough.

Then a nearby metropolitan social services department ran an advert for an open evening for people interested in fostering and adopting and I decided to go. After the meeting I approached one of the social workers and told her that I was in a lesbian relationship. I said if this was going to be a problem then I'd rather be told outright than have our hopes raised unnecessarily. She said that approving a lesbian couple would not be a problem. In retrospect, this was something of an understatement! It wasn't a problem in principle but in practice seemed to cause some difficulties. The social worker said that she would contact our own local authority first but if they weren't prepared to take us on, her authority would. Either way, at long last we had a commitment that the process of our approval could begin.

The assessment took the form of home study and attendance at group sessions. The home study lasted for twelve months and the group was for about ten evening sessions, two whole Saturdays and one Sunday. Our home study started first as we had to wait for about six months for a group to start. The first visit by the social worker was very business-like. She told us about the process and the types of children that might be available; she confirmed that there would be no possibility of a baby.

We had already decided on a sibling group. We knew that as a lesbian couple we would only be considered for the most difficult-to-place children – children with learning difficulties, severe physical problems/illnesses, or sibling groups. Neither of us wanted an only child, nor did we relish the idea of going through the process twice to get a second child, and as it appeared that sibling groups were difficult to place, this is what we asked for.

Needless to say, we were the only lesbian couple in the assessment group – the others were four married couples and two single women. The group was led by two social workers, neither of whom were our social worker for home study, and our participation in the group was being assessed. The group assessment resulted in a five-page report on our attitudes to issues around race, gender, birth parents, abuse, etc.

After the group finished, our social worker apologised for putting us in the position of being the only lesbian couple because, as such, we had been used to test out the attitudes and prejudices of the rest of the group. We had survived this well and performed a useful role for them but they acknowledged that this shouldn't have happened and not everyone would have survived that experience. Having to answer questions from other group members about our sexuality and how we had come to that choice could be seen as useful preparation for being bold about our sexuality with our children and people we encounter through them!

The local authority had only ever approved one other lesbian couple and our social worker arranged for us to meet them. This was the first time we had encountered lesbians who had either fostered or adopted children. The social worker felt that they had been easier to approve as they fitted into more stereotypical male/female, butch/femme roles which the adoption panel could relate to. We did not present this type of relationship so we underwent a lot of questioning around how jobs around the house were divided and also how we would provide positive male role models for children.

The discussion about male role models went on for some time. For some years our social circle had been entirely female. I even worked in an all-women environment. We told the social worker that we had no male friends but that we had reasonable relationships with most of the male members in our families. There were also lengthy discussions around the gender of the children we wanted. We initially dodged the issue, feeling that if we declared an interest only in girls, this would be disapproved of, but after two sessions the social worker herself said that she felt we had far more to offer girls than boys and that she would be recommending that we be considered for girls only. I had also felt very uncomfortable about expressing a preference as if I had become pregnant, I would have not had this option.

It's very important at this stage that you be honest about what type of children and behaviours you are willing to deal with as you are the ones who will live with the children. No matter how prepared you think you might be, there will always be things that crop up that you feel ill-equipped to cope with.

The social worker was still concerned about male role models for girls, however, so we struggled to put a list together of men we might be prepared to develop some kind of friendship with. For our referees we chose the heterosexual couple next door and one of my work friends.

The whole process was so long and stressful and put an incredible strain on our relationship. We had told friends and family and work colleagues and they were always asking how things were progressing. After a year of our relationship being put under the microscope, we withdrew our application, just three weeks before going to panel. Shortly after this Lou and I separated.

If you get pregnant, even if it has taken some time to come to that decision and for it to happen, once it's done there's not much you can do apart from wait for it to be born. But when going through a lengthy process of other people questioning your lifestyle, relationship and personality, it can really make you begin to doubt that you have anything to offer.

After a couple of months I moved back in with Lou and we started to pick up the pieces. Two years later I moved to Manchester and, after a further year, Lou got a job in Manchester and joined me. We now felt ready to start again and, fortunately, this time around we chose an authority that had much more experience of approving lesbians and gays.

Our new social worker contacted our previous authority, who had kept all their assessment reports on us and sent copies to her. This meant that only an update was needed before we could go to panel. The updating process took just six months of home studies and no more group sessions were needed. This time, considerable pressure was exerted to persuade us to consider boys. We agreed to this but on the basis that we were not prepared to accept boys only.

In November 1994 we were ready to go to panel. We were kept advised of potential panel dates where our social worker was trying to get us a space. We felt vulnerable because we were not going to be there to present our case but she reassured us that it was her job to do so. She had been extremely positive with us throughout and, besides which, we had no option but to trust her to do the best she could. She eventually got a date for mid-December and in the afternoon she phoned us both to say that we had been approved as long-term carers for sibling group of up to three children aged ten years and under.

Although when we started out it felt as though being approved at panel would be the final triumph, the winning of our battle, we now know differently. For a start, it had taken us eight years from our first enquiries in 1986 to get to this point. Second, we had by now met other lesbians and gay men who had been approved but were still waiting for a placement, so it now felt as though approval was only the first hurdle.

We immediately started to apply considerable pressure to our social worker to find us a placement. We knew that she didn't want to have done the work only for us to have children from another authority. Whenever we'd speak to her about children we were interested in and that we had seen advertised in the PPIAS (Parent to Parent Information on Adoption Service) booklet, she'd ask us just to hang on a bit longer.

Only four months after being approved a match was found and this had to be put before the panel for them to approve. Within one month of finding out about the children, they had moved in. The introduction process was very quick but planned. On the day they were to meet us the children's social worker did some work with them around different types of families and what they wanted. We had made a book of photos of ourselves, our home and pets for them to look at beforehand. They found out about us just the day before we met them. After this there was a programme of visits to their house, trips out and visits to our house which culminated in them moving in a fortnight later.

The children have been with us for over 18 months and I am in the process of adopting them. Lou and I will also apply for a joint residence order so that we both have equal care and control of the children. I have already been approved for adoption at a third panel early in 1996.

During the whole process we had become very used to 'coming out' constantly to people who started out as virtual strangers, so once the children arrived and were 'outing' us to their teachers and school friends we pretty much took this in our stride. Recently we were due to attend our son's parent evening in his first term at junior school. The teacher asked around the classroom whose parents were coming and he announced to everyone: 'My two mums are coming, they're lesbians'. Now the children call us both mum it is also more apparent to people generally in shops and when we're out and about.

As with all children in care, our children have had experiences which have been damaging. Where we once looked forward to the day where we would have children of our own and would leave social workers behind us, having support from social workers over these first 18 months has been a comfort to us. It has helped us in securing some of the help our children need as well as providing us with support and affirmation for the parenting we are able to provide.

The children have had some taunting and bullying at school because they have lesbian parents but we continue to discuss the issues around choice and people's right to be different with them at every opportunity. Hopefully, as they have started this process at such a young age, they will grow up with a sense of their own individuality and an ability to stand up for the rights of all of us to be different. And maybe, as they grow up, we can all grow to be proud of each other.

'Out of Step'
Paul and Richard's Story

Paul and Richard are white gay men now turning 50. They have been together as a couple for 25 years. Patrick, who is now 11 and every bit as lively as he has always been, has been living with them for the last two years. Paul is a financial consultant and Richard is an independent social worker. It took eight years for them to achieve their dream of becoming foster carers to a child in care. Richard has written their story.

I have a clear memory of when it hit me as a teenager that I would not be able to have children of my own. Embarrassing as it is to admit it, I remember crying about it on one occasion in bed at night. It seems amazing now, more than thirty years later, that I could have had such a clear perception at that young age. Like a lot of teenagers, I was struggling with issues of 'abnormal' sexual feelings and sexual identity 'problems'. They sound more manageable and reasonable when phrased in these objective, adult terms but carry none of the horror and desperation that you can remember feeling at the time.

It must be better for young lesbians and gay men growing up today. The misinformation and the void beyond have surely been replaced for most youngsters, with much more information mixed with the misinformation. Do some young people who are 'different' sexually still think they are the only ones?

Anyway, back to the subject of children. I decided that even if I couldn't have my own children I would be able to work in the child-care field. (I am sure some readers will groan about this, but there are a lot of lesbians and gay men in social work for good reasons.) I had the considerable asset of a loving family and a secure home background to draw on. Even though while at university I decided that my religious beliefs were a sham, I retained 'do-gooding' ideas. I met other gay people for the first time and, at 24, met the man I've been living with for most of the last 25 years.

I trained as a social worker and, being sufficiently 'long in the tooth', I even saw the tail end of one of the old Children's Departments which existed before social services departments were set up at the end of the 1960s. Foster carers, or foster parents as they were called in those days, were more scarce than today, with many more children's homes in existence. I almost always enjoyed visits to foster homes, whilst secretly envying the foster parents' freedom to care for other people's children.

Fostering and Gay Rights

I'm not sure when it first dawned on me that I might one day be able to join the ranks of foster carers. I suppose there were two parallel developments going on in the world – one to do with fostering and adoption, and one to do with the identity and expectations of gay men and women. Both ended up affecting me very personally.

The early 1970s and the developing 'gay liberation movement' very fortuitously coincided with my reaching adulthood (21 in those days). I became involved in the Campaign for Homosexual Equality and dragged my partner in as well. I remember taking my courage in my mouth and asking work colleagues, including my boss, to support a vote at the AGM of the British Association of Social Workers to include sexual orientation in a non-discrimination clause of their code of ethics. Although risky in those days, it was quite a satisfactory way of 'coming out'.

In 1976 I was a member of a small national group of Gay Social Workers and Probation Officers (GSWPO) who had signed a letter in a social work journal. Those names were obviously burned on the memory of the Assistant Director of the department I next applied to work for. Before being offered the job, although I'd not breathed a word about GSWPO at my interview, I was told by my future boss that I'd better be careful not to use any work time on such organisations.

After sampling the 'joys' of a managerial post for a number of years, I decided to go for a post in fostering and adoption. The developments in family placement, as it was now termed, had also been considerable. 'Catch all' foster homes were being replaced by a plethora of differentially defined family placements. There were not only short-term foster homes but task-centred foster homes. Children and young people who had not been considered suitable for placements with families were now being given that opportunity. Teenage and professional fostering schemes were being set up. The orthodoxy of transracial placements was being challenged by schemes to find black families for black children. Permanent placements were being heralded as the right of all children and young people in the care system. There was even a change in the law to allow single men to foster. The latter rang a particularly personal bell, as you can imagine.

The two parallel developments finally came together in 1987 when a London-wide working party was set up by the London Strategic Policy Unit, the rump of the old Greater London Council. The task of the working party was to look at fostering and adoption policies and practice, throughout the capital, as they affected lesbians and gay men. My boss in the Family Placement Unit, not surprisingly, asked if I wanted to represent my authority on the working party. The working party produced the first account in this country of issues on this subject – *Fostering and Adoption by Lesbians and Gay Men*, edited by Jane Skeates and Dorian Jabri and published in 1988.

Applying to Foster

Just prior to this, Paul and I had already started telephoning agencies that were seeking permanent foster carers or adopters for particular children. It felt like we were doing something unacceptable and you had to take more than a few deep breaths before dialling each number. Mostly, we had embarrassed responses. One outer-London council said that they had difficulty enough getting their fostering and adoption panels to accept single carers let alone gay carers. Another council wanted us to explain, when we responded to an advert for a particular boy, why we were interested in fostering boys. She had agreed that we wouldn't be considered for girls! (Although Paul and I had done a lot of caring of a relative's daughter.) Quite often we were told that the child concerned wouldn't be able to cope with having gay carers on top of everything else he or she had experienced in life.

Fortunately, after about a year of 'banging our heads against a brick wall', we got an offer to assess us from one of the few boroughs who had a statement of anti-discriminatory childcare policies. We received a general assessment with no particular child being considered. A year later, in August 1988, we were finally approved for a permanent placement of a child aged nine years and upwards. We felt that this was a major achievement in the climate as it was then and thought our 'approval' would stand us in good stead for being accepted as suitable carers for a particular child. We should have known better.

The authority that had approved us did initially go ahead and consider us for a possible placement of a much younger child. However, when the child's mother was asked what she would think of her son being placed with a gay couple, she gave us the 'thumbs down' and their legal department didn't think we stood much of a chance in a contested court hearing. After that the authority never approached us again.

We hung on for some time waiting to hear from them but eventually 'got the message' and realised that we were going to have to approach other agencies if we were going to stand any chance of success. For the next two-and-a-half years we touted ourselves around fifteen or more agencies following up adverts for particular children or asking the agencies to consider us generally.

We finally agreed to take a homeless teenager from the Albert Kennedy Trust. This is an organisation that specialises in placing lesbian and gay youngsters with older settled gay people. Richard (he had the same name as me) decided that he wanted to come and stay with us after visiting from Manchester. However, once we had helped him get a job he started disappearing more and more into London and eventually decided he wanted to go into bed and breakfast accommodation. It all happened within a period of two months or so and left us, and particularly me, feeling pretty drained. Paul concluded it wasn't the sort of placement we had sought anyway and that we should go back to focusing on a younger child.

At around this time I was asked by a female friend of mine if I would consider becoming a sperm donor for her so that she and her girlfriend could have a child. Although there was the expectation that Paul and myself would have a part in the life of any child that was conceived, I knew that this would be insufficient involvement in parenting for me. Also, I wasn't wanting to bring another child into the world when I knew there were so many children in need of substitute homes. Thus Paul and I continued our search.

Some agencies gave us a reasonable consideration and at least met us. Most didn't. However, as a former fostering worker (I use the word 'former' as I had by this time moved on to work in a Family Centre) I knew that many many couples flog themselves around agencies asking to be considered for particular children. Most of these people, though, would be restricting themselves to very young children. There are few such children compared to the number of people offering them a home. Paul and I were offering ourselves for the so-called 'hard-to-place' older children where potential homes were few and far between. Nonetheless, it seemed that a children's home was preferable for some agencies (and probably for many more if the truth was known behind the reasons they gave) than taking the chance of placing with a gay couple.

What was the chance that they would be taking? Mainly, I think, facing the prejudice of a hostile, sensation-making tabloid press. The government had set the tone with Clause 28 of the Local Government Act in 1988. Even reasonable people in social services departments, or on their fostering panels, didn't believe that they could look at the situation after that with an open, enquiring mind.

Back Door

At the end of 1991 we again considered doing something which wasn't what we had been approved for. One agency that had responded more positively to our general enquiries asked if we would consider doing some respite care. Basically, as many people will know, this is providing a break to carers of difficult and/or demanding children and young people. The child concerned was a six-year-old boy called Patrick who had recently been placed with his sister in an adoptive placement and was giving his carers 'hell'.

Paul said that this wasn't at all what we were looking for. However, I was equally determined that if no one was going to ask us to do anything else, at least we could help out someone and not go completely to waste. Paul reluctantly gave way, but he had been right. We made lousy respite carers. We ended up not providing the support that the prospective adopters needed. I had the benefit of my training and work experience and understood what I was meant to be doing. Paul didn't stand a chance. He took to Patrick like 'a duck to water'. He is a bright boy and Paul really enjoyed everything about him and tended to minimise his problems. As a result the prospective adopters thought we were critical of them.

Paul realised on one level that he shouldn't be getting emotionally involved. However, when Patrick went to a specialist residential establishment with schooling on the premises and no plan that he should return to his former prospective adoptive home, the inevitable had already happened and Patrick's move changed the basis of our involvement. The community home and Patrick's local authority kept us at arm's length about what the future might hold. However, they did encourage us to become 'social uncles' to Patrick and we were allowed to take him out for the day once a month.

Patrick gave us a hard time, as he always had done. He was angry with everyone in his life. Fortunately, he was receiving a lot of intensive help from the staff of the residential establishment. Contact was re-established with his mother and he began to understand more, if not come to terms with, all the separations in his life. Our contact was eventually increased to a weekend once a month when we stayed with Patrick at a flat belonging to the residential establishment. The local authority also updated our assessment report and we were then also approved as foster carers by Patrick's local authority. We were not, however, approved as his future foster carers.

Patrick had been at the community home for two years before that decision was finally taken by his local authority. During that time we had to deal with a lot of resistance from one key manager in the local authority and some homophobic attitudes from a residential worker. It felt like a constant battle for a long time. It is arguable that the two years of uncertainty was justified whilst plans were worked out for Patrick. However, for us, it was very painful. We gave an enormous amount of our time and emotional energy to Patrick and all the meetings connected with him and there was always the possibility at the end of that time that he would be placed with someone else. Our relief and pleasure when the decision was finally made was, literally, a dream come true.

Foster Carers at Last

Six months later, Patrick came to live with us on a permanent basis. He was upset at leaving the other children and staff he had become attached to, although he said it was different from other separations in that he was moving to familiar people and a familiar place. (He had, by then, been visiting our home for some time.)

It certainly hasn't been 'plain sailing' since then, although the sense of fulfilment for both Paul and me has been enormous. As a child who had had difficulties at school, we had to get Patrick 'statemented' and get a school to accept him. He had been six when we first met him but he was nearly ten by this time and had four more terms to do at junior school. More recently, getting a secondary school to suit his needs was also a struggle. However, he is now successfully coming to the end of his first year there.

He has now been with us for over two years. He has decided that continuing to see his mother just gives him grief. He does, however, still regularly see his sister with whom he was previously placed. Like her, he now also wants to be adopted and we are about to embark on negotiating this with the courts.

General Issues

Turning from the personal to more general issues, I'm sure that a lot of people will question how appropriate it is for a gay couple to adopt a child as young as Patrick. Issues to do with our sexual orientation have not been to the fore. The struggles we have had have been much more those of any couple taking on the task of parenting a child in care with all the problems their past brings with them. We are part of large extended families and Patrick has also been settling in as part of our families.

Generally, I think, male parents, whether straight or gay, face much more suspicion than female parents, who are regarded in society as 'natural parents'. Thus men seeking to parent alone or together are still likely to be scrutinised more closely or rejected more quickly than lesbians in a similar position.

There is also a vulnerability that you feel as a male parent. The issue of men showing affection to children has been hedged around with so much media suspicion that you need a lot of confidence in your own ability to nurture and care for a child to counteract this. As a gay male parent, there is the added pressure to put all sexual activity 'in the deep freeze'. One focuses so much on being accepted as a parent that you feel added pressure to minimise that part of yourself of which society disapproves.

I don't think that Paul and I would have persisted in trying to become foster carers and finally been successful but for my knowledge and experience of social work. Nor would we have had the enormous amount of time to devote to the whole process but for the fact that I was working part-time and Paul was self-employed. There must be any number of potential gay male foster carers going to waste because they don't have the 'know-how' to challenge the system or all the necessary time and energy to devote to the struggle. More importantly, there are a lot of kids in care who are missing out as a result.

What has been the reaction of other people to Paul and me fostering? One reaction that has surprised me, in particular, has been that of other gay men. Many have been interested, if surprised, that we have finally been successful. Some good friends have been very supportive. However, we've met more hostility than I would have anticipated and I think there is a good deal of self-oppression within the gay community. 'Gay men can't be trusted to be parents' because that's what we've been taught.

However, people's attitudes generally have been much better than we feared. We have taken the line of expecting to be accepted and neighbours, other parents at school and school staff have generally been positive, although sometimes it would have been interesting to know what was said behind the scenes.

Patrick asked us years ago, when Paul and I were talking about our first holiday together, 'Why were you such good friends? Are you "gays"?' When we told him we were, he looked a bit worried and I asked him what he had heard about gay people. He said that he'd seen something in a sex education book he had looked at at the children's home. He didn't seem to want to talk any more about it at the time. This was a year or more before he came to live with us.

Since that occasion, when there has been the opportunity, we have talked of how some people are attracted to members of their own sex, although most people are attracted to the opposite sex. Patrick understands that Paul and I love one another. We have always thought it important not to hide our affection. We will give one another a cuddle or a kiss as the occasion warrants, as we would do in front of members of our extended families.

Patrick himself is an affectionate child. He wasn't when we first knew him but has become much more demonstrative over the years, more confident that he is loved and is lovable.

Greater coverage in the media about homosexuality has helped and it has hindered. It has helped in so far as there is more about people being gay and more acceptance. For example, it was Patrick himself who related the news about the age of consent debate in Parliament in 1994. However, the media also reflects and, to a certain extent, perpetuates the prejudice and negative views about lesbians and gay men. As Patrick says, the term 'poofter' is a term of abuse at school (as it is in society at large). How do we help him with this?

Patrick is happy to bring friends home from school and is learning confidence that name calling from other children will be dealt with firmly by school staff, as it was on the two occasions it has happened in his present school. It is complicated in that issues often get mixed up. For example, on one of the occasions another child had made fun of the fact that Patrick had, as she conjectured, been rejected by his mother. However, she then went on to imply that his mother couldn't have thought much of him, leaving him with two gays.

Paul and I have put in a lot of work to ensure that the school staff will not allow discrimination to go unchallenged. We have taken time to make ourselves known at both Patrick's schools, joining in the PTAs and school events as well as getting to know school staff. Paul has also got himself elected as a parent governor. It has helped that Patrick has always had a helper in class because of his statement of educational needs. This has been the person with whom we have had the most direct liaison and it was the current helper who ensured that the year head spoke to the children involved in name calling. One of the children, who had previously been friendly with Patrick, apologised directly to him as a result.

Concluding Comments

We are generally hopeful that with a good solicitor and the backing of Patrick's local authority, both of which we have, we will be successful in our adoption application. This is particularly as it is in line with Patrick's wishes. With the present state of the law, only one of us can adopt but we will also be applying for a joint residence order so that we both have parental responsibility.

The fact that an adoption order was granted to a gay male couple in Scotland in 1996 must be a good precedent with emphasis being placed on the needs of the child. However, it would be reassuring to know if there are any similar cases in England which have managed to avoid publicity.

A final concluding comment that both Paul and myself would like to make is on the general acceptance that we have found. Our experience has been that when faced with the reality of a gay household with children, people are much more ready to accept us on our own terms than the worst tabloids would have you think. We feel that it is now the Clause 28 Tory MPs who are totally 'out of step' with the everyday reality of our experience.

'The Eye of the Storm...'
Barbara's Story

Barbara is a 40-year-old white lesbian who lives in the north of England. She has fostered almost sixty children, at various times, over a period of about 13 years. She has fostered both as a single person and with her ex-partner, with whom she remains in contact. Currently, she has a partner who is not living with her and is not involved with the care of the children. Barbara has worked in the Armed Forces, as an ambulance driver, and is now a freelance Reiki Healer. She has adopted three of her foster sons.

Before fostering, I worked with young people in youth clubs and then I was unemployed. I was interested in fostering but I almost ended up doing it by accident! I went with a friend to a meeting about fostering organised by the social services department in 1983. I didn't think they'd consider me because I didn't think single people could foster, but I ended up getting approved as a foster carer that same year! I started fostering teenagers at the beginning and the first one came for six months. He was called Ian and he came from a children's home. I was approved to care for up to three long-term foster children at any one time. My motivation at that time was that I wanted to offer young people a home until they were able to move on to their own independence.

When I made the application to be a foster carer, I didn't tell them I was a lesbian and it was never talked about, although the social workers were well aware of my sexuality. This was in 1983 and my local authority didn't have any other gay carers then that I knew of. Anyway, if I'd have come out then it would have been a big problem to the authority. As it was, there were no problems with my approval. The social workers did talk to me about my past relationships but I only told them about relationships that I'd had with men.

I had been fostering for about one-and-a-half years when Susan moved in as my partner. We had a new social worker then called Rachael who was aware that we were lesbians. Susan made a separate application to foster short term. This was in 1984, but again nothing was said about our relationship, even though we were living together. I often look back on that and think 'why?', why didn't they discuss it with us?

Although some of my social workers had always known about it, four years ago I came out as a lesbian to the social services department. The social workers just said: 'We already knew!' That was actually very disheartening for me because I'd really worked myself up to telling the social workers and facing them with the truth. The Director just wanted to know if I had faced any prejudice and that was that. But it was a really big issue to me and they all just said: 'fine'! Maybe things are very different now. The authority has four sets of lesbian or gay carers now that I know of.

In 1987 Sean and Matthew came to me as a long-term placement, with the view to their being eventually placed with another family for adoption. About a year later they were still here and we all felt that it would be a good idea for me to adopt them. My approval to adopt them was very quick and the social workers just upgraded my Form F for the adoption panel in 1988.

I adopted Sean and Matthew because it seemed the right thing to do and because they wanted me to. Later on, I adopted another boy, Marcus, who has cerebral palsy. He came to me five years ago as a 'hard-to-place' child. The plans were for him to be adopted but no carers could be found, despite advertising. Marcus was seen as having very great needs and the prognosis for him was very poor. They said he'd never sit up, that he was totally deaf and that he'd never walk. When I said I'd adopt him, the social workers made it very clear to me that I was very lucky to do so because they wouldn't normally allow single people to adopt! They had no other options for Marcus, needless to say. Anyway, we've proved people wrong because he is doing great now. His communication is good, he walks fine and he now attends a mainstream school. He's seven years old now and probably functions educationally at about four years, but he's doing really well.

I asked the social workers to re-approve me again, for various reasons ... because I had come out as openly gay and I was now single again after Susan and I split up, but also because I had adopted three of the boys. But the social workers just said it was too much work to resource. When I went to the adoption panel about the boys I didn't come out and the social workers advised this because of the panel itself! This was in 1988. The only thing that was really checked out was with my referees, who were asked whether the adopted children would be clear that I was their mum. Again, things are different now and someone has gone through the adoption panel as an open lesbian.

The fostering panel were a different story and they have always been very open and welcoming to me. When Susan and I were together and both fostering we were used a lot – we've fostered over 50 children and we took a lot of sibling groups that are very hard to place. These were groups of about three or four children. We did a lot of work to reunite children with their families, bringing sibling groups back together again, preparing children to be adopted and taking children from placement breakdowns. We were a bit like a rescue service! I remember one Christmas we had nine children! They often came in groups of three siblings and so we had to get a minibus! Susan took younger ones and, in 1986, I changed to take short-term placements of children up to eight years old. Susan was approved to take up to three short-term placements up to age eight. I think the hardest thing we had to do was introduce children to their new adoptive parents when they had to move on. We did a lot of this but I always found it hard to see them go and I always worried that no one could look after them like I could!

Susan preferred younger children and babies, but I wasn't into that to begin with as I had always taken older ones. I remember one time when we had to take some premature twins, a boy and a girl, and I was terrified! It was awful and we had to do nightfeeds every two hours between us. But it was incredible and this eventually gave me the confidence to handle babies, so I got used to them. Those twins stayed for about five months and then moved on, mainly because Sean couldn't cope with having them around. I remember another baby boy that we collected straight from hospital who stayed seven months. We did work to reunite his siblings with him in preparation for adoption. We cared for about five newly born babies, at different times, and many more aged up to two years.

After that, we started to take older children and I have always found it easier to take boys – maybe because I grew up in a family of brothers – so I've always taken boys. I was happier taking boys and felt I had more to offer them in terms of experience and things that I was into. But just recently I've taken a brother and sister, Rebecca and Paul. Susan was the one who always dealt with the girls but I was approved for either sex. Now I am approved for one or two long-term placements of boys but Susan and I still do some co-care and we support each other – we live next door to each other!

When I said I wanted to care for boys, the social workers made a thing out of saying I had to provide male role models. Actually, I think that's rubbish because the boys get loads of male influences in many areas of their lives. But the social workers wanted me to name some specific men that I knew. But at the time, all that I was able to say was that I would find them 'godfathers'. The social workers said that they needed to say all this to get me through the fostering panel and so they just said that I was aware of the gender issues and would address it. Otherwise, it's never been a problem with boys and I've never felt uncomfortable with it. Two years ago my fostering review made the decision that I should be approved just for boys, but they've since broken that rule when they placed Rebecca and Paul here. Now some people in social services have been saying: 'Is it appropriate for a lesbian to care for a girl?' and 'Why do you want to care for her?' That is just awful and it makes me sick!

There is a shortage of carers here and social workers still phone me and say: 'we've got so-and-so, can you take them?' and sometimes they do overload me. This is a general problem with all carers who tend to get overloaded with placements and can lead to breakdowns and allegations. I'm involved in supporting other foster carers here and I attend the Fostering Liaison Group (with the Director, Assistant Director, fostering officers, etc) to represent my area (there are three areas). I'm also involved in carers support groups, so that means I'm very involved politically and people come to me if they have allegations made against them. My role is to support the carer against whom allegations have been made and to make sure the process of investigation is fair, whether the allegation is true or not. I've been doing that for eight years and I have been the Vice Chair of the local Fostering Association.

Have there been any problems about my sexuality? One or two social workers have questioned whether it is safe to place children with me and the fostering officer told them that was ridiculous. Some social workers have refused outright to place children with me. Others have just been downright rude and that is just to do with their prejudice – no one has ever said my child care is poor! Many regard me very positively and some social workers actively seek to place children with me or Susan.

I have had an allegation of sexual abuse made against me by a doctor but it was dropped when he found out I was gay. He said that a boy in my care had been sexually assaulted but he withdrew the allegation at a case conference when he said that the evidence was of penetration by an adult male penis. As it turned out, there was no evidence anyway but the whole thing was awful. No one supported me and it made me question everything about my care of children. I know how people feel when they have allegations made against them.

I've also had a problem recently with a principal fostering/adoption officer who was recruiting people to assess carers for NVQ (National Vocational Qualification) awards. I said that I'd like to be an assessor for the scheme and she said: 'you do realise that it's a sensitive thing going into people's homes to assess them'. She wouldn't openly say that she had a problem with my being a lesbian but I think that's what it was.

I've also been doing training for foster carers, especially around protecting children who have been sexually abused. We used videos and case studies, one of which was about a boy who had been systematically abused and was questioning his sexuality. There was so much homophobia from foster carers on the course, which really hurt me personally because they all know me and they must know I'm gay. Also, it's very worrying because they're caring for teenagers. We referred the issue to the department and their response was to drop me from doing the training! The training is now done by a fostering officer and one of the male carers who was so homophobic! The issue just has not been dealt with. The department deals with all other child protection issues but not gay ones. Also, my carers support group has got five gay people in it, but this is never mentioned!

I came out to my boys four years ago. I felt it was probably obvious to them but also there were some issues to do with school, so I decided to tell them I was gay. We just had a normal discussion about it and about sexuality generally. One of the boys said that children at school had been saying that I was gay but he didn't tell me because he didn't want to upset me. There's never really been any trouble at schools about it but I remember the first day that Sean went to high school and one child said: 'your mum must have a lot of sex to have all those children'! Matthew was also at that school and I was worried that he might use the fact that I'm gay to get at Sean, so I went to see the school bursar to explain about myself. From that point on Sean's teacher refused to make eye contact with me and he stopped communicating with me. I remember when they did sex education in Personal and Social Education and they discussed homosexuality in detail and Sean got distressed. I went to try and talk to the school about how to be sensitive about it but they wouldn't discuss it with me and just said: 'is there a problem at home?'

The primary school is very different. It's Church of England and I went to see the Head to explain that I was gay. He was fine and said thanks for letting them know. They're very supportive and the Head has actually helped me deal with some of the personal stuff that affects the boys. That school has taken all my kids and they even have a 'carers day' instead of 'mother's day' for my children and they ask me how to approach stuff about 'the family'. That's great! The boys themselves don't say that much to their friends about me being gay and they deal with it themselves in their own way. One has chosen to say: 'My mum is divorced'.

My fostering placement worker has just retired and they've just left me to get on with it! That's not very good really because they still give me loads of kids to care for. I will speak up when I need help but that's not the point really. When I asked for my re-approval, which, as I said, never happened, the social worker talked about what would happen if I got another partner in the future. She said it was just for information and she said: 'if I'm being too personal let me know!' and that was fine. That social worker has had three gay carers so she's used to it!

I do have a partner now but she's not involved with the care of the children so I'm still registered as a single carer. As a single carer it can be hard because you don't get so much support. I had a support worker and social worker and some friends who were also fostering, but they were all in couples. I never went to a support group and I had no idea there were groups for gay carers. I certainly wasn't keen on the idea of going to a support group that was all heterosexuals and me! When I found out about the northern support group it was great. I read about it in the gay press and I really enjoy going. It's nice to meet other gay carers and some of us have been away on holiday together with all the kids, which was good fun. Also, it's nice to get out of my local area and meet up with others and talk about the problems and the good times.

Why do I foster? I just do it because I love the kids to bits. I'd have hundreds if I could! And if you get a social worker who is prepared to work with you, we can do marvels really, whatever the children's problems. We've been able to get some kids far more accepted by their peers, even despite them having huge emotional problems. And, sometimes, the problems have been huge! I have had to deal with some very difficult and, sometimes, violent behaviour and, at times, the house has been in turmoil. There's a saying isn't there about 'the eye of the storm', which is the really calm part amongst all the chaos and destruction. It's the centre that holds everything together, that drives the whole thing, and that's what I feel like sometimes.

'..."No one ever learned us"...'
Dfiza and Anne's Story

Dfiza and Anne are a lesbian couple who live in the north of England. Dfiza is black African and Anne is white Irish and they have been together for fourteen years. They are adopting two African Caribbean mixed-race sisters, Carla and Tanya, and also co-parent Elliot and Ella, a brother and sister of African heritage who lived with them for six years and now live mostly with their birth parents and partly with Dfiza and Anne.

We first thought about adoption years ago, even when we were trying to have a birth child. Dfiza had always thought about adopting. As a child, her parents had considered it and since then she had always wanted to adopt a black child because she knew there was a shortage of black adopters. Anne had never thought about adoption before but she had always loved children and she herself had come from a very big family.

The first time we did anything about it was when Dfiza went down to an 'adoption shop' when we were living in London. The woman who worked there insisted that we would be ideal for teenagers and she wouldn't listen to anything about younger children. We decided to drop it for a while. It felt hard to push things, even though it was what we wanted. We knew that being lesbians didn't make it easy. We eventually contacted another borough by phone but when we told the social worker we were a lesbian couple she told us not to tell anyone and one of us should go forward as a single person!

The next contact we made was with another city. We saw a black child with Downs Syndrome advertised and when we contacted the agency they sent for us immediately to come and meet the child, although we weren't even approved. The foster parents she had been with from birth brought her to the office. This was about eight years ago and she was about eighteen months old then. They said they had to start our assessment. They visited us in London a couple of times and then contacted our local social services. The local social services sent two social workers to visit us and it just felt like they'd come to look at the freaks – there was no purpose to the visit, they didn't do anything. After that we never heard anything more. We kept writing to the agency responsible for the child but the worker who first contacted us had gone off on maternity leave.

Around this time we were asked to take Elliot by his birth mother, a relative of Dfiza's who had gone back to work full time. He came to us when he was four months old and his birth parents led us to believe that it was intended to be for life. But in the traditions of that part of Africa you never give up your child, so it was never formalised and there was always the possibility hanging over us that his birth parents would take him back. They said originally that they wanted to see him once a year but we made sure they saw him on average once every three weeks because we thought if they ever decided they wanted him back we wanted him to know them. We moved north and, twelve months later, they had another baby, Ella, and she also came to us when she was four months old. They stayed with us until Elliot was six and Ella was five and then their birth parents took them back, but they still come to us every school holiday and we're very strong about them still belonging to this family.

It was an enormous shock to us that they wanted the kids to live with them in London. We gritted our teeth and encouraged the kids to see their move as a positive experience. We went all out to stay with them in London and gave them extra reassurance and support. It was a difficult time but after a few months they settled into a new school and life there. They live with us all school holidays and whenever possible on top of that. The two of them are at home in both their homes and adjust to each with confident ease.

After we got Elliot we still wanted to adopt. About a year later we got a letter from the agency placing the Downs child telling us they had decided not to place her with us. They gave three reasons: one, we were living in a white area; two, the child has Mosaic Downs Syndrome which means she has the appearance of a Downs child but no other symptoms and was reaching all her developmental milestones, so to put her with a lesbian couple would further disadvantage her; and, three, because she was really quite dark and as we were a mixed-race couple it would not be appropriate. She actually looked as if she were African and Asian mixed race. We had a similar response later on from other adoption agencies who implied that we would not be considered for black children who were not mixed-race because we're a mixed-race couple. We wrote a strong letter back, arguing with all these points. By this time she was three and the white family she had been with from birth wanted to adopt her. The social workers told the family they were getting too attached and moved her to another white couple. They still haven't placed her permanently, even though we would have adopted her years ago.

We contacted the local adoption agency when we moved up here and a man came to see us and said it wouldn't take long to assess us. He never got back to us. We rang up a few times but it just felt like no one was interested in us. Then, four years ago, we went to the LAGFAPN conference in Manchester and after that a social worker friend, Jean, kept saying to us: 'You should apply, they'll snap you up'. Then, the summer before last, we decided let's get on with it. We first contacted one of our local authorities and they just seemed out of the ark, so we went to an authority in a big city. The original agency contacted us later pleading with us to go to them because they wanted to make us a test case, they'd never approved any lesbians before. But we didn't want to be a test case so we stuck with the city authority, where we also felt we were more likely to have black kids placed with us.

The six-week preparation course was really enjoyable. There was a very friendly and supportive atmosphere. There were about forty people in the group – black and white, single carers, couples, some who had their own kids, most without, a disabled person and no other gay people that we were aware of. There were three social workers running it for three hours a night, one night a week, for six weeks and you couldn't fault them on anything, it was all inclusive.

Not long after that they came to do our assessment. Anne was working temporarily in London at the time so she took a week's leave and they did our assessment in a week. They gave us the Form F to fill in beforehand. Anne wrote nineteen sides of A4 and Dfiza wrote nine. The social worker said that this made her job a million times easier because normally it was like trying to get blood from a stone getting people to write anything down for these questions, which are mostly about how you feel about things. It was a really nice week. Doing the form was quite cathartic, like, for Anne, her father had died a couple of years before and it made her think things about him that she hadn't thought about properly before. We were quite amazed at what a positive experience it was and how we never felt any hint of homophobia or prejudice throughout the whole experience of assessment.

They approved us to adopt up to four children aged seven and under. Very shortly after we'd been approved, they rang up and said they knew we wanted black children but would we take these four white boys? We said no. It felt a bit insensitive – they make out there's this desperate need for black carers and Dfiza being black and Elliot and Ella here for more than three months of the year and they're asking us to take four white children. They wouldn't tell us if they were considering any children for us until they had actually picked some out for us, so we were left hearing nothing for months. We kept ringing and they wouldn't say, which was very frustrating because we are adults and we can take disappointment if something falls through. Dfiza went down to London and an authority there came up with lots of possibilities and kept ringing us up but we felt we should wait a bit longer for our own authority to come up with something. It's quite an emotional business. You can't help feeling bad turning them down, even those four white boys, and wondering what will happen to them.

We phoned various agencies about children we saw in the adoption magazines. We always told them we were lesbians and there was always some excuse why they wouldn't consider us. There was one case of a brother and sister in separate foster homes who they wanted to be adopted together. When we offered to adopt them they said they wanted a straight couple. Now the older one has appeared in the adoption paper again, alone, and it says he needs to be in contact with his younger sibling who has already been placed for adoption, so they've ended up placing them separately, even though we were offering them a home together.

About four months after we were approved we were contacted about Carla and Tanya, who are African Caribbean mixed-race sisters. They have had many moves and, therefore, had many behavioural problems. Their social worker said that they had considered quite a few heterosexual couples for them but when she read our Form F she knew we would be perfect for them, partly because they had been cared for by lesbians before and also because the girls had such strong personalities that they needed two strong people who would take equal responsibility for them. We do work well together and we have our experience with other children to help us.

The introductions were supposed to be really quick. We made a photograph album for them all about ourselves and that was good for them. The first few meetings went well. Then they came to stay overnight and the next day the social worker phoned to say that the foster family were very distressed about them leaving and could we come to a meeting. A meeting was held in the foster home, in front of the children, at which the foster mother said that she had been crying all night and she couldn't sleep and couldn't bear the thought of them going. She told a story about when she had been in foster care herself and had been taken away from a foster mother she really loved and put somewhere she hated and how she had run away from the next place. The children were sitting there listening to all this. The social worker said that it had been decided that we should go a bit slower and asked the foster carer to explain this to the children, so she said to them: 'You know you said you don't want to go to Dfiza and Anne, well you don't have to go yet, you can tell us when you're ready to go', which was totally inappropriate, they were only five and six. We were absolutely livid but we couldn't say anything in front of the children so we rang up our social worker and said that it wasn't on. They arranged another meeting with our social worker, the children's social worker, the foster carer and her social worker and it was decided that we should go ahead as quickly as possible. That foster carer had only cared for the girls for two months and obviously had her own agenda and problems.

After that, they were terrible with us. The foster carer really put a lot of emotional pressure on them to be loyal to her. The way she was with them made it feel like a death had happened in that family. It was extremely hard and when they came here they talked about her constantly, wanted to ring her all the time and ran down the road shouting her name. She gave them no support whatsoever in their move. Her behaviour was not how foster carers usually act, especially as they had lived there for such a short time and she knew it was a pre-adoptive placement.

The first six or seven weeks were so unbelievably difficult. We used to wake up in the morning and our hearts would plunge. We used to think: 'what on earth are we doing?' They were really acting up and threatening to harm themselves. They're very strong personalities and they were quite horrible to each other as well as towards us. In the end, we really came down on them like a ton of bricks, stopped doing anything except a really strict routine, stopped any cheekiness and tried to establish very clear boundaries. We had to take control for them as they were so out of control. The whole thing just turned around, they just blossomed, it was amazing. We don't put up with anything and it's worked and they're happy. The firmer we are, the more they like us and they treat each other much better. They did try to set us against each other but they do it less and less because we work really well together. Often, when we tell them something, they say: 'It's not our fault, no one ever learned us this'. They're learning really quickly, they're lovely kids.

They've lived with us for sixteen months now and are much more settled with us and at school. Elliot and Ella were with us for Christmas and we all had a wonderful holiday. As time goes by we are all beginning to see the funnier side to things. We are building on all their coping skills for life. It is hard, challenging work, but well worth it.

It's a real backwater round here, which does make us a bit paranoid about being lesbians sometimes. But we feel quite strongly that our sexuality is no one else's business. We always told people that Elliot and Ella were ours but we didn't go about in the community labelling ourselves as lesbians. If people put two and two together, that's fine. We're nice to everyone and people are nice to us. We always talk about 'our' kids and people make of it what they want. We don't know what they say about us behind our backs.

They didn't give us a choice about who would be the named adopter when it goes to court. They say it has to be Dfiza as the black parent. We'd already decided that ourselves and we don't tell people who the adopter is anyway. We say we're both adopting them and we will be doing a joint residence order at the same time as the adoption. We are getting an adoption allowance now. They put us on a fostering allowance to begin with because Anne was a student and not getting any money for a while.

The past sixteen months have been totally rewarding, positive and *draining*! The girls have come on in leaps and bounds. It feels like nothing could have prepared us for the reality of adoption in terms of the reality of giving two very vulnerable, damaged children a permanent loving secure family. We've all still got a long way to go but it feels like we're over the worst.

Postscript: November 1997

We had decided we would like a younger brother or sister for the four kids and we saw a mixed-race baby with Downs Syndrome advertised for adoption. We made enquiries and the social workers took us on as prospective adopters. He was attached to an outer-London borough and when our case went to panel we were the first lesbian couple they had had to assess. They were very homophobic but our social worker did an admirable job in convincing them that our sexuality was irrelevant as we met the child's needs on all levels. We were approved and he joined our family two months ago and is settling in very well. The other kids think he is truly wonderful (as we do) and we can't believe our luck.

For Carla and Tanya, his presence has given them a further sense of permanency and has taken out some of the intensity of their relationship. Having a baby of their own is helping them make some connections to their lost past.

For us, having these children in our lives is such a powerful, positive experience. We have chosen them and it is like it is meant to be and we love them all unconditionally and dearly. It is, and has been, hard work, but we wouldn't be without them.

'Caring Across the Spectrum'
Mark and Paul's Story

Mark and Paul are white gay men who have been together for ten years and live in a three-bedroom terraced house in south-east London. Both work full time and are employed in the caring professions. Mark is a senior social worker, working as a counsellor in an adolescent counselling project and as the co-ordinator of a sexual health project for young people. Paul is a support worker in a residential establishment for adults with learning disabilities. They decided to foster eight years ago and were approved by one inner-London council for the care of children and by another council for adults with learning disabilities. Altogether, they have had eight placements, of both adults and children, and these have varied in length and time. John, a 28-year-old man with moderate learning difficulties, has been with them for seven years. Mark tells their story.

We met at a youth club for people with learning difficulties, where we both worked. Both of us had always had a special interest in working with young people and had also been involved in playschemes and after-school clubs. I was keen to foster and Paul agreed it would be a good idea and once we started living together we actually moved house to accommodate those we wanted to look after. We felt that we wanted to offer our services as a foster placement that wasn't seen as a traditional family unit, since many young people or children in care have difficulties with traditional family units and often want a break from these. We also felt that we could offer a good placement to a young person which would be supportive and consistent with their individual needs and demands.

Both our sets of parents supported the placements in their own way but Paul's sexual identity was never openly discussed with his family. I was able to discuss being gay with my family but they did not approve of my lifestyle. My family come from a Christian background, my mum being Church of England and my dad Roman Catholic, and I think this affects how they feel. Most of our support has come from each other and our friends in the gay community. Neighbours have helped out from time to time as well.

Our original assessment as carers was initially delayed due to the worker wanting a gay colleague to carry out the assessment with him. However, once this was sorted out we were approved as foster carers. Later, we decided that we wanted to care for adults with learning disabilities too and so we had to be assessed for that as well. We made this decision because one of the young men we had cared for, Robert, went back home but needed to continue coming to us for respite care. When he became an adult, we wanted to offer him a continuity of care. We both have a commitment to seeing people move on into independence and we didn't want to 'drop' Robert just because he was no longer a young person.

So we went through assessments to care for adults as well as children. This was very confusing for us because we had to keep getting to know new social workers! However, this also created some problems because the fostering and adoption unit that had approved us to care for young people said that it was not their policy to allow carers looking after children to have dependent adults in the home as well. They had to check that the adults for whom we were caring did not have any offences against children and made it clear that they weren't happy with this. One social worker, who was very religious and also homophobic, came round to do our regular review and told us that they were going to deregister us as the carers of young people. We were upset by this and pointed out that when the young people became adults we wanted to continue to offer them care and help them move on into independent living. We made an official complaint about the attempt to deregister us, saying that social services should reconsider their policy. The complaint took two-and-a-half years to investigate but found in our favour. The local authority changed their policy to allow us to care for both adults and children.

We now have three link workers from different sections supporting us – one from adult care, one from the adult respite service and one from fostering. At times, this gets confusing and the social workers can be unclear about where we should draw our support from. We are also approved by the Albert Kennedy Trust, which is a voluntary organisation that places homeless young lesbians and gay men with adult lesbian or gay carers. However, we are only approved for three placements in all and we are currently full!

James, who was in his forties, was our first placement. He was an adult with learning disabilities and he had stomach cancer. He used to live independently in his own home but his condition and care needs increased and he was unable to remain at home. He did not want to move into a hospice and so he came to live with us with the support of community nursing. He had special dietary needs which involved liquidizing his food and he needed to take morphine on a regular basis to alleviate some of his pain. The level of medicine he required increased as the placement went on and his condition degenerated until, eventually, he needed to be admitted into a hospice. He wanted to come home for weekends with us but, unfortunately, due to his condition, it was not possible. He died approximately two weeks after being admitted.

Paul and I felt relieved that James had only spent a limited amount of time in the hospice and was able to remain with us in the community as he had wished. James was a very religious man and this brought us face to face with various religious contacts. Because he was unable to go out to various churches, the churches came to him in our home. We remember one Christmas Eve having a house full of people in our living room holding a service for James, which he appreciated greatly. James' funeral left from our house, as James had wanted it to, and we had the opportunity to meet some of James' extended family that we had not met before.

Peter, a boy of 14 years of age who had Laurence Moon Bardet-Biedle syndrome, came to us as a short-term placement but stayed long term. He is now aged 19. He was born with the syndrome but it was only discovered and recognised relatively recently. There is a support group for carers of people with the syndrome and Paul and I are members of it. Peter has suffered from liver and kidney problems from birth. He is overweight and has a compulsive eating disorder. He also has retinitis pigmentosa which means that his retina are slow in adjusting to changes in light, hence he is almost blind in the mornings when the sun rises and late afternoon when it sets. The syndrome is a degenerative condition and Peter's percentage of sight loss per year is high. He is registered as blind and now resides at an attached annexe to a Royal National Institute for the Blind college where he can stay indefinitely. He is delayed in his sexual development and the possibility is that he will not reach full maturity. He can often be hyperactive and aggressive, rude and obstinate if not set firm boundaries about bedtimes and dietary restrictions.

Peter is still in contact with us and stays one weekend a month. At the beginning he presented a real challenge to us and required constant care. He often displayed difficult and disruptive behaviour in the early days but is now able to control his behaviour at home. I think really that we gave Peter our attention and time and were willing to listen and talk to him, all of which he had not had before. Peter listens to people who have genuine time for him, otherwise he can be rude and obstinate. Schooling for Peter was a major problem in the early days and taking him on holiday could be quite stressful due to his requiring 24-hour attention. On his first day at school Peter told his teacher that his two foster dads were sleeping together. The school informed social services, who confirmed the fact that Peter's carers were gay!

As you can imagine, his disability affects Peter greatly in a variety of situations and individual circumstances. He has reached adolescence, which has brought another area to the forefront of his care. Peter wants to be doing things that other adolescents do, like staying out late, going to the pub and generally enjoying himself. However, his condition limits some of these activities, which Peter is struggling to come to terms with. His weight has increased greatly in the past few months due to alcohol consumption and Paul and I are particularly concerned about the effect this will have on his health and life expectancy. However, we have shared our feelings with Peter but he is still struggling greatly with this dilemma.

John, who is now 28, has moderate learning difficulties and has been with us full-time for seven years. Like Peter, he also has retinitis pigmentosa. John had been living by himself in a flat in the community but he was abused by a man from the local area. The man used to tie John up and would only free him to allow him to draw his benefits, which he then kept. Eventually, this was discovered, but it made John very nervous and frightened of living alone. He came to us on a short-term basis but decided he wanted to stay. We've worked with him so that he can wash, cook and clean for himself, but he is still very frightened by his experiences. John works in a garden centre and, sometimes, at a supermarket. He keeps in contact with his Mum and there is a court protection order on him to safeguard his money. He knows that we are gay and he is okay about it, but he would not feel comfortable coming to a gay bar with us. John buys pornography, which he is into. We've talked to him about this and we've had debates with him about how degrading it is to women. Our attitude in the house is that he has to keep it to himself.

Each year we go on holiday to Gran Canaria and whoever is placed with us at the time is very welcome to come with us. Roles are shared at home and both of us teach those living with us to be self-sufficient and independent. I was seen by Peter as more authoritarian and I do tend to be more organised than Paul. Paul is more spontaneous and is more flexible around some things than me – like chores in the house, for example. I try to set very firm boundaries and expectations, which I see as very important, whereas Paul is far more laid-back and doesn't take it so seriously.

Most people who come to live with us are aware that we are gay, although Peter was not informed until he arrived! One man in his thirties only stayed two nights because he was afraid of being sexually attacked by us. He had been told about our sexuality but the more he thought about it the more uncomfortable he felt. He therefore decided to leave and we really feel that the social workers should have spent more time preparing him for the placement.

Generally, it has been a struggle to go through the bureaucracy of assessment and approval as carers but, once through, it has been an enjoyable and challenging experience. We feel the positives have outweighed the difficulties. I strongly feel that if you are not happy about something, it is better to say so as professionals are not always right, in our experience. It has been an advantage for me to be working in a social services setting and to know how things operate. This made it far easier for us to stand up to social services and to complain when we felt we were being unjustly treated. I can imagine that for others, who are not used to the system, this would be just too daunting and they might just give up.

We have experienced an allegation being made about us but we did feel fully supported by the social workers. The allegation was made against Paul by an adult, who said that he had touched him inappropriately. In fact, Paul had just given him a hug but he made an allegation that someone had touched him. Initially, he didn't say who, and so everyone, including the social workers, was under suspicion. There was great relief from many people, including myself, when it emerged that the allegation was about Paul, but that was very hard for Paul. It was thoroughly investigated by the social workers, who talked to the man and to us, and was found to be false. We felt that it was quickly dealt with in a professional manner.

The authority that investigated the allegation have recently made a new placement with us, a fifteen-and-a-half-year-old called Michael, who needed to be placed on an urgent basis. He was living at home with his mother and stepfather but felt unable to live there any longer and wanted to go and live with his father and stepmother, with whom he was in regular contact. However, social services needed to complete an assessment before this possibility could be properly considered and it would appear that, due to a variety of reasons, it is not appropriate for Michael to live with his father. We are near to Michael's father's home and Michael can visit as he wishes and can still have a home base with us. Michael attends mainstream secondary school and does not have a learning disability. He is chatty and very interested in doing things outside and inside of the home with and without Paul and I. He is particularly into animals and brought with him two gerbils and a budgerigar. He has asked us if it would be possible to have a rat, something which we are currently in negotiations about!

Michael was told about us being gay but he has never had a problem with this. He is very into sport and he said to the social workers: 'Well, it's like this, some people like football and others like tennis. I like football but I know they won't force me to like tennis'. He sees it as just different. He's never used it against us, even in anger, which is often when these things come out. Michael's social worker has asked us whether we would be able to care for him on a long-term basis until he is eighteen years old. Paul and I have discussed this with each other and feel that we would very much like Michael to stay with us. However, for some reason we did feel that there was some hesitation from the local authority unit about making the decision to place him with us.

When we took Michael in, it had been nearly two-and-a-half years since our last placement and so we are enjoying his stay with us. We enjoy the experience of looking after somebody and, at the same time, encouraging them to be independent and take responsibility for their own actions. We like to offer people care until they reach what they feel is their independence, so in that sense we are caring across the spectrum of ages, of abilities, and of need.

Postscript: September 1997

We continue to care for Peter (now 20) on a respite basis, Michael (now 16) on a full-time fostering basis and John (now 28) full time.

'Single Black Lesbian'
Olivette's Story

Olivette is a forty-something-year-old black lesbian who lives in London. She has two children, Emil aged eleven and Louise aged eight. Louise was placed with Olivette for adoption when she was two.

I decided to write this for a variety of reasons but largely because I know I have two loveable, delightful, determined, individual and, sometimes, difficult children who have given me much joy and also because I think that if people are considering adoption and want to weigh up the pros and cons, perhaps this will assist them. Let me say from the onset that as a lesbian I am still pro-adoption and pro-being 'out' – though it is not always plain sailing.

I knew I wanted to have children when I was in my teens; the why is debatable, the how was almost unthinkable, but that is what I wanted. I wasn't thinking about having a child when I was young, given the prejudices that were around then and still exist now in relation to lesbians and gay men caring for children. I thought it would be much better if I had something behind me first so that there was less room for criticism. I discussed it with my mother and my first option was adoption. I applied to adopt in my late twenties. I was already a confirmed lesbian but, given the prejudices and my perception of the difficulties I was likely to encounter, I decided to pretend to be straight! It was a nightmare!! I was assessed by someone who was homophobic. During the assessment he was clear that the one thing he did not want to know or find out was that I was a lesbian. This appeared to be part of his prepared speech and he went on to talk about sodomy and how it is unlawful in biblical terms and referred to lesbians and gay men in a derogatory manner. I still managed to get through the assessment process and was approved by the adoption panel. I had contact visits with the young person I was going to adopt and everything seemed to go quite well. The weekend before she was due to be placed with me I was told it was no longer going to be possible because the young person in question needed more preparation. I was totally devastated.

Following that experience I decided to conceive – something which I had never wanted to do. I had neither the desire nor the inclination and I also knew there were lots of children waiting to be adopted whom I could provide a home to, but, having gone through the experience of being assessed, pretending to be 'straight', looking over my shoulder and feeling very anxious if I went to a gay club or bar, I decided I had to do things differently. Artificial insemination was my next choice, although my mother was not at all keen on this option. Given that I knew my mother would play a large part in my child's life, I paid some attention to her views, although I went ahead anyway. I went to consultations at BPAS (British Pregnancy Advisory Service) along with a friend at the time. My friend conceived and I did not so I decided it was not meant to be. I finally conceived after a lot of angst in a process which I consider was 'stage-managed' and I had a beautiful son.

I never intended to have only one child and if I had been rich and with a committed partner, I would have liked half a dozen children, but this was not the case so I decided to go for adoption again but this time not pretending to be straight. One of the things that spurred me on to apply to adopt at the time I did was that the political climate was such that some boroughs were being proactive in encouraging lesbians and gay men to foster and adopt. I approached one of these boroughs and attended a preparatory group prior to being assessed. Having worked as a social worker in a fostering and adoption unit, I felt I was in a strong position as I knew the general criteria that were required of prospective adoptive parents and felt I met those with ease. I had also assessed prospective adoptive carers in the past and so did not feel at all phased by the assessment. Incidentally, the young woman who assessed me had never carried out an assessment before.

Ultimately, I went to a borough where there were lesbian-friendly staff and so the initial processes were much easier and smoother than others have encountered. The main difficulties I experienced were around the politics, with councillors being over-anxious and staff at a managerial level not fully understanding the issues and thus over-reacting. Another difficult area is to do with which children are placed with lesbians and gay men – they are largely children who have difficulties that a heterosexual couple may not care to deal with.

I was offered a child who was aged one year and nine months. However, I had heard of her when she was six months old. A heterosexual couple were considered for her and it was only after they decided to withdraw that I was considered. After introductory visits with both myself and my son, and preparing the little girl who is now my daughter for a move at a particular date, this all changed at the last minute because the hierarchy felt they needed directions and guidance. Whatever they felt, I believe the truth is they were anxious and did not want any bad press so delayed the move by going back to the courts, which was unnecessary. At the time, another local authority had been blazoned across the press for 'allowing' two gay men to foster. Fortunately for us, the courts felt there were no reasons to delay the placement and I had my daughter approximately two months later.

My daughter was adopted approximately two-and-a-half years from the date of her placement. This took much longer than was necessary because of councillors and officers being over-cautious and debates around the birth mother's 'need' to know that I was a lesbian. I had an excellent solicitor who was well versed in these matters, which made it much easier for me. I also had a great deal of support, both practical and emotional, from family and friends, which was a tremendous help and it was a great relief when the adoption order was finally granted.

In the fostering and adoption process there are many facets that need to be considered. In most instances you will have a social worker assigned to the foster carer or prospective adoptive parent and a separate social worker assigned to a particular child or family. The attitude of the workers is crucial because if they are homophobic, it makes it extremely difficult for the assessment process to proceed in a fair and balanced way. If there is a homophobic manager, this can also hamper the process as a worker will be taking the questions and queries, as well as the draft report, to the manager for discussion and approval. Some authorities have policies which state that anyone can be assessed, but these are sabotaged by those carrying out the assessments or by their line managers.

The practice of placing 'hard to place' or 'difficult' children with lesbians and gay men has been going on for years and that is what happened in my case. Before lesbians and gay men were coming forward as prospective carers in larger numbers, there were those who quietly applied and were given children who had severe mental or physical disabilities. For those of us who have wanted a child regardless, we have gone on to accept who we have been given, despite the fact we might be faced with severe difficulties. I feel the reason for this is that once we have got through all the hurdles, it is a 'sigh of relief' and even, perhaps, euphoria that we have been approved. To then be offered a child with a view to them being placed with us, something which we have perhaps waited a long time for, is something we gladly accept.

There does seem to be a pecking order of the 'deserving' and 'not so deserving' and, in my experience, it is rare to find a very young child or baby placed with lesbians or gay men. I attended a conference a few years ago organised by a fostering and adoption agency. During the day, one of the participants asked if I knew of any carers for a six-month-old black child. She told me she was having difficulties finding a placement and then went on to say that she wanted a mother and a father because she wanted the mother to be at home and the only people who had come forward had been single parents or working mothers. In this instance a lesbian or a gay man would have totally been out of the question.

When my daughter was six months old there was a couple who were earmarked to adopt her. I was later told that they decided not to pursue it because, amongst other reasons, she had a very obvious squint. When I was in the preparation group I was told there was a black baby girl of six months who was available for adoption. I ended up having the same young girl when she was just over two years old. When my daughter was placed with me, I realised that she was extremely behind for her age and, after asking for her to be assessed, it transpired that she had moderate learning difficulties. I have to ask the question that, no doubt, many other lesbians and gay men have asked: If there are such anxieties around our sexuality and we are considered to be inferior or second-class citizens, why place children who need extra special care and attention with us? I would like to believe that it is because social workers feel we may empathise more because of our own experiences of being treated differently. However, I wonder if that is really the case or are we seen as the last resort?

Society's attitude to lesbians and gay men has changed over the past few years and, this is due, I believe, to several factors, particularly the persistent challenging by direct-action groups and pressure groups – Outrage! and Stonewall, to name but two. Political activism by lesbians and gay men has put the issue on the agenda. Specific issues have received widespread coverage by the media – for example, partnership rights and lesbians and gay men in the armed forces. Socialists have often joined with lesbians and gay men on issues of human rights. However, when it comes to parenting issues, homophobia is rife. I have heard childcare workers state quite categorically that they would not place children with gay men and I know that when it comes to assessments there seems to be a bias on sex and relationships. Given that professionals have such a negative attitude, it is no wonder that when a poll was undertaken recently by *Panorama* to elicit the views of the public on various issues, the majority of the sample were against lesbians and gay men fostering and adopting[1]. In the chat shows, again, the homophobia around parenting rears its ugly head and arguments that perpetuate homophobia are constantly used.

1   BBC 1 *Panorama* (1997) 'Gay Times', in which a telephone survey found that 64% of respondents did not support lesbians and gay men having equality of opportunity in the

I believe that on the whole lesbians and gay men are quietly getting on with parenting their children, whether fostered, biological or adopted, and I know that, like others, I look to my family and friends for support, as opposed to agencies. I have been involved with the Stonewall lesbian and gay parenting group and it has renewed my faith in people to a large extent. It is heartening to see children running around playing with each other, squabbling with each other and having fun in a lesbian and gay environment. My one regret is there are not more forums where children of lesbian and gay parents can meet, talk and have a bit of fun without the fear of being pathologised or victimised.

I would say that my experience of adopting was, ultimately, a positive one, although there were several issues that came up initially because of homophobia, including over-emphasis on sex and intimate relationships, anxieties around the birth mother and her views in relation to my sexuality and pandering to the whims and fancies of the press by, perhaps unwittingly, allowing them to dictate at what point a child can be placed with a lesbian or gay man.

I am happy with my daughter and she is very much a part of the family, not just my biological family but the extended lesbian and gay 'family'. There are issues around her having learning difficulties and she attends a special school where there are various 'professionals' involved. Somewhere in the reams of paperwork it is written that I am a 'homosexual'! There is sibling rivalry and, often, other children without learning difficulties find it hard to understand that there are certain things that, at this stage, my daughter cannot do. This is frustrating for her and, no doubt, for the other children as well.

I would say to anyone thinking of fostering or adopting: Don't be thwarted by initial negative responses. If one agency does not respond to you, write back and question them, challenge them and take it further. At the same time, apply to other agencies. There are people who may attempt to undermine you or question your motives. Once you are clear about what you want, hold your ground. Speak to others who have fostered or adopted, ask questions, talk through the assessment process. Be realistic. It is unlikely that, in the current climate, prospective lesbian and gay carers will get babies if they are looking for long-term/adoptive placements, though black carers are more likely to be offered younger children because, statistically, there are more younger black children available.

To conclude, there are battles to be fought and obstacles along the way but, ultimately, if you have love, warmth and security to offer a child, it is worth going through the process. As a black lesbian I have experienced lots of prejudice, discrimination and obstacles. I experienced discrimination at school, in the further and higher education systems and in the workplace.

Furthermore, there are many people who are homophobic and this became more apparent to me as I 'came out' in different circles. I had friends – or people I considered friends at the time – who stopped talking to me once they realised I was a lesbian. I have also found that some people find it hard to understand that lesbians and gay men would like to have children and others truly feel that we are undeserving and should definitely not have children.

Having gone through these experiences, I was prepared for anything. So, for me, the process was relatively painless overall. I would not only encourage others to go ahead but would offer any support I am able to as I believe lesbians and gay men can and do provide excellent care to children and young people. I feel it is important for us to be positive about ourselves, our parenting skills and what we have to offer children and young people and, ultimately, for this to be encouraged by childcare agencies.

'The Impossible Dream'
Sarah and Christine's Story

Sarah and Christine are two white lesbians who live in London. In 1993, after a five-year search and wait, they finally had four sisters aged between five and nine placed with them for adoption. Now they live with three of the girls in a large house with a cat. They are currently waiting to adopt.

Introduction

Sarah: We came to parenting in very different ways. I was heterosexual when I was younger and very much involved with campaigning for women's reproductive rights, but bringing up children myself didn't ever seem much of an issue. In fact, ironically, I only started thinking about parenting when I had my first serious relationship with a woman. We discussed the possibility of me having a child and her supporting me. I don't think she was very into kids but she would have gone along with me. When I met Christine, it was pre-Clause 28 and lesbian parenting seemed very possible. Fairly soon after, both of us were expressing interest in having kids and it was not too long before we were thinking seriously about adoption. When I realised it might really be possible for lesbians to adopt, I felt I would rather adopt a sibling group than bring a single child into the world. I also felt, as an only child myself, that I wanted a sibling group.

Christine: When I was heterosexual, I'd always assumed I would have children. In a reverse to Sarah's situation, when I became a lesbian, I found that parenting went on the back burner to a certain extent, although when one of my straight women friends said: 'well, you can't have your cake and eat it' – in other words, you can't be a lesbian *and* have children – I was incensed, which suggests that it must have been something of an issue for me even then. Later, I got involved in a group that did work around lesbian parenting issues, including lesbian fostering and adoption. That was something of a spark for me. When I met Sarah, we talked about having children and then I said to her that I'd decided to adopt a child. At first I thought of adopting on my own, but Sarah said that she was interested too, so we decided to try together. That's how it all started.

Once we'd finally made the decision to adopt, we kept it pretty much to ourselves. Those people we did tell were fairly relaxed about it, but perhaps they didn't really believe it would happen. Even when the process eventually did get underway, people never really believed that we would get children – it took so long, they probably felt justified feeling that way. As far as we know, when we applied, there were no out lesbians who had adopted. We started off in October 1988 by listing various agencies we thought would be likely to take us on, dividing them between us and phoning them up, which gave us a list of 'no's' and 'probably not's'. The tone was frequently off-hand and, sometimes, very negative. On one occasion we were even told that unless we were married there was nothing they could do for us, which seemed a rather bizarre suggestion to make to two lesbians. Surprisingly, some of the places which we knew had a positive fostering and adoption policy for lesbians and gays were equally off-hand. One authority, however, was more positive and invited us along to a pre-placement group and, although the information on offer was mostly about babies, which wasn't all that much help, it was good that the process had begun to get underway. Eventually, in April 1989, we had a social worker assigned to us. We were approved a year later and, after a lot of hopes raised and a lot of disappointments, the girls – Sally (nine), Wendy (eight), Rachel (six) and Nicola (five) – were finally placed with us. In the end, the agency that placed them was different from the one that approved us. All in all, from when we first started approaching adoption agencies to having the girls placed with us, the process took five years.

Relationships with Professionals

Our experience with social workers throughout this process has been mixed. On the one hand, the woman who was the girls' social worker for the first two years was lovely. She used to come every third week on Saturday morning to see the girls, spending a little time with us first. Plus, the woman who effectively placed the kids with us was great, as were her manager and colleagues. They talked very carefully with us about the girls' extremely difficult and painful pasts. In fact, more than half of the social workers we've come across have been at least reasonable.

However, our recent experience with social workers has been just dreadful and, we think, anti-lesbian. Last summer, the girls' social worker changed. They were assigned to a new team, who, basically, don't know what they're doing. They just leap in, do things wrong and then don't even bother to apologise. We have to attend review meetings every six months where decisions are taken and, though they expect us to abide by them, they don't stick to decisions themselves when it suits them. They've made a whole catalogue of mistakes and we're considering making a formal complaint. For instance, they recently turned up at Sally's school – she's the eldest – without checking with us first or even letting us know. Fortunately, she was very sensible about it and even when they asked her wind-up questions like: 'Why don't you ever phone your sister Wendy any more?' she stayed calm. She knows we're not allowed to contact Wendy. It could have been awful. In fact, the next day, Sally did play up to a certain extent, but that's not surprising because she's trying hard to fit in at school, she doesn't want to stand out from the crowd, and having your social worker come and see you at school is not exactly going to help with that.

Other professionals haven't exactly been anti-lesbian but they haven't always been particularly supportive either. For example, the children were part of a therapy research project, which was one of the conditions of their placement with us. The project required the girls to attend a large number of sessions and we were led to believe that once the sessions were over they could get some extra help and support if they needed it. But that didn't happen. The girls were left stranded, help given one day then taken away the next. Rachel found it particularly difficult. After thirty therapy sessions, the help she was getting suddenly came to an end just as her teacher changed. As a result, she went berserk at school one day and threatened to throw herself out of a third-floor window. We feel that the girls were treated like guinea-pigs – experimented upon and then dumped.

Doctors have generally behaved better, although when Christine took them for their medical last summer and the girls were in the room, the doctor asked when the adoption would be going through, which was unfortunate because it was about four days before Wendy was leaving us. It was a very delicate time. But the community dentist is very good, although the staff there seem to have a slight problem getting their heads round the concept of four girls with two different mums. It's not an anti-lesbian thing necessarily, they just get confused about who's who. You can tell they're thinking: 'I've seen these girls, but I don't remember their mum. Have I talked to this person before?' Teachers have been great, especially in primary. In secondary it's been generally good. When Sally was being teased about us being lesbians, we had a promise that the issue of lesbian parents would be raised in class as part of a broad 'families' curriculum project in such a way that the children wouldn't link it to Sally and possibly make matters worse.

Personal Relationships

Our relationship has changed since the girls have been living with us. It has brought us closer. Before, we were two separate people doing our own thing, coming together for nice times – meals out, a night at the pictures, that sort of thing. We even lived separately to a extent, on different floors of the same house. We do still have our own bedrooms – our own space is still very important – but so much else has changed now we live together as a family. For the first six months of the placement, although it was a very difficult time with the kids, the two of us enjoyed a kind of honeymoon period. It was great finally being the family we'd always wanted to be. And now we still get along very well together. We laugh, otherwise we'd have gone up the wall years ago, especially about the difficulties we face with the children and professionals, and we don't disagree very often – the kids know they'll get more or less the same line from both of us. We're a good team working with the girls – people seem to acknowledge that – and it's strengthened our relationship but we do appreciate the time we have on our own together. We spend a lot of time with other lesbians and gay men who have foster or adoptive children. We also have some very good heterosexual friends, some of whom have their own children, who are really supportive.

The two younger children accept our relationship. They know that we're lesbians. They understand that on their level. A boy in Rachel's year four class teased her about it but she didn't find it a problem at all. She sat between us and explained what had happened in such a straightforward way, it was obvious it wasn't an issue. She just accepts that she's got two mums. Sally finds it more difficult. She even has a go at us about it sometimes. But when she does, the others are supportive to us. For instance, one time Sally was in a really foul mood and was describing us as dirty lesbians. Rachel said: 'that's not very nice about Paul and Richard!' (two gay male friends of ours) and Nicola said: 'nor Sarah and Christine either!' Sally is older, so it's perhaps more understandable: she absorbed the prejudice from her background and it gets reinforced at school, plus she's at that age where she wants everything around her to be absolutely 'normal'. She does want to be here, she just wishes we weren't lesbians sometimes. The birth family know we're lesbians too. Their mum wanted to meet us before the girls came to live with us to see if we had horns or something. She had a look, saw we were okay and said: 'You'll give them a good education, won't you.' It was really good that we met her. The kids have even got a letter from their birth mother saying: 'Be good for your two mums'. It makes such a difference for them to know their mum knows and is in favour.

Sarah: In terms of our families, mine has been very supportive on the whole, although they were all a bit taken aback when they heard we were adopting four. My dad has always been worried about the over-population of the world, so that's one of the reasons he approves of the adoption! He and his partner take the girls out on their birthdays and at Christmas to buy presents, which is very special for the girls, especially as the birthday thing is reversed – the girls choose the present and wrap it up so it is a surprise for everyone else. My mum has been great too. She has them to stay and, in general, is incredibly supportive both to us and the girls.

Christine: My family has been more mixed. When my brother heard about the placement, he sent a long letter giving his views on 'female only' families and why they were a bad idea for children. But since then he's behaved like any other uncle – he buys Christmas presents, he makes us all lunch when we go and see him, he does quite well really. My other brother and my father have been very supportive but my sister has had more difficulty.

Our neighbours have been fantastic, especially considering some of the things they must hear through the walls – the girls shouting, screaming, swearing, throwing things around! Our walls aren't that thick. We wouldn't have been surprised if one of them had called social services. But they've only been supportive and really friendly. One side even gives Easter eggs and Christmas presents to the girls.

Conflict

One big area of conflict, in terms of our adoption experience, was whether to move on to the adoption in the light of how Wendy was behaving. Wendy was the second eldest of the girls placed with us and she never really settled. All the girls have behaviour problems but, while the others gradually became attached to us, Wendy didn't seem to bond at all. We realised she had an attachment disorder, which basically meant that all her relationships were superficial and would remain so. There was a certain attachment on her part, nevertheless; but she couldn't settle, her behaviour was always a lot worse than the others' and constantly challenging. Even at the best of times, her behaviour was still difficult and in the end the situation broke down. The crunch came very quickly. We all went away for the weekend and Wendy was dreadful the whole time. She sat in the middle of the road, she was violent, she pulled our hair, kicked, bit and 'snotted' at us. Eventually, we got back home and hoped she would then calm down, but she didn't. A horrendous scene in the library shortly afterwards, where she kicked and screamed at Sarah, was the last straw. Wendy herself was phoning her social worker saying that she didn't want to live with us any more; Sarah already believed that Wendy shouldn't live with us any longer. But Christine continued to agonise about it – she was having great difficulty saying 'Wendy has to go'. Although she gradually accepted it, it was still a very difficult conflict between us. Eventually, we were both thankful that it was Wendy who made the decision to leave herself.

A counsellor, who was doing some work with us and Wendy, told us that with extremely disturbed children, it's often the mother who gets the brunt of the anger. He pointed out that because in our family there were two mums, Wendy had had to make a choice between us. From everything that had happened, it was obvious that she'd chosen Sarah.

Sarah: She made a bee-line for me the very first day and started clinging on to me, in a positive way, following me round, but then started taking things out on me. I bore the brunt of Wendy's anger, not that Christine didn't experience exactly the same abuse, but it was always worse, always more intense between Wendy and me.

Christine: So I started spending a lot of time with Wendy – quality time – in order to balance things up and, in the process, got very attached to her, which caused problems later when it came to Wendy going.

Sarah: Yes, I kind of wondered whether Christine really believed how awful Wendy could be to me sometimes. Their relationship was so very different. The scene in the library was the last straw: I was in tears, with the other girls hugging me. We knew then, really, that Wendy had to leave in order for us to survive as a family. We still think that it was the right decision – though it was a very difficult one – and, in retrospect, we're angry that Wendy was placed with us at all. Especially given that at Wendy's disruption meeting we were told that because the girls' needs were so great, the original recommendation was to place them separately. The social workers never seemed to realise how different Wendy was. She was still hooked on her birth mother and if somebody had bothered to sit down and talk to her in any kind of depth, they would have found out that she never really wanted to be adopted at all. That would have stopped her being placed with us and could have spared all of us some really terrible times. It still affects the three other girls – on Wendy's birthday, for example, they play up and get upset – and it's something the two of us feel very distressed about even now.

The girls can be awful when they're determined to play up. The social workers told us before the placement what their behaviour might be like, in general terms, but they didn't go into the specifics of what that behaviour actually entailed. On balance, over the years, though, things do seem to have become better. Sally, in particular, is quite good at talking things through now.

She's learned that talking really helps her calm down. And once she's got past the anger and we've talked, a lot of bonding goes on. Now when they calm down, they do so quite quickly. Christine's cat, Tao, helps with this too. The girls really like her, especially Sally and Rachel, who have something of a competition over her. And even though Wendy used to kick her, she's very good with them. If they're in a bad mood, sometimes they'll go and find Tao and give her a cuddle and talk to her, which really helps.

Talking is a big part of what happens at the dinner table too. One sadness is that although we do have good conversations – really great conversations sometimes – they're not the conversations we would have had if the girls had been with us from the very beginning. That's a big disappointment. The conversations we have are always informed by, ruled by, the girls' past and the dynamic of that past. They're never very inclusive. A lot of the time, it's just us two having a conversation or else it's the others talking amongst themselves with nobody listening properly to anyone else or with Rachel constantly interrupting what everyone else is saying.

Christine: Class has also been a very big issue in the placement. The girls come from working-class backgrounds and their foster carers were working-class too, but we're middle-class. That was certainly very significant for Wendy. In fact, it's one of the reasons she didn't settle with us. She found changing class very difficult. The other girls have changed class without too much difficulty. Sally is aware of it. Sometimes, she'll shout 'I don't want your fucking education!' when we're reading with them or something. But the younger two don't seem to be so aware of it.

Sarah: But it's more of an issue between our different backgrounds. I mean, I notice you've identified as middle-class on my behalf...

Christine: Between the two of us we're middle-class...

Sarah: Well, yes, you're right, but if I feel like a fish out of water with your family, God knows what they must feel like! They've certainly commented on your family's house – big house, massive grounds...

Day-to-Day Living

Sarah: When it looked likely that the kids would be placed with us – although I am very out at work – I felt I didn't want people to know I was adopting because I felt that, ironically, that might mean that the wrong person or people could get to know that a lesbian was having children placed. I was particularly anxious about it on the children's behalf as there is more prejudice against lesbians and gays adopting than anything else. So, when eventually the girls were placed with us and I was given special adoption leave, I told my colleagues that I was taking a break to finish a course I'd been doing. Only my boss and his immediate boss knew what was really going on and they were only told because they had to approve the leave. When I came back to work, I told my immediate team as I wanted them to know, although I still asked them not to tell people about it. But you can't keep four children quiet for very long! Since then, I've been in and out of job-shares and although ideally that's what I'd want to be doing, I'm back full-time at the moment.

Christine: I used to job-share before the children arrived but that was for a number of reasons, not just because we were hoping to adopt. I've changed work since but I've stayed in job-share because it really suits me.

When we're not working, we do like to get away. We go camping once a year, though we don't go on trips to China and other exotic places like we used to. We stay on a large campsite with organised children's activities – which is great! We get a chance to have a break from the girls, read our books a bit and appreciate their company when they come back, and they get a chance to take part in organised children's activities, which they love.

Sarah: There are a lot of funny moments – at least funny in retrospect. For instance, we bought Rachel some jelly-shoes for holiday and told her it was okay to go into the sea wearing them. But once she got into the water, one of the shoes slipped off and she lost it. An incredible performance followed, which lasted a long, long time. So much upset over one shoe! People we've told about it have said: 'why didn't you just go and buy her a new pair?' But we trekked around every shop in town on the hunt for jelly-shoes – we tried so hard – but it was the end of the season and they had all sold out. We can just about laugh about it now, although Rachel can't and still complains about her lost jelly-shoe over a year on.

Christine: Another funny-in-retrospect story concerns Sally. Sally normally goes straight from school to a playcentre but on one occasion she announced that she was going to go to a friend's house instead. This worried us – the friend lived a long way away – so I went to school to make sure that Sally would turn up at the playcentre as usual. When Sally saw me standing there at the school gates, she was absolutely furious. She shouted 'You fucking well get into your fucking car, now!' as a whole crowd of other girls stood around watching. We can laugh about that now too. I was just another ordinary parent come to collect her daughter and there was Sally swearing away!

Sarah: We do have a boundary that they're not allowed in the bedroom, which means that they're not allowed to come into bed with us. For my own space, that feels right and appropriate. But it's also a sadness because that's something that would have happened with a birth kid so naturally. There's my stuff too, imagining social services coming round saying: 'Here you are – lesbians – and you're having them in your bed!' Also, there's the other way round. With a birth child, being in bed with me might have been a nice thing but their experience of beds and parents may well have been different because they were sexually abused, so that complicates it too.

In terms of talking about sex, we have talked to them about sex and when it has happened, it's happened very naturally. I'm in the shower and they're talking to me and I just answer their questions. But we haven't really done it the other way round, with us sitting down with them and telling them.

Christine: With nudity, I didn't like them to see me in the shower when they were first living with us. But now it seems pretty natural. There I am having a shower and there they are in the bathroom. I gradually became less worried about it.

The Adoption Process

The adoption process which led to the girls being placed with us was a very lengthy and extremely arduous one. We used to answer adverts in PPIAS (Parent-to-Parent Information on Adoption Service) and *Be My Parent* and then follow up by phone, but as the responses we were getting were fairly negative, in fact, often unpleasant, we decided to write instead, using a word processor. This went on for two years. At the beginning we were seriously considered for two girls aged ten and eleven, only for social services to realise that the grandparents lived in the next road, so, obviously, the placement couldn't go any further. This was very disappointing, especially because when we'd been thinking of moving into the area, we asked our social worker whether living there would make a difference and she said it wouldn't. Next, we were considered for two boys, which was strange because we were initially approved for two girls. We agonised all weekend about whether we should say yes but they were eventually placed with another couple – two lesbians. Actually, we were quite pleased about this because it showed us that adoption by lesbians was acceptable, at least to this particular authority. We did have to wheedle it out of them, that it *was* two lesbians. They were very reluctant to tell us as they thought the lesbian community was so small that we would know them. But it really helped us to know that it was possible for out lesbians to adopt.

The next possibility was four children. We were on a short-list of two and, eventually, we were turned down. But we don't believe that the decision was essentially an anti-lesbian one because the family who were approved had more experience of working around learning disability, which was important for the placement, and, furthermore, the social workers there were really excellent. At that time, we went back to panel and were approved for up to four children. It's unusual for panel to change what you've been approved for before children are placed, so we were lucky. But then, unfortunately, we did have an awful experience. We were being considered to adopt a boy and girl from another authority and two social workers came on a visit. It was clear from their questions and general attitude that they had made up their minds about us before they even got through the door. Given that they said the boy needed a father figure, we wondered why they bothered to visit. They just weren't interested and the whole experience was awkward and very unpleasant. On another occasion, we might well have had another four girls placed with us but the agency that approved us told us that the authority wouldn't provide post-adoption care – social work resources, in other words – which was essential in this case as the girls had been severely traumatised by their past experiences. Finally, we went to see a girl at a special school. We were very taken with her and her social worker seemed very taken with us, but then her senior started asking lots of questions and making difficulties and as it began to seem very likely that the girls we have now would be placed with us, we decided to leave it.

We had written to one particular authority about two sets of children – two and three girls, respectively – and, fairly soon afterwards, the social workers came to meet us. We had a very good meeting with them and, just before the end, they asked us whether we'd also be interested in having a group of four girls placed with us. Christine had previously felt that she didn't want to take on four but, gradually, she began to come round to the idea. Then the social workers told us that they were interested in placing the girls with us. What happened next was amazing. Two seemingly straight social workers – a man and a woman – arrived on our doorstep for the assessment and did an interview with us that seemed to go very well. At the end, when we asked whether they wanted a tour of the house, the woman said it wasn't necessary for her but that one of us might show the man, who was the girls' social worker, round the place. Once the two of them had left the room, the woman leaned over to Sarah and said: 'I wasn't sure whether I should tell you this, but I'm a lesbian too!' She went on to be hugely supportive throughout the placement process and got really involved, perhaps too involved because she was taken off the case sooner than she might have been. She even came out herself at work to help our case. She basically said to those of her colleagues who were questioning our fitness to adopt when we were still being considered: 'Look, I'm a lesbian. You think

I'm all right. They're the same. There's nothing wrong with them'. She has been fantastic. We've always thought of her as our fairy godmother.

The girls have been with us for three years now and we're waiting to adopt. Ideally, we'd both like to be legal parents but, unfortunately, the law, as it stands at the moment, means that only one of us can adopt. One decision we made fairly early on – years before we were even offered the girls – was that we weren't going to tell the kids which of us will be their legal parent. They've got two mums, that's all they need to know. They don't need to know the legal details.

Looking back on the process and on the placement itself, it's surprising how awful things can be when they're really awful. Some of the horrible, terrible experiences and feelings we've been through we could never have imagined. Nevertheless, it's surprising how well the girls have slipped into being here, in spite of all their difficulties in the past, and also how fulfilling the girls' living here has been for us, how wonderful it has been. We did some work recently at the post-adoption centre on imagining our ideal kids and that was a real eye-opener. We found that a lot of the characteristics we valued in our ideal children were already there in the three girls we've got now. That was an extremely positive experience. We found out what an incredibly good match we are.

'Things Might Look a Little Cloudy Now, But...'
John and Rob's Story

John and Rob live in a comfortable semi-detached house in the south of England. John is 37 and Rob is 28 and they have lived together for about five years. John worked as a residential social worker previously but now does consultancy and training work. Rob has his own curtain design company. Their foster son, Ismail, is now 22 years of age and has recently returned home to live due to financial difficulties. He has his own flat which he is planning to return to soon. Ismail is of Turkish Cypriot origin, John is white, but with a mixed heritage as his mother came from the Seychelles, and Rob's heritage is Indian. Their story is told by John.

About eight years ago, when I was thirty, I applied as a single person to foster Ismail, a fourteen-year-old Turkish Cypriot young man, who was, at that time, resident in the children's home where I was officer-in-charge. The whole process started in May 1989 and took about a year, as Ismail moved in to live with me a year later. I met Rob five years ago, in 1991, and he moved in to live with me and Ismail that same year.

It was really a case of Ismail and I both choosing one another. I had said that I wouldn't be able to foster any of the local authority's children as I worked for the borough. However, when I was leaving the local authority, Ismail saw his chance. He was upset and shocked at the prospect of my leaving. He had lost his father at a young age (eight years) and I'd lost my mother at the age of three. We had that in common. We probably both still function at those ages! Anyway, I put in my application to foster.

I had checked out the idea of fostering Ismail with the rest of the staff group and they were positive, initially. They saw that Ismail needed something different from what the home was offering. On the face of it, things seemed pretty straightforward. Certainly, that is how the home saw it. There was industrial action in the department at the time and, as a result, Ismail came to stay for three weeks. Overnight stays had already been agreed. The rest of the children in the home either went to their own families or were cared for by the skeleton staff group because of the strike.

The department's plan was to find an independent social worker to assess me. This caused delays but I felt that it didn't matter as Ismail was already living with me. Once the industrial action was over, he was actually spending four nights with me and three in the children's home.

However, there was a change of senior management in children's services at the time and the new service manager said that the 'charge and control regulations' had been broken by Ismail coming to stay. For example, no checks, police or otherwise, had been carried out. On the one hand, I understood their position, but I had, until recently, been the manager of the children's home where Ismail lived. In this role I had been police-checked! I had worked for the department for five years and was a qualified social worker. Ismail didn't understand their objections either.

To make the situation worse, the department decided that access should be cut down and, at the same time, Ismail's key worker should be changed as that member of staff had previously been supervised by me. This all happened without consulting Ismail.

I felt it was the department's responsibility to manage the situation better. I hadn't been through the process of a fostering placement with any of the children in care before, so I didn't know the procedures. All sections of the department had agreed the process in the beginning but Ismail and myself were having to carry the burden of their mistakes. By that I mean that they should have carried out an assessment and checks before allowing Ismail to come and stay with me.

Then it became an escalating situation. The local authority explained that their actions were for our own good and that was why they were doing it this way. No one apologised for the mix-up of allowing Ismail to come to live with me and then changing their minds. I was getting it from everyone that their hands were tied and it was an instruction that they had to follow the 'charge and control regulations'. No one was willing to say it was their responsibility. We were made to feel it was our responsibility. Suddenly, things were formalised between me and the home, right down to when Ismail and I could have telephone contact. Lots of boundaries were being put down over contact and access was stopped altogether.

Ismail's field social worker was allocated to do the assessment of his needs. Also, the new key worker at the home was asked to do the same. An independent social worker was appointed to assess me and was excellent. She was very understanding and did, in fact, work for the local authority but didn't know me.

Ismail's new key worker started to be extra nice to him, spent money on him and took him to see an 18-certificate film at the cinema. I didn't approve of that because he was fourteen. She took him out for meals and spoilt him. It did soften the blow of him not being able to see so much of me though.

I asked for an advocate for Ismail as my hands were tied and I had no say. This was in spite of the fact that I knew a great deal about him and knew his history. When he had any problems at school, I wasn't allowed to have any input. From someone with lots of power, I became very powerless. My request for an advocate for Ismail was, in fact, ignored and a voluntary child advocacy project couldn't get involved as a result.

Ismail refused to see his field social worker as he blamed that person for what was happening. The social worker's office was on the estate where Ismail had been brought up. Ismail wanted to stay away from there but this was sabotaging his assessment. If the social worker had realised that Ismail was blaming him, he would have realised that he needed to bridge the gap and build up the relationship. His previous social worker had left without saying goodbye and the new worker was getting the blame for that as well. Basically, Ismail was very angry with the way he'd been treated.

I went to NFCA (the National Foster Care Association), BAAF (British Agencies for Adoption and Fostering) and the Children's Legal Centre to get advice and support for myself as I felt really isolated. The local authority hadn't offered anyone for me to talk to. The children's home staff were instructed not to speak to me, although one did 'off the record'.

Ismail's school situation had always been precarious but he now started to 'create' and the school situation broke down. I was called to a meeting and the department were looking to move Ismail to another home for adolescents as they felt he had outgrown the present one. I'm not sure, but I think they also gave the reason that it would be easier for me as it wasn't the children's home where I had previously worked. Later, they said that was one of the reasons. The move was planned for two weeks before the fostering panel met to decide whether I could foster Ismail or not. This made me feel that they had already decided against allowing me to foster. Ismail was getting more out of control and these decisions were feeding into that by saying ever more loudly that he should move. His social worker was saying that he didn't think he could do an assessment as Ismail was so angry. Ismail was encouraged to go to see the new home to see what it was like. He was then told it was going to happen anyway. Both of us felt that the department were against the idea of him being fostered, why else were they choosing to move him two weeks before the fostering panel met?

On the Friday that he was due to move, Ismail ran away to my home. I had got advice from NFCA that, under emergency fostering arrangements, there was a six-week period during which the assessment could be done. When I suggested this to the head of services, he said that Ismail had to go to the new residential placement and that I had to get him there. I was told that, otherwise, I would be 'harbouring' the child and the police would be informed. They weren't sympathetic and didn't appear to understand.

I took Ismail to the new placement and cancelled the forthcoming slot at the fostering panel. Fortunately, on the day he moved, Ismail was allowed to have the independent advocate represent him. The first thing Ismail's advocate did was to put a complaint into the department and another to the ombudsman on Ismail's behalf. The complaint was that Ismail had been moved from one children's home to another against his wishes, that there had been a change of key worker without consultation, that there had been a suspension of opportunity to stay with a potential foster carer, that Ismail's request for an independent representative was not listened to and that his complaints about all of these points had not been listened to. All of these complaints were eventually upheld and the council was found guilty of maladministration. Ismail received compensation but no personal apologies.

A meeting was held concerning the 'charge and control regulations' over access. Both children's homes were represented, the headteacher of Ismail's school came, the field social worker and his senior, the independent advocate and myself. As a result of the meeting, overnight access was granted and Ismail was allowed to come to stay for Christmas with me, contrary to what a lot of people wanted. The headteacher had been very supportive of access and the decision went in our favour, even though there were objections from all the social workers. I felt that what really helped us to succeed was the support of the independent advocate from a voluntary organisation for children in care. It was the first time that we felt that things were going our way.

In February the fostering panel finally met. The report from his old children's home was against Ismail being fostered by anyone. However, the report had mostly been about difficulties they had with me and very little about Ismail's needs. It had been written by the new key worker he had been allocated. The independent advocate tore it apart when she presented her report to the panel. The new children's home were in favour of Ismail being fostered and the panel went ahead and approved the placement. Their only concern was that Ismail was of Turkish Cypriot origin and Muslim in religion. They said that I would need support in these areas as he was of a different religion and racial background, though this support was in fact never addressed.

The report on me said that I had been in a heterosexual relationship but was now single. I had not come out as gay at the time that the assessment was done. The underlying assumption was that I was 'straight', which was not surprising in view of the fact that up until then I had always had heterosexual relationships. I thought some people in the department had suspicions that I was gay, but I was never asked. I do not believe that Ismail would have been placed with me if I had declared that I wanted a gay relationship. Ismail always knew I was gay and was able to talk to my ex-girlfriend about this.

Ismail was fifteen when he moved in with me. He had no school support and was appointed a new key worker from the second children's home. I got him into college and he then found work at a do-it-yourself store. He has remained in work ever since – although in other jobs. The first thing we did was to go on holiday to Kenya. I wanted the department to pay for us to go to Cyprus but they refused.

It was the following October that I met Rob. When I told the local authority about the relationship, they ran in the opposite direction! The social worker started asking me questions about my relationship with my foster son. I was very angry about this and told the social worker that he needed to think carefully about what he was asking, especially if he was going to talk to Ismail. The social worker said that they would have to assess Rob, but they never did so. They did do police checks on Rob but only after it emerged in a review that these hadn't yet been done! None of us received any support toward helping us to adjust to one another.

I met Rob in another London borough where he had a contract to do the curtains in their family centres. Both of us were invited to the opening of one of the centres. When we became a couple, Ismail was not at all pleased. Although he knew I wanted a gay relationship, this was not generally known by anyone else at the time and Rob coming into my life was a shock for family and friends alike. Ismail was worried about the effect my news would have on everyone, especially his friends! Rob moved in quite quickly and, although I sat down and discussed this with Ismail, it was not up for debate and Ismail had little say around Rob moving in. They avoided one another in the beginning. Rob kept out of Ismail's way and Ismail spent most of his time out. Ismail found himself a new girlfriend soon after I met Rob and spent much of his time with her. At one point, he was hardly at home and I was concerned that Ismail was gradually rejecting us.

On meeting Ismail, Rob tried to be nice but Ismail ignored him. 'This is my house and what are you doing here?' was Ismail's attitude. I arranged for a trusted friend to come over to talk with Ismail. The friend helped Ismail explain how he felt – that is, that he was being pushed out.

Rob was not confident with Ismail for some time and, although I was encouraging of him to get to know Ismail, Rob was very reluctant at first. Ismail's relationship with his girlfriend ended and he started to spend more time at home. Gradually, his friends began to come over and were introduced to Rob, who made them welcome. By this time, Rob was wanting to look after Ismail by doing his washing and cleaning, giving him lifts to work and cooking for him. It was Rob's way of getting to know Ismail and wanting to be accepted by him. Given that Ismail had been taught to do all of these things already and was fairly independent, I initially overlooked these changes but I was concerned that Ismail might take advantage of Rob or become used to having things done for him. Rob would get annoyed with Ismail over some of his habits and put pressure on me to do something. My view was that Rob should say something. In the end, it led to many arguments. I felt in the middle, trying to maintain the peace, though I suppose we all felt in the middle at times. Eventually, from pure frustration and concerns, I decided to hold family meetings, sometimes in the middle of the night, to resolve disagreements that arose. I would inform both Ismail and Rob how I felt and ask that we work together on improving relationships. Neither Ismail or Rob could be direct with one another about how they really felt. I was having to tell both of them how they each felt about the other. I even wrote each of their feelings down once and gave them a copy.

Rob felt that Ismail and I raised lots of feelings for each other. We had both lost parents and were still dealing with the pain of this. Ismail losing his dad was brought back by Rob 'taking me away', as he initially saw it.

Rob was without a role in Ismail's life. Rob felt most comfortable looking after both of us – doing all the washing, cooking, cleaning and gardening. He didn't know how to fit in when he first moved in. I had been firm with Ismail about sharing jobs but suddenly neither of us had jobs to do because Rob was doing it all. It was like having a mother come in to look after us. Rob said that his mother was so good that he was happy to provide that for other people. It released me to become more of a father to Ismail, though Rob said that he found Ismail and I were always arguing, which he didn't like. Nevertheless, we were also very close. Certainly, Ismail and I had always been very straight with one another, even if it meant conflict.

For a while, Rob had the dilemma of whether to be a friend or parent. Initially, Rob found the parent role difficult because his own parents divorced when he was twelve. Rob was still dealing with how his parents split up and had said that he was never going to have kids! When Rob first moved in, he didn't like the idea of having a child but, eventually, he worked Ismail out quite well and how to get on with him.

There was one time when Rob decided to put a lock on the bedroom door. Ismail used to take Rob's things deliberately to get at him. I was unhappy at Rob doing this because I had never locked anything up from Ismail. Rob felt unable to confront Ismail about things so chose to put a lock on the door instead. Ismail discovered a way in by using the back door key that happened to fit the same lock! He then left the bedroom door open for Rob to see that he could get in. It was never locked again! Ismail was showing Rob that he couldn't lock him out. We found out that whatever age you are, everyone has to be treated fairly. You can't treat a younger person in a different way. It has taught us a lot about the way one looks at people.

Rob says that he's become a much more positive person through taking on a foster child, but it took a long time to work the relationships out. It took nearly a year for Ismail and Rob to spend genuine time together and it helped enormously when Rob took Ismail out to work with him. I was able to relax then, pleased that the two of them were now getting on and enjoying one another's company.

Generally, I feel my relationship improved enormously with Ismail when Rob moved in. This was not apparent at first but the type of arguments Ismail and I would have subsided and finally disappeared. Having someone else around made an enormous difference. Obviously, Ismail did not get the amount of attention he was used to when Rob moved in but then he eventually got the attention of two people rather than one. There were some things Ismail spoke to Rob about rather than me because of my position as his foster parent and being older. Rob tended to 'mother' Ismail whereas I could then concentrate more on being a father figure to him. This had been hard before because I had tried to fulfill both roles. In most cases I became more flexible with Ismail and more understanding. Rob would often point things out to me that perhaps I hadn't seen before and I would reflect on this and try something different. We were all learning from one another and responding to one another's needs. As the oldest, I felt the most responsible and I would endeavor to maintain open communication between us all. We had our rows but there was never a time I would choose one above the other. I loved them both and hated to see us not get on.

Holidays were taken separately when Rob moved in. Rob and I would go away together because Ismail was now at an age where he preferred to go away with his mates or his girlfriend. Eating habits changed too. Rob and I gradually started to eat less meat and varied our menu. I think Ismail missed some of the meals I used to cook!

We are quite a cosmopolitan family. Rob's parents originated from India and Ismail's from Cyprus. Rob and I were both baptised Catholics and Ismail was a

Muslim. None of us followed our religions or parents' cultures. My mother came from the Seychelles, which are islands situated in the Indian Ocean that are both English- and French-speaking but include many races. Eventually, Ismail and Rob had no trouble getting on. Although Ismail used to be quite discriminatory toward Asian people and even gay men and lesbians at one point, he never rejected Rob because of his race and culture. Really, they were in a similar position, having parents who were from another country, but happy to see themselves as British. Neither related to being called 'black'. In this respect, both rejected their original cultural roots because they identified themselves as British. Being a social worker, I would correct both Ismail and Rob over their language and attitude sometimes. They would gang up against me in return, uninterested in my 'political correctness', and even tease me!

Issues of 'race' and culture had been raised by the fostering panel in relation to Ismail but this was never addressed again by the social workers. However, it did come up later when Rob and I wanted to foster Ismail's sister, Nazan. She wanted to be placed with her brother but she was placed in a white middle-class family instead because they decided that her needs would be better met by a female. As a male couple, we couldn't compete. This made us angry as it seemed to matter not whether we could meet any of her needs or that she would be living with her brother. None of us were consulted about Ismail's sister's placement, including their birth mother.

I later lodged a complaint against the council for not properly considering my earlier complaint about the implementation of Ismail's care plan. This was upheld by the ombudsman and amounted to maladministration for the second time. I complained that the department had not properly considered my complaint that I was dealt with inappropriately when I disclosed my sexuality. Again, the council were found guilty of maladministration. I argued that they had not properly considered our request for Ismail's sister to come to live with the family. The ombudsman concluded that the decision to place Nazan elsewhere was reasonable and not taken with bias. However, the process involved amounted to maladministration. Finally, we received compensation.

I therefore feel that I was treated unjustly by the local authority and the ombudsman found in my favour. Unfortunately, I felt that bias did play a part and I found that some council officers even lied to the ombudsman to cover their backs and their prejudices. I requested an advocate for Ismail's sister but this fell on deaf ears. The people who mattered in this saga were not consulted or listened to. Why? I am a qualified social worker, groupwork trainer, ex-social services manager and successful foster carer. I wasn't listened to. My partner, Rob, was totally ignored and, at one particular meeting, was asked, by Ismail's sister's social worker, what he was doing there! Ismail was ignored, as was his mother, his brother and, most of all, his sister, who had no say with regard to where she wanted to live, which happened to be with us. The damage the local authority have caused through their ignorance and prejudice is incalculable. None of the officers involved will ever be made accountable for their actions and will continue to make the same decisions elsewhere until they are taken to task again. Hopefully, this state of affairs will eventually change and, although we have not been seen as able to offer a home for my son's sister, others will hopefully be given the opportunity in future.

We wanted our story to be told, hoping that future placements with gay carers will be considered seriously alongside any other placements. To be not considered at all is not only unjust but it can go against the child's wishes and the wishes of the people close to the child, such as family, and this brings the Children Act into disrepute. The Act clearly states that the child and members of his/her family should be consulted. The local authority in this case should have learnt lessons from the first complaint. I'm still aggrieved that we had to complain twice and we are still not satisfied, even though both our complaints were upheld. Has council policy changed? I doubt it.

There should be a happy ending to this story but I have to tell you that Ismail's sister's placement ceased because her carers chose to retire. We were offering her a home for life! She is now living in a young women's hostel. Many gay carers do not have children of their own and anyone we choose to foster is like our 'own'. We – gay and lesbian carers – are a valuable, under-represented resource that could, and should, be tapped into. Local authorities need to 'wake up' and use us as potential placements. No child need be without a loving home.

Postscript: November 1997

Ismail is now living back in his flat. He lived alone for a year, then his girlfriend joined him. He sees his sister and the rest of his family regularly. We're very proud of him and look forward to being put in the role of grandparents one day!

'A Family, Not Pretend But Real!'
Jean and Trixie's story

Jean lives with her partner, Trixie, and they co-parent four children. Jean (aged 40) is a college lecturer and part-time social worker and Trixie (aged 36) is also a social worker. They live in West Yorkshire and have been together for five years. They are both white. Trixie has two birth children, Georgia (aged twelve) and Max (aged eight), each with different fathers. Georgia sees her birth father on an irregular basis and Max has shared care and regular contact with his father. Jean fostered Claire, who is now fifteen, from the time that she was six years old, but Claire has recently moved on into a residential setting. The plans are for Claire to receive some form of adult care after her sixteenth birthday. Jean and Trixie maintain regular contact with Claire, seeing her as part of their 'family' and taking her on holidays. Joshua (aged eight) lives with the couple on a residence order. He was conceived by self-insemination and his birth mother, with whom he has regular contact, is Jean's ex-partner. Jean also fostered James, a two-year-old boy with profound disabilities, until his death more than five years ago. Jean tells her story, followed by Trixie.

Jean

It's difficult to explain the make-up of our family without having to expose our 'lifestyle' (as lesbian chic magazines have described it), our pasts and our vulnerabilities. This in itself can cause problems for our children and for ourselves as an innocent question about our 'family' requires a complex explanation! The younger children, however, will meticulously explain the make-up of the family, happily using the 'L-word', often to the astonishment of the enquirer.

Each of the children has a different surname and different contact arrangements with the non-resident parts of their families. We have tried very hard to bestow a feeling of 'specialness' on each child, so that they feel they are individuals with their own history and background that they can bring to the family in which they live and belong.

Each child seems very clear about their own background and how they came to be living with us and they are at pains to explain the differences and similarities between themselves and their siblings. They know that their family is somewhat different from those of many of their schoolmates but schoolmates often have family trees which are difficult for others to grasp too. We are presently making adjustments to cater for the excruciating embarrassments that *any* family causes for teenagers and we are struggling to accommodate how they wish to present us to others!

When Trixie and I first began our relationship it was difficult to consider living together. Apart from the usual issues about putting our children together, the added dimensions due to the involvement of social services seemed daunting. We had to let them know about us and how our relationship was being presented to my foster child and, as things developed, we had to discuss with the social worker the implications for us moving in together. It felt worse than coming out to our parents, in that a professional assessment would have to be undertaken and police checks made. Our relationship, and Trixie's past, would have to be discussed and our children interviewed. At least, with our parents, we could adopt the 'it's our lives and if you can't cope with it, it's your problem' approach! The process just had to be gone through and we tried to be as stoic as possible about the matter.

The social workers visited us – Claire's to determine the effects on her of having an 'instant' new family and the family placement worker to assess the situation. Trixie had no aspirations to be a foster carer and becoming Claire's foster mum was inappropriate for Claire at that time. It was decided that Trixie should be checked as a member of the household for the time being, until such time as we felt comfortable to proceed further. We couldn't help feeling that our relationship was about to undergo a test but we decided not to dwell on this and got on with the challenges of our new family life.

Shortly after we all moved in together, Trixie and I decided to take the children away for a few days. Georgia was a bright and precocious eight-year-old to Claire's chronological ten but functioning five-year-old. They shared a room with a double bed. The next morning we discovered Georgia encased in a sleeping bag zipped up to her chin on the floor. Claire had tried to 'touch her up' and had also wet the bed and Georgia's utter disgust was palpable.

As the weekend progressed, Georgia attempted to dominate the bigger girl in every way. She particularly demonstrated her verbal skills, since Claire has a language disorder and her speech is poor, wittering on at Claire in a disdainful way at every opportunity. We tried to referee as much as we could but when they were alone together, in the kitchen making a drink, we heard their usual 'banter' getting louder and louder. Finally, a shriek was heard as Claire, thoroughly sick of Georgia's verbal barrage, retaliated by dumping her apple juice over Georgia's head. As parents, it was difficult to determine who we most sympathised with so, inevitably, they both got it in the neck. Nothing if not even-handed!

It was soon apparent that Claire and Georgia were destined to have a stormy relationship, but Georgia was generally astute and mature enough to withdraw from most conflicts with Claire. At one point, though, we felt that perhaps we ought to issue her with a kettle and a rent book as she spent so much time in her room.

Claire thrived in the company of the two little boys, loving their toys and games. Max also withdrew from any inappropriate behaviour, particularly that which was sexualised, and we worked with both boys on identifying such behaviour and dealing with it. Joshua, however, had grown up with such behaviour and regarded it more as the norm. As Max usually told us when such behaviour was happening, we began to see just how frequently it was occurring and had been occurring and that no matter how vigilant we were, we never could protect the other children from it completely. It was apparent that Joshua must have indulged many times with Claire in sexualised behaviour in the past. The matter of teaching the children how to protect themselves became ever more important.

It was harder, however, to know how to deal with the effects of the other types of anti-social behaviour which were the norm for Claire, such as stealing, telling lies, having tantrums (on a massive scale) and truanting from school, as well as destructive behaviour and some self-mutilation. Whilst Max and Georgia withdrew from the scenes when they arose, Joshua, for whom Claire had been a role model since birth, was clearly following her example.

We certainly needed some help with this but we did hesitate in raising issues with the social worker, although, to be fair, neither our family placement worker nor Claire's social worker were anything but helpful. I think that we exerted pressure on ourselves and I think that this is true of any foster carer who is attempting, inevitably, to be a better parent than the child's birth parent. I believe, however, that the pressures become more for lesbian carers due to the questions that always arise during discussions on the issue. For example, people say: 'I'm sure you'd be wonderful parents but our concern lies with the children, children who've been through the care system and have so much to deal with that they need ordinary families so that they have as many chances as possible of reversing the damage.'

We became so incredibly sensitive to any difficulties which might mean that we would lay bare our vulnerabilities and inadequacies. This is particularly true when our children are teased about living with lesbians. Strangely, though, this has been an area which, in our experience, has actually been positively helped by being foster carers. It is almost impossible not to be out to the professionals involved in your foster child's life due to the reviewing process. With our birth children, we at least had the choices that we all individually make about if and when to make our sexuality clear. As we are so exposed, it forces other professionals to deal with the issue and, fortunately, this has been a positive experience for us. Teachers become aware of any teasing about sexual orientation and it is stopped immediately. When family tree projects are undertaken, they are treated with great sensitivity by our children's teachers. In fact, the only concerns about behaviour bordering on bullying reported to us from schools have been to do with issues of being fat or having poor handwriting. The reality is that teasing is inevitable during childhood and each and every child has something about them that can be picked on. It is our job as parents to try to give our children the security to deal with this and enough trust in us to feel that they can come to us if it's a problem. Children who have been through the care system are damaged and, therefore, need extraordinary families in order to be given as many chances as possible.

Georgia was possibly most affected by the spectre of bullying and, again, this had nothing to do with our sexual orientation. She was living in dread of having to attend the same school as Claire. Luckily, this was relatively easily dealt with in our education district and they attended different high schools. We then set about trying to impress on Georgia the positive side of sharing her family with Claire. Georgia got to go places and have treats that she might not have if she hadn't had an elder sister to go with. They certainly didn't have to associate with each other when they were there but each girl knew that they wouldn't have been allowed to go without the other.

What about networks of support? This is an inevitable question in any carer assessment and one which is generally answered and asked about in terms of 'family' first. This can cause worry for those of us whose families cannot, or will not, accept our sexuality. In my case, although Trixie's family are utterly brilliant about us, my own is problematic. My mother, particularly, will not have any mention of my 'Queer so-called family nor my Queer so-called friends', although my father and brother's family are as accepting and supportive as they could be in the face of my mother's hostility.

I know that my networks of support lie with my friends. My views about whether there was a supposed 'lesbian community' and whether it would support me as a parent were somewhat cynical, but I knew that most of my friends were lesbians and we certainly supported each other as much as we were able, in my experience. I was unsure whether this constituted a 'community' though. I suppose that what changed my view of this was when James, my foster son, died.

I will not dwell on his death here because I was caring for him five years ago and this is, perhaps, another chapter for another time. He was a profoundly disabled boy and was placed with us for long-term fostering. Soon afterwards he was diagnosed as having a degenerative condition that was terminal. He actually died quite suddenly and unexpectedly from a chest infection.

To be honest, my memories of that time are somewhat blurred – a feature of the shock, devastation and the complexity of the situation. With all these feelings there were still practical tasks to be completed, legal and ethical minefields regarding these, and the reactions of the children to be worked through. Perhaps it really is best not to go into it all now. However, the point I wish to make, and I feel is perhaps the most significant thing I can take away from that experience as I see it now, is that there *really is* a lesbian and gay community and it *really does* work for us.

People who I knew vaguely, and their friends and partners and children, appeared and consulted with those I was close to. *They really helped.* They took the children out and made practical arrangements that were tedious and unthinkable for me at the time but were necessary. They sent cards, sent 'rescue remedy' and all gave what they could and *it really helped.*

I have brought away from that experience a real sense of respect and belonging that I never had before. I *know* there *is* a community which will help me on my terms, when appropriate, and not make demands on me afterwards. These people are not my 'family' but offer a network of support that is real and tangible and must be assessed as such. I have close friends who are indeed my first line of support, but the 'community' is important and demands to be taken into account in any social work assessment. Don't underestimate the power of friendships!

As time went by it became apparent that Trixie and I and the children were functioning as a family and our identity as such was stronger. Trixie began the assessment to become approved as a foster carer and, when the approval was given, we had a tea party. It was an occasion that needed to be marked, not for becoming Claire's foster mum (as adults, we rarely use the 'M-word' as it's so loaded in our family and we let the children use it as they wish) but because it was important to acknowledge what we'd all been through to achieve the status, in at least the fostering panel's eyes, of a family, not pretend but real!

Trixie

I took quite a vicarious route to becoming a long-term foster carer because I fell in love with a woman who was already fostering! I'd known Jean for a while because we both lived in the same area where there was a fairly small lesbian community. I knew she had a foster child, Claire, and our kids had met each other. When Jean and I began our relationship, I had to think about the idea of taking on a foster child. This wasn't really my 'ideal', but that wasn't to do with Claire being a foster child, it was more that I didn't initially want to take on any more kids as I already had two of my own! I could see my precious child-free time vanishing before my eyes!

However, I took it in my stride and the fact that Claire was fostered was neither here nor there to me at the start. Later, it became a big issue as I suppose I hadn't really realised just how profoundly damaged Claire was by her past. The other thing that I had to get my head around was the continuing contact with Jean's ex-partner. Both Claire and Joshua were still having regular contact with her but she began to undermine their stability at home by saying things like 'they don't care about you' or 'they're going to get rid of you'. She even threatened to kill herself, all of which had devastating effects on Claire and Joshua. Eventually, social services decided to cut all contact between her and Claire because it was just too emotionally damaging. Joshua continues with his contact as she is his birth mother.

We decided that Georgia, Max and I should all move in to Jean's because it was just easier to cope with all the kids together and, also, my house was not big enough! So we moved in about five years ago. At first, though, I kept some distance and just spent two nights a week at Jean's. This was because I wanted my kids to get used to the relationship and, also, I needed to check out if Jean's relationship with her ex-partner was really over. It was a bad time for Jean because James – her foster son – had just died and her ex-partner was making suicide threats. After about four months, though, we decided that we should live together. I also think that it was better for us to move in to Jean's because she needed to maintain some stability for Joshua and Claire at that time.

We wanted to 'own up' to social services about the relationship as soon as possible, so we told them when I moved in. We asked the social worker to come to the house and we explained it together. The social worker wasn't phased and handled it well. Jean had been previously assessed as a foster carer as part of a lesbian couple, so it wasn't news to social services. Initially they did basic police checks, but we made it clear that we didn't want to go for the 'just a friend in the same house' thing but eventually wanted to be re-assessed as a co-parenting couple. So, within about a year I was assessed as a foster carer too.

Social services re-did the Form F assessment from scratch with both of us. Also, the family placement officer came to talk to the kids about how they felt. Because all our children are so clear about their individual parentage, birth histories and contact arrangements, the social worker was quite amazed that they all had such a good grasp of who they were and where they came from! The assessment didn't take long really because Jean was already seen as an excellent foster carer and I was seen as very supportive, and so, I think, social services just thought things could only get better. However, it took a year before I got any training as a foster carer. I made a fuss about this and said that they should have sent me on training. Eventually they did send me on the three-day foster carers' preparation course and then an HIV course, but this was all ages after the assessment was completed. The assessment itself was no big deal really, it wasn't traumatic and not really that memorable because the social workers didn't really seem that bothered about me. There were no problems with our approval at panel.

The big trauma for me was the impact of moving in together. It was a big shock for the kids too. I think the major thing was living with children where you just don't know their full history. There are still bits of their lives quite unknown to me! And I think this did turn out to be one of the major differences about having a foster child. It's a bit like taking on a stranger and I would say that you really have to learn to love them, which is not that easy. However you get kids, there are different emotions and you have to learn to love all kids, but with foster children this is especially important. I can't say that I just loved them from the start, I had to learn to do so and we all went through major life changes. Just in terms of the house itself, we had to cope with breakages, stealing, and so much clutter of toys, clothes, mess...

Claire has been very damaged by her past abuse and that was difficult for me because I hadn't lived with it before. It helped that I had my own children but I think the foster parent role is different from the relationship I have with my own kids. I'd kill for my children and I would also protect Claire and Joshua, but the reasons are slightly different. In some ways, the fostering role is more powerful because they need an advocate, someone who is passionate about them but it is also one step removed, so I think it is different from having birth children. As I say, one of the things was having to cope with Claire's behaviour, which dominated the whole family at times. This included sexualised behaviour and we had to come to terms with difficult behaviour being the norm.

We always referred to me as 'Trixie' with the children. 'Mum' is just too loaded a word for some foster children and I didn't want to be seen as replacing anyone. The children themselves do use the word 'Mum' when they want to and Joshua will happily and readily explain the whole family set-up to anyone!

My birth children, Georgia and Max, knew that Claire had problems and I explained the different family histories to all the children. Having a foster sister didn't really phase my children, it was the fact of having to move in with other children that was the major change. Georgia was quite used to having me to herself. She'd been 'Queen Bee' of her own home and she basically met her match in Claire! They never really got on but we all just had to deal with it. In the end, Georgia had to get a lock on her door to prevent Claire stealing things. Claire's stealing was very difficult because you never felt there was any privacy and it wore us down.

As I say, at times, Claire came to dominate everything. It felt like everything was revolving around her and her arrangements, which caused stress. She would regularly run away three times a week and we had to involve the police and go out looking for her. She would skive off school and disappear. At one time we had the 'challenging behaviour' team in working with us. We also had to cope with her physical violence. This is all about being realistic about damaged foster kids who've been through the care system and have histories of abuse and placement breakdowns.

I think Jean and I are quite similar in our parenting approaches, which is good. I'm definitely the stricter one and when I say 'don't do something', I mean it! But I'm also the more cuddly type and am very affectionate with my children. When we moved in with Claire, though, I had to really think about this because if you were to cuddle her, she would start to make it into sexualised behaviour. Our roles have also changed drastically. I was used to being a single working parent with my own income, but when we moved in together we couldn't afford to pay childcare and so I gave up employment to become a full-time mother and student. Suddenly, I was unwaged and the main childcarer while Jean worked full-time. This was a big shock for me. I did use the time to study for my social work qualification but my identity had changed so much. I developed diabetes and, at one time, thought I was getting really depressed because I had changed from a working independent woman to full-time 'mum' and cook! Now things have changed again and I'm working full-time doing social work and Jean does most of the childcare, which is now hard for her. I think that roles are very important and, while we try to share tasks, the issue of feeling that you don't have any financial independence can get to you. We get our main support from each other and complement each other in our parenting. If one of us has had enough or 'loses it', the other will step in and pull things through. And no, our menstrual cycles have not coincided either, that's just rubbish!

My parents are great. They visit and we visit them every summer. Neighbours and schools have been fine with us. I'm very out at work and I think what's the point hiding it? Jean's mother is not supportive and won't talk to me but her brother's fine. Jean goes to the LAGFAPN support group for lesbian and gay foster carers but I prefer not to go, it's not really me! The kids like going because they go to the crèche and it means I get child-free time. We have lots of friends who help out and do childminding so we do get some time to ourselves. We used to have a lodger in the attic and he would care for the kids sometimes.

What I want to emphasise in this story is the impact of having foster children. The 'rosy' image of it has to be challenged. I don't mean don't do it or that it's not rewarding, but the impact is earth-shattering! I knew that our foster child was damaged and I thought I was prepared for some of the things that might happen, but multiply it all by at least one hundred and you might get some idea! Foster children can have very difficult histories and behaviour and so people need to ask themselves 'why do I want to do this?' I think lesbians, of necessity, have to ask themselves why they want kids because it's not so easy for them to have children so it has to be a conscious choice. I had my kids when I was in heterosexual relationships and I often wonder if I would have done it otherwise.

My children have not reacted totally negatively to living with other children, including a foster child. They've learnt some good things from each other and we are a 'family'. We certainly feel like we are. I didn't just wake up one morning and think 'we're a family now', but I've noticed that the children come up in conversation pretty quickly with me and that's because they're my first love I suppose. My birth children were my family and then it just grew. Jean and the kids were an extension! I would say that my children are really important to me, but I mean all of them. In everyday conversation I just say that I've got four kids and I don't start making distinctions between them. I'd like them all to get to adulthood with as few problems as possible. Yes, they drive us mad sometimes and we them, but overall we love them and wouldn't have it any other way.

'Matched'
Kath's Story

Kath is a white lesbian living in the north of England who was not out as a lesbian when she was approved as a single adopter. She has adopted a white girl called Rosie who was eight when placed and is now ten.

I always knew I didn't want to have my own birth children. I had a number of friends who had babies quite young and the struggles they had dispelled any illusions I might have had about having little babies. Also, I feel there's something about the state the world's in that means that if there's a child there who's got a life already who I can offer something to, I would rather do that than go through the whole process of having a baby. I had a lot of relationships with children and I knew I could offer a lot to a child and could gain a lot from having a child in my life. I also knew there were a lot of older children around needing families and I felt confident that I could attach to an older child and, in some ways, would prefer that. I felt that, as a single lesbian, I wanted to adopt on my own and I could be clear about that.

For a long time I knew it was something I wanted to do and I kind of worked towards it by choosing to live in households with children before moving to my own place but, for some people, it was still a surprise. Some people were really positive and others were protective of me – like my mum, who was quite concerned I might not be approved but, once I was approved, she was right behind me. Some people who were parents themselves were worried at what I was taking on. Others were worried about the game I was going to have to play in not being out through the process. I had lots of struggles about that myself but, in the end, as I was on my own, I felt that what I was presenting more than anything else was a single parent. I felt that the social worker assessing me might have had her suspicions from the start and was almost warning me off saying anything to her directly because of what she knew about her particular agency.

The assessment itself did have its difficulties because I felt quite vulnerable but, generally, it felt empowering and my social worker was right behind me.

She was quite astute and I really enjoyed our discussions. You could say she didn't do her job as well as she should have but I suppose I pre-empted some of her questions by answering them before they were asked in my thinking beforehand and, sometimes, in practice as well. Sometimes, I felt she was playing the game, but you can find out later that that wasn't the case at all. From the beginning she was quite clear that she thought I was worth getting through the process and she was going to do her best to get me through.

When I first went into it I considered a range of family options and children with different special needs but discussions with my social worker clarified that it was more likely to work with one girl and she was always pushing the strong single woman model. In the end, I was approved for one girl aged between five and ten.

Where I live there's a lot of poverty and it's a very mixed community. I have very close relations with my neighbours, including Asian families in the area. My social worker saw this and my relationships with their children as very positive, both in being good experience for me and also networks for a child coming to live with me. But when children's social workers came to see me I received some very negative feedback about the area. Although I knew this was their problem, it still had a big impact because of the power they had in choosing families.

There was a lot of pressure on me to demonstrate good support networks because I was on my own, and some pressure to provide male role models. But although there was some brief mention of limited contact with men on my Form F, both my referees were women single parents and the support network I presented was very female.

It went through panel with no problems and the whole assessment was very quick, less than five months. But looking for a child took much longer and the waiting was excruciating. After a few months I was approached about a child but there were lots of potential problems regarding the child's birth family. This child was around in my life for a long time and I really took her on board emotionally, but in the end I said I didn't want to pursue it. I followed up one or two adverts for children in newsletters and was approached about another child. Often, huge assumptions were made about me based on very little contact and it was hard not to take this personally, especially being on my own with it and in the vulnerability of not being out. At the end of the day, I think this was down to the inexperience of the social workers in assessing families for the children they had to place, and their own agendas. I certainly felt, in a couple of instances, that there was little understanding or sensitivity to my situation – by one social worker I was described as strong but lacking in humour and by another, "lovely, but not sure she'll be strong enough"!

Then there was an ad in one of the newsletters for Rosie. The write-up appealed to me immediately and they were clearly not looking for a family where men were a big presence. I also remember Clare from the support group ringing me up and saying she'd seen this child in a newsletter who was just for me! There was quite a lot of interest in her but they picked out my form and came to visit me.

The next step was when I went to see the foster carer, who was very positive about me. Different people seemed to have very different views of this child. I think I'd say to anyone 'get as many views as possible of the child and don't take any of them too seriously, remember they'll be different with you'. The sort of things the foster carer described to me about Rosie were quite different from how she was when she came to me and a lot of this was about the carer and the kind of household it was. Any doubts the social workers had were dispelled by the meeting with the foster carer and it was decided to go ahead to the panel. There were a lot of delays around that and I felt I had been hanging around a long time waiting for her. We were matched at panel and then discussions about introductions started, which they envisaged as being quite a long process, they just weren't committed to speeding things along. I ended up writing a letter of complaint. This was well responded to and I got what I was asking for and we went very quickly into introductions.

Again, I was in the position of playing a game because Rosie's social worker was certainly wondering about my sexuality and, possibly, the foster carer. During some chat with the social worker I was talking about having friends in Huddersfield and she said: 'Oh is that so-and-so?', who just happened to be a lesbian couple. There were suspicions and there seemed to be a message that it was all right, but for me to have actually come out would have been quite difficult. I found that whole experience of not being able to be open and suspecting that everybody was colluding didn't sit very well and I wish I could have felt able to be out in the first place. If you're in a system where you, as the potential adopter, are playing the game and it's only you playing it, that's one thing, but the fact that a lot of people working in the system are playing it as well just seems even more ridiculous.

The other controversy was about how the introductions would be done. Because Rosie had had so many rejections in her life there was an expectation that I should go along at first as a friend just dropping in, not as the prospective adoptive parent. But I was very clear that I wanted to be introduced as her adoptive parent and that she should see the album I'd made about myself first to get an idea of me before she met me. In fact, that worked really well. They were terrified about broaching the subject with her but she was over the moon when she saw the album. The actual day I met her was absolutely wonderful. I would never have imagined it could be like that. There was an immediate something and it felt quite easy, even though I was terrified. One good thing was that I was able to move into the foster home to some extent, even staying there for a weekend, and I got to know the other children there a bit and got a real picture of where she was living.

The introductions were incredibly tiring because of all the travelling and, emotionally, it was a complete whirlwind. It took about three weeks. I did feel quite fearful that if a child came to me and had particular problems and outed me to social workers, that was a vulnerability hanging over me. But it was never an issue with Rosie because from very early on she was introduced to my lesbian friends. Whenever we talked about anything around sexuality or families I was very clear that some of my friends are lesbians and that if I ever intended to go out with anyone it would be a woman, and she took that on board quite easily. I think that was partly because she was watching things like *Brookside*; it was a time when lesbian relationships were on the television and there has been a shift in children's awareness because of that.

Rosie had had a lifetime in care and she'd had enough of social workers. It was agreed that they wouldn't come very often after she was placed. They were very supportive of the placement and very happy for me to go for the adoption order quite early on. I didn't feel particularly that I had to prove anything once she was placed with me, but now we have had some time post-adoption, Rosie and I feel a kind of liberation.

It was about fifteen months from when I was approved to Rosie moving in and about six months from first seeing her in the newsletter to her moving in. The adoption process was a bit drawn out and there was a problem with the court because, although there is a new court here, like several other new courts there's no facility for keeping parties apart in the family court. Otherwise, it was very straightforward. The actual hearing was quick and we went home and had a party afterwards.

There was a lot of pressure before the adoption. Because Rosie had had so many moves and had had pre-adoptive placements before, the adoption was a huge big deal for her and it was something else she'd not been through with another family. She went through months of saying I was going to die when I was forty, which I worked out was when she would have been with me two years, which was the longest she'd ever lived with anyone. So, in some respects, it gave her some sense of security to feel that the way she thought I was going to go was to die, not to shove her out. She has incredible fears and insecurities. They don't come out now in the same way but they're still there. It has been quite hard and it has felt like an enormous responsibility because she has had so many upheavals and a catalogue of bad judgments and mistakes and it sometimes feels like you've got to make up for it all and you can't, you can only do what you can do.

I'm absolutely besotted with her and we have so much fun together. I couldn't, in my wildest dreams, have ever imagined a better match. I think she's absolutely incredible. But I don't think I expected to feel quite so overwhelmed by her story. That's partly because I am a single parent and partly because there is so much in her story and I had to be clear who I was going to talk to about some of the things in Rosie's past. You can make plans for that but then things change, like friends starting relationships or other people who've got a real commitment to Rosie having a hard time in other ways, like a relationship breaking up, so I've protected them from some of the things I've needed to talk about. I think support is quite difficult because it doesn't matter how much you plan for support, you can never really envisage what you're going to need and it's never going to be exactly what you think it might be.

The biggest thing for me is having someone to share the pains your child goes through. Every time something happens to Rosie that's painful for her in her life now, in my mind there's this whole big scenario behind it and I feel like saying 'hasn't she been through enough?' There are lots of people who care about her but they're not able to share that feeling in the same way. If I was going through it again, I would seek out one other person who would be given all the information, whether a friend or my mum or whoever, so that there was someone else who has the same kind of background information on the child's story. You can end up taking on so much and, at least, if there's someone else who's done that, you've got someone to share it with and you don't have to go over old ground or explain yourself. I'm lucky that I know some other people who have adopted and I've got a lot of support from friends and family, but the load is spread a bit and it's having one place to go that would make a lot of difference.

She felt safe with me very quickly and she quickly transformed from this child who had been described as 'biddable' to testing me out in lots of respects. She is very strong-willed and very strong physically. We have periodic episodes of violence, which are incredible power struggles. They don't happen very often but when they do they are extreme and aren't very manageable. Thankfully, I have people I can ring and sometimes they have come down. Just having someone else there can change the emphasis. When I talk to her about it she says she feels she could have stopped things in her past happening and there's anger there and the feeling that she was responsible, and that comes from having had so many rejections. She can't quite handle the dependence she feels upon me and she needs so much reassurance. I know there aren't any easy answers, you just have to do what you can to get through it and talk about it afterwards. Although there are odd times when I feel out of my depth, these are fleeting and my experience of professionals has led me to believe that they are generally more out of their depth. Usually, they have not dealt with some of the things that I have.

There have been many occasions where I've had to take risks and push for Rosie's needs to be met, and, sometimes, my own. I think you have to be prepared to do that. If you're clear about what you want and what you think is right, you've got to be prepared to push, write letters of complaint, challenge social workers, write to the court about their inadequate new building, request financial help, whatever it takes. Through contact with other people who have adopted, I know I'm more fortunate than some. Before my child was placed I was told I'd have times when I would wonder what I'd done adopting a child. I haven't! I was prepared for a tough time and I know there are tough times to come. But what I receive from Rosie and our life together is much more than I've put in, and that's a lot. I think that what I provide Rosie with more than anything is total commitment. Children's needs do differ, but, in this case, as someone once said to me, 'what children who have been in care really need is someone to stick to them like glue'.

'A Great Asset'
Mike and Brian's Story

Mike and Brian are a white gay couple now in their mid-40s. They live in a small, modern, suburban housing development where everyone knows one another. Their home is not unlike thousands of others with family photos displayed on the bookcase in the living room. Brian is involved in cricket and football and Mike works in a bank. The only thing that makes them stand out is that they have lived together as a gay couple for the last twenty years and, for the last six of those years, have fostered fourteen teenage lads.

Brian: We were both coming up to forty at the time that we discussed fostering and decided that either we could grow old, fat and boring or could do a bit more with our lives. Once a couple have struggled to get a home together, build up careers and put themselves on a sound financial footing, that becomes a dangerous time. You are tempted to get involved elsewhere and you start taking one another for granted. Alternatively, you can let the years pass and you look back asking what you have done with your lives and what you have added to the world. One of our strengths as a couple has been that there are things that we have wanted to work on together.

We'd always been used to dealing with teenagers. I work in the transport industry and trainees from other parts of the country need lodgings in the city, thus we'd got used to always having someone staying in the house. Then we saw an advert from the local council – 'Would you like to foster teenagers? – Single people can apply'. At the bottom of the advert it said that the council was an equal opportunities employer. That started us wondering if they would accept a male couple as foster carers. There was only one way to find out, so I rang them and asked. The response was that they would have to ring back. Surprisingly, they were true to their word and did.

We were told that it was 'no problem' and someone came to visit and started filling in the forms. We joined in the next set of training groups. Three references were taken up and they also met my Mum when she was visiting. The whole process must have taken about a year from when we first saw the advert.

The Media

You need to be highly suspicious of the media. When we were first approved as foster carers, the local paper was featuring the issue of gay fostering because a case in Manchester was reported in a Sunday paper. They asked readers to write in with their comments. The letters that were printed in the newspaper were quite disturbing. There were supportive letters but the ones that stuck in my mind were the vitriolic ones of the sort 'How can you let dirty perverts get their hands on children!'

Soon after this there was a one-day course organised by the National Foster Care Association on the subject of fostering by lesbians and gay men. The press had been informed about the course and several right-wing MPs, including Norman Tebbit, had been quoted in the papers as being outraged that such a disreputable event was being organised. It didn't do much for our confidence. We discussed it with our fostering officer and thought that, with all the publicity our case had already had, it was wisest that we didn't turn up. The press might have been lying in wait.

As I have been in a reasonably powerful position, I believe that, previously, I have been cushioned against potential discrimination. I have been captain of the local cricket club and chairman of the sports club and at work am established in a responsible job running my own training consultancy. People have known about my sexuality. When placed in a position of responsibility, in a way, people may want to keep you there as they would suffer by your demise. People who have not come out are more vulnerable. Coming out depends on having strong people around you, good relationships and a strong family. Personal confidence comes from how you feel about yourself. 'Outing' annoys me, as people do what they feel able to do. So many things are important other than sexual matters.

Mike: We're not hugely demonstrative to each other – not in company. We give each other nice surprises and the odd cuddle at unexpected moments. When we started having boys placed with us, we couldn't go away suddenly and other impromptu things were less possible. However, we appreciate the time that we do have to ourselves more.

My position is different from Brian's. I've been working in a large international bank for eighteen years. It's a fairly mundane job. Some colleagues know that I'm gay, but not the senior managers. I have, however, taken Brian to the annual dinner and dance. The emphasis is on talking, eating and drinking and when we have occasionally hit the dance floor it has been with women! I took Brian the first year that we met, in June 1978.

Neighbours, Family, Friends and Social Workers

Brian: We live in an end-of-terrace house in a small modern housing development around a green. We could afford to live in larger accommodation but are on friendly terms with all the neighbours and would miss that. This is the right sized community with eleven houses and people make a big effort to get on. Everyone sends each other Christmas cards. One older neighbour helps a child fix a bike. One of the others is a builder. When one of our boys damaged the house, the builder did the repairs and charged us very little. Our animals meant that we got to know our neighbours, but it happened a lot more with the boys. We apologised to our next door neighbours for all the loud music and noise, but they've never complained. When we were going through a problem with one of the kids, one of our neighbours said: 'I do admire what you do with these youngsters, I really do'.

Most friends thought we were mad to consider becoming foster carers to teenagers because of the risk of bad publicity with it being such a controversial subject. They also warned that the kids were likely to display disturbed patterns of behaviour and might well make allegations against us. One couple of friends decided that they couldn't risk seeing us any more. One of them was the managing director of a large firm and felt that there might be allegations and scandal if he was linked with the household.

Generally, though, friends and family have been very supportive. I have sometimes taken the boys to work when they have been 'kicked out' of school and get them to take messages and do minor jobs around the office. Work colleagues say: 'Couldn't do what you do' and seem to respect us.

My family always asks after the boys and are very positive in their attitude. Some of the boys have stayed with my sister, who lives by the sea and has teenage children herself. Also, my mother comes to stay on occasions to give us a break. My parents separated when I was in my teens and, on occasions, it has been helpful to say, particularly to the boys who have experienced difficult relationships, what happened with my Dad and how I coped.

Mike: There were a couple of social workers in one of the children's homes that some of the boys had been in previously who were pretty negative. However, generally, social workers have been positive. We never really considered doing anything other than fostering teenagers. We didn't want to go for something long-term as we didn't know how it was going to work out. Matching is so difficult. You can only tell two years or so later whether it has really worked out. Our local council has kept us very busy with placements and some have worked better than others. Our fostering officer has told us, particularly when the going has been tough, what a great asset we are to the department.

Brian: When making placements, it has often been considered whether or not it would be helpful for there to be a female figure around. Where in previous placements the young person's difficult behaviour has focused on women, or it has been particularly mothers who have let the boys down, there can be advantages to having solely male carers. In a lot of instances the boys haven't previously had fathers around or there has been a bad relationship with a stepfather. Generally, there is such a diversity of kids needing foster homes that you need a diversity of placements to meet their needs.

How the Boys View our Relationship

Mike: Generally, we haven't changed how we organise the home. We both do much as we did before the boys arrived. Having grown up in a crowded household of seven brothers, I was delighted to have my own home and am more interested in houses generally than Brian is. He takes responsibility for the garden, the holidays and the car, but also cooks twice a week, which includes the evening that I'm out. We try to get the boys involved in family activities and Brian is building a bike stand with the lad who is with us at the moment.

Usually, before they are placed, the boys will visit and stop overnight to get a feel of the place and see if they are going to like it with us. They know that the placement is with a gay couple before they visit. They may check the idea out with their friends but may also be careful which friends they tell. All of them have been happy to have friends back here. In some ways, it may seem quite a 'hip' thing to have gay foster carers. We have always made sure that their friends' parents know the situation here before their children visit.

Brian: There have been a couple of occasions when we've learnt that critical comments have been made to the boys about us, but they usually take it 'in their stride'. Either we or they say that people will always pick on something to be critical about and if it's not being gay, it will be something else.

One of the first boys, David, still sends us Fathers' Day cards saying how much he appreciates us both. He's now 22 and we're going to his wedding.

Young People that Stick in your Mind

Mike: Shane was the fourth or fifth lad we had in placement. He was a tough, thirteen-year-old skinhead. All his brothers had been in trouble with the law. He was quite wild when he arrived. He'd use his hands as spoons, like shovels, for eating. He was told he had to eat at the table. His clothes were in an awful state, his personal hygiene non-existent, occasionally he would wet the bed and he smelt. As a result, he was ignored or taunted at school.

It was obvious that more and more vicious anger was to come out. On the second night he had to be physically restrained. He'd done karate and wouldn't give up. He was very wound up and, eventually, we sat him down and asked him what was wrong. 'When are you going to have an argument?' was the response. He had been so used to living in the midst of conflict that he couldn't cope with the uncertainty of waiting for it to erupt again. After six weeks or so he realised that what we said was true, that we don't really have arguments but discuss things out. He then started to relax and enjoy things.

Brian: One funny incident I remember involved the neighbours on the other side of the green. They are a nice, refined, fairly reserved elderly couple. Their daughter had just come back from a trip to Bali, had a great tan and was wearing shorts and a sleeveless Tee shirt. We had just arrived back in the car with Shane. He spied the young woman, strode over to look her up and down, and said: 'Gawd, you aren't harf brown!' 'Oh, thank you, I've been away actually.' 'But bet your bum's white!'

I took him to my sports club and the reaction from the other members was 'What on earth have you brought in now?' Shane was so aggressive and angry. However, underneath it he was quite a nice lad and his behaviour improved quite quickly. People in general were very supportive and Shane really responded to their interest.

It had only been a three-month placement but we had been able to offer him a different environment altogether. We saw an enormous change in him, which people started to remark on. He started making friends at school and he was even invited into their games. People's reactions had changed. He started to become demonstrative. He would give you a hug when you were sitting down and put his arm round you. He wanted to be hugged and cuddled himself.

We don't really know what had gone on before. His father had hit him a lot and he'd suffered lots of different types of abuse probably. His social worker referred to sexual and emotional abuse. When he was with us, it was the first time he felt wanted and safe. People started spending time with him rather than shunning him.

However, there was a 'sub-plot' going on all the time. His mother wasn't going to take him back until she got a new council house. Then, one night, she walked out with him, even though she hadn't been able to get a council house.

She had been coming round to our house two or three times a week. She had been 'nice as pie' to our faces but behind the scenes she was saying that it was not appropriate for her son to be placed with two gay men with 'one of them buying flowers for the other' ! She later intimated to us that she'd been forced by the situation with her accommodation to place her child in care and she didn't want that to be with gay foster carers. We found that very undermining.

In the end she was confronted about her attitudes and it was then that she removed her son. She told Shane that we had thrown him out and, as we've never been able to see him since, he probably still believes that to be true. It is also frustrating to think that he would have deteriorated again. It's as though it was all for nothing. We'd got attached to him. That was one of the times when we thought 'Why are we doing this?'

Mike: Another placement we particularly remember was Sachin's. He was a fourteen-year-old boy from Mauritius who had been brought here by a distant relative in order to give him a better education than his brothers had had. She must have brought him on a holiday visa, probably for six months. Unfortunately, she had him running around like a slave, with no intention of getting him an education. However, he refused to put up with the bad treatment and in the end she had marched him into social services. A lot of people wanted to prevent him being deported and that's how he came to be placed with us. He was used to hard work and had worked as a panel beater back home. He spoke Creole French and would shorten words. Fortunately, I speak some French. When he arrived and saw our cat, he wouldn't leave poor Sam alone. He also got on well with Duke the dog.

Brian: On one occasion I was digging a pond in the back garden and needed to dig down about three feet. Sachin offered to do it. I marked out the area and then went to work on my car over the other side of the green. I chatted with neighbours and forgot all about what Sachin was doing. When finally I came back into the garden, there was a pile of soil four feet high. Sachin wasn't to be seen, just the glint of the shovel coming out of the hole. He was sweating profusely and smiling and the hole was already much too deep for the pond. I didn't have the heart to tell him and had to try to gradually fill the hole back in without him noticing. To this day, it's still too deep.

Sachin had never seen cricket and he tagged along and managed to work out one or two things about the game. I put him at the safest place where he wouldn't get hurt or get the ball in his direction. The other team's star player had been batting for fifteen minutes and was going to win the match if his innings wasn't brought to an end. He hit the ball in the direction of Sachin's head. I tried to shout to him to get out of the way but Sachin caught it right in front of his face. Everyone was clapping him on the back. It had been a marvellous catch for his first match.

At the end of Sachin's placement, his status in this country was becoming increasingly precarious. With the immigration authorities 'closing in', we told him that if he wanted to come back to visit sometime, he ought to leave the country voluntarily. If he became an illegal overstayer and was deported, that would never be possible. He was losing the battle. We both took the day off to take him to the airport. It was an emotional day. He keeps his English up and remains in contact through phone calls. He's now about nineteen and a carpenter. He was upset to hear when our cat died.

Difficult Behaviour

Mike: When we began fostering we were warned that we might find such things as excrement or rotten food hidden in drawers. We haven't had that so far. Wet beds is the worse we've had and that was with Shane. He was told, when it happened, to just put the bedding in the washing machine and no one would mention it. He had a plastic mattress cover and knew where clean sheets were. It happened on two or three occasions but had slowed down. It had been going on for thirteen years but it stopped within a month of him being with us.

One of the most difficult situations was when Colin was placed for a period of assessment whilst we had another lad here called Jimmy. We were told that Colin would need psychiatric help and he was certainly very difficult. Doors had to be replaced upstairs after he had smashed them with training weights. He'd been sent to his room to calm down! He started being violent to Jimmy and pulled a knife on him on one occasion. For the safety of both of them, Colin couldn't stay. He went to a children's home and it was decided that he wasn't fosterable.

Coming from a large family has made me more tolerant, although silly little things will wind me up more than they will Brian. For example, after Christmas there was quite a lot of turkey over and I told everyone not to touch it as I was going to make a curry. Tony couldn't leave it alone and kept taking large strips out of it. I lost patience with him but, in retrospect, I should have just discussed it. When I'm cross I generally tend to be 'off' with the boys and they soon realise. Brian calls it the 'silent treatment'.

Brian: I'm probably less tolerant than Mike. However, I'm into Buddhism and that possibly makes me less judgmental. I will take a more confrontational approach though. For example, Richard was a compulsive thief and liar and I challenged him about this and still he lied. In the end I got angry with him and it was all over and done with. One of the worst difficulties is when a boy constantly lies. You don't know what to believe or know which of their problems to believe.

Mike: When you take on young people you are also taking on their families. Tony would come back from visiting his family and he would be so depressed.

I felt so sad that they could treat him like that but, as a foster carer, you can't really get involved with the family. You just try to help the young people themselves.

Attitudes to Sex

Brian: When we were preparing to go on holiday to Tenerife, a few years ago now, the three boys who were with us at the time were boasting in the back of the car. They said how they were going to 'give the birds a right good screwing'. I stopped the car at a chemists and said that in that case we'd better go in to get some condoms. Having shocked them by my seeming acceptance of what they had been saying, I was able to take the opportunity, subsequently, to get a discussion going about attitudes to relationships with girls and safer sex.

Conclusions

Mike: Currently, we have Anthony with us. He moved in six months ago and will soon be fifteen. He could be with us for two more years and by that time we will have been fostering for eight years. We will probably be wanting to have a break or stop fostering by then, maybe continuing to do some respite care. Although teenagers seem to fit in with our way of life remarkably easily, the stresses and strains and uncertainties of fostering take their toll. We have found that social workers, parents and, above all, the teenagers we have cared for have largely been without bias or, at least, visible prejudice about our being gay. However, one hears of other, straight foster carers getting accused of all sorts of things, usually because of the problems of the particular child, and you feel it is only a matter of time before we suffer the same fate. You feel more vulnerable as a gay foster carer.

Brian: Generally, though, we feel that our experience of fostering has been very worthwhile. Dealing with emotionally disturbed young people and inadequate parenting, you can be involved in highly volatile situations. It is this which stretches your skills to the limit. You find out more about yourself and meet so many different people with different experiences of life. This, coupled with the lads coming back to see us, some now with their wives and their own children, is what makes it such an enriching experience. This is something very valuable that we would have missed if we hadn't decided to foster.

'You May Have to Count to Ten, No Twenty, Sometimes…'
Sandra's Story

Sandra is a white lesbian who lives in the south of England and is studying full time. She has two-mixed race birth children, aged seven and nine, of African Caribbean and English heritage. She has been doing short-term and emergency fostering of teenage girls for some years and has had two long-term placements. Her current foster child has been with her for eight months. She and her children and their cats live in a big house in a multi-racial inner-city area.

I suppose I grew up feeling that having babies and parenting was the be-all and end-all of life and that's what was expected of me. I've always really liked having a big family around and when I was growing up I wanted more brothers and sisters. I had my own children and then a social worker I knew introduced me to the idea of fostering.

When I decided to foster and contacted a local agency, I wasn't out as a lesbian, I was actually still dating men. When I finally came out it was to my link worker on the doorstep of my house and I found it extremely difficult to tell her. I do feel my link worker and I haven't clicked and she suggested herself that we don't get on. She reacted really well at the time, outwardly she appears not to have a problem, but I don't know if I could say that underneath she hasn't got a problem with it.

I felt I was assessed quite quickly, in about three to six months, and it was really interesting going through my own 'history' and seeing how it benefits my understanding of what children in care might be going through. I feel a lot of my past and childhood contributed to what I was going into. I've only ever had one-to-one fostering training about abused children, so I don't know what they say to other foster carers. I don't know why it was necessary to do it one-to-one as it was very time-consuming and expensive for the agency and in a group you can share ideas and thoughts and feelings. I think I would have preferred that.

I had a child placed with me quite quickly as well. Because I'm a single parent with two young children, it was suggested to me, and I agreed, that I foster young teenage girls and that I wouldn't take boys or children with learning difficulties or other disabilities because I've also been at college all the time that I've been fostering. Having said that, the first child I got had mild learning difficulties, which was fine, but she needed a lot more input than I could give her and the placement didn't last very long. If she had had one-to-one attention and more assistance, she would have been able to stay in a family environment longer.

In the main, you get a child's history after they've been placed with you. Both long-term children I've had came initially for one night only as emergency placements and ended up staying for two years and I've learnt their history as I've gone along. Even with emergency care you're supposed to know some of their history before you take them, but it doesn't often happen.

My friends have been marvellous about me fostering, more so than my family. They've accepted that I've got three or four children, whereas my family have been more rejecting. My father has been really, really good and he plays a big part in this family unit's life here at home. He treats everyone equally but the rest of the family haven't looked on the foster child as being part of the family, which is important. They don't include them or see them as part of the family in the same way. They wouldn't expect to include that child on an outing, whereas my father wouldn't consider not taking that child as well. Some of my family might be confused by how openly I speak to my children about being a lesbian. I came out about three years ago and my mother thinks it's a phase I'm going through. I think she's concerned that I could make a child be gay or lesbian.

I haven't lived here very long and, gradually, my neighbours have found out about my sexuality but no one has said anything derogatory, which is quite unusual. I've had quite a lot of dealings with outside bodies and I feel that people like counsellors are more approachable than social workers or link workers. They're more relaxed about sexuality and more used to talking about things like that. The social workers have to try and be right-on about their attitude towards us but maybe underneath they still can't grasp how not to let their own personal views of lesbian and gay fostering and adoption get in the way. I've told the school I'm a lesbian because I've been called in on a number of occasions with my children using the word 'femidom'. We have a teenage foster child with us at the moment and she's been given condoms and femidoms which the kids have picked up. I've told the school that I don't hide anything like that from the children, except perhaps from Joanne who's seven, but Michael's nine.

I don't really know why I only do short-term fostering. It often starts off short-term and ends up long-term, like the child I had before this one was for two years and the child I've got now I've had for eight months and they're going to class as long-term. It's very difficult when they leave but I think I prefer long-term, it feels healthier mentally and emotionally for everyone concerned – for me, my children and the child that's coming in. But it doesn't always work out. I've probably fostered about six children this year and one of them is still here and they could all have been potentially long-term so it's quite sad I think. One of them was almost permanently on the run, one has gone back to the birth mother and some are with other foster carers.

Fostering is very different from my life before and it can be quite stressful. I feel like I only half belong to social services and I'm doing a lot of work that I've never had any training for and I have to cope with it on a daily basis. We're not supported enough and, especially, the young person in care is not supported enough. It feels like there's this big company up there with all these standards and when they want you to act you have to act immediately and they don't really realise what's involved in the day-to-day care of that child. My holidays in Lesbos, camping on women-only sites, have caused a bit of trouble about taking them to where there are lesbians and people worrying about me turning them into lesbians and so on. But we've got loads of ambitions, we want to go to India as well, and no one's going to hold us back. We have house meetings around the dinner table and if we're not talking about school, we're planning other things, like where we want to go. Conversations at home do change when you've got a foster child, especially where there's an age gap with the younger children.

My children really like us fostering, especially when the foster children are nearer to their age. My son wants me to foster a boy so I'm trying to get my category changed. I have fostered boys on emergency placements and it's been brilliant and really good fun for all the children. They really enjoy having a teenager around who likes to play loud music and put on make-up and dance to *Top of the Pops* in the front room. I remember as a kid having teenage cousins coming to stay who were my idols. My children get very upset sometimes when the foster children run away or stay out at night and they hear me talking about it and, obviously, when they leave they miss them. Generally, spaces and gaps we've had without a foster child have been nice in some ways but we've missed having other children around. They can feel jealous of the foster children but then you overhear one of them calling her 'my big sister' or something, which is really nice. I think it's natural for children to feel jealous of each other at times, even when they're biologically related.

My children are black and, sometimes, if we foster white children, they don't like West Indian food and we have a problem with that. The foster child I have at the moment is white but has previously been placed with a black foster family and they taught her how to cook a few West Indian dishes, so that's brilliant. Because we eat more curries and food that white foster children aren't used to, it can be unsettling for the foster children at first. I usually take them shopping with me to find out what they like and I will cook something different for them. They can hardly believe it the way we go round the supermarket piling things into a massive trolley and end up with an enormous bill! We've recently moved into a much bigger house and every bit of space is taken up by something. We moved to an area with more black people because we were dealing with a lot of racism where we were before. There seems to be a better mix here and people are more culturally aware.

I'm really surprised that I'm not allowed to foster black or mixed-race children. I have before but because there's a same-race placement policy and I'm white, I'm only supposed to be given white children and it's not enough that my children are mixed-race. The children do see their father and he is a positive role model for them and I have lots of black friends. I have been praised for the work I did with one mixed-race child who I fostered for two years. I feel it's sad that you hear that there are so many black children in care that they can't find placements for and I'm sitting here. Also, I've had really sad things happen, like white foster children's use of racist language, that I've had to deal with. I feel I'd like to give another mixed-race child in care the chance to come into an environment where we're so positive about identity and hair care and food and culture.

Sometimes, you feel like you're living in a goldfish bowl and everything you want to do you have to get permission for and you live by fostering and adoption's morals and standards. You do have to adapt to their way of thinking, their Victorian outlook. My fifteen-year-old foster child and I have a lot of discussion on the fact that everything she wants to do she has to ask them and we have to fight for everything. We both get really fed up of the bureaucracy, begging for things like clothing grants and holiday grants. She's involved with a youth project so she has to ask if she can do things with them, go on the radio, it's all so unnatural. It puts a lot of strain on our relationship because she can never get a straight answer from me. I have to say to her: 'You know I have to ask "them"', which is sad really because other kids can just ask their parents 'can I do this tomorrow?' and they'll say yes or no straight away.

I feel you have to tell social services straight away if you've got a new partner or someone who may be a new partner, so I sit there thinking: do I tell social services that I've been to the pictures with someone or had a meal with someone? knowing myself that it may not be a new relationship, just being closer-than-usual friends maybe? I always think it's going to be easy to ask friends if they will be police-checked but as you go to say it, it's like you're asking them if they've got a criminal record and you haven't really got to know them that well yet. Both the new partners I've had while fostering have been police-checked but it was worrying for them being investigated in that way. They were taken out for a coffee by the link worker and talked to without me being there. That's quite a lot to ask someone to do at the beginning of a relationship. They're probably wondering: 'what am I getting into here and how good do I have to be, do I have to give the right answers?' It's very stressful.

Our lifestyle and standard of living has been an issue where a child has not been used to having pocket money, being bought new clothes, being taken out, having fruit around, things like that. Politically, a white child coming in using racist language, we'd have to talk about it and sort it out. I think my lifestyle is an issue with birth parents sometimes, the way I dress, the style of house, stripped floors and so on, maybe going to festivals. I am described as being quite young at heart by my link worker and other social workers. Usually, when they're placing children, they'll say to them: 'You'll have really good fun in this house. They do lots of exciting stuff'. But parents aren't used to that, going to festivals, planning camping trips abroad, things like that, and they're suspicious. When there is a lot of involvement of birth parents, their jealousy can create hell. With my present foster child, her parent is changing his attitude towards my fostering skills and I think this is because this is the first place she's really settled down and he's probably feeling a bit jealous. It would be so easy to deal with if only the social worker would say to him 'maybe you're feeling a bit jealous', rather than him getting angry about other issues.

Because I'm fostering teenage girls who have all been sexually active, how to talk about sex has been a big issue in the house. There have been visits to clinics for venereal diseases and open discussions about condoms and femidoms, which the younger children have talked about at school and then I've had to go to the school to explain. Sex is sometimes discussed on a daily basis. The type of children I've fostered really need to know how to protect themselves.

I felt different about nudity in the house after the training I had about the experiences of the children I might get and after I had an allegation made against me about nudity by a girl I was fostering, which I think was influenced by previous informal carers she had been with for a long time. I feel it's really sad that we have to hide our bodies from each other and I don't agree with a lot of the policy of fostering and adoption, but I have been talked to about it and told to uphold it. The policy is that you must keep the bathroom door locked, you mustn't walk around with no clothes on and you mustn't have children running into the bathroom when you're in the bath, which I think is impossible and an unnatural environment. I can't understand why they're so worried. I agree with some of what they're telling me about abused children and nudity but I think I know what I'm doing if someone walks into the bathroom when I'm not fully dressed. I feel abuse and nudity are separate issues. It makes you feel like an abuser just because you've been seen with no clothes on. Children are so vulnerable and confused, it's positive for them to understand how our bodies change. When I was a young woman I felt really lonely and confused and horrified by the changes in my body. I'm glad my daughter and son know what's going to happen to them when they grow up.

I had an allegation made against me by the parents of one girl I fostered. The girl used to turn up at a local gay and lesbian club I went to as she was going out with the bouncer, who was heterosexual. I was accused both of making her sleep with men and of trying to make her into a lesbian by taking her to the club, which I never did. When she went missing or didn't come home sometimes, I would call the police and one time they told me that they preferred that she was at the club because she was safer there than anywhere else. It was a local club and lots of my friends would be in there. The girl was going out with the bouncer and they knew she would be looked after and brought home. When a parent finds out that their child has been placed with a lesbian they tend to start to complain about other issues. The latest complaints have been that I had no carpet because my floorboards are stripped and varnished and that I was a single parent. Parents have also complained that they think their children will be abused by me. You have to be quite strong and not listen too much because it feels like you've got to prove to that parent that you're an okay person. The social workers always say: 'Oh, they've been told you've been police-checked and you've been fostering for some years'. They don't tackle the parent's attitude that all lesbians are abusers but just try to convince the parent that this particular foster carer has been properly checked. If they countered the abuse issue head-on, it would be much more helpful.

In the two long-term placements I've had I've only had positive responses to me being a lesbian, although one of them was influenced by her birth parents to make negative comments. I feel it helps them to open up and talk about sex with men because maybe it doesn't seem so close to me and they're not so embarrassed about talking about it. They're obviously interested in what I get up to and maybe that pushes them to start asking questions, which leads on to safer sex and other stuff. I always say to them 'you tell who you want to tell, you don't have to tell everyone'. My younger children have been called lesbian and gay in school but I think that happens to all children and I try to tell them that they don't have to tell people about me. I think our household is generally more open and we're a more socially and culturally aware family than most because we've got mixed-race children, a lesbian mother, and a white heterosexual foster child who is going out with a black guy, so we're all inter-connected in some way in our experiences of discrimination.

I'm the sort of person who blows up and calms down. I've had to deal with so much challenging behaviour over the last year – stamping feet, slamming doors, manipulative behaviour. I start afresh with each child and I'm a bit slow to realise what they're actually doing. Some of them have learnt the system, what they can do and get away with – I'm talking about fifteen-year-olds who don't come in all night and don't care. The child I've got at the moment started off like that but has really, really settled down. Like with the child that made a lot of allegations about me, I just stick by them and don't mind if they slam doors occasionally and talk back. They can have a bit of a debate with me, I'm quite easygoing. With stuff like staying out all night, I was really one for grounding and stopping pocket money but I've stopped that now because it doesn't seem to make much difference. I just talk and try and tell them how important it is for them to communicate with me if they're not coming in because, otherwise, I'm worrying myself sick. It's part of them making a commitment and they can be really proud of that. One important thing is that a foster child will test you to the limit to see if you'll say right, that's it, you've got to go. They're treated like a parcel, one child said to me that she felt like a pass the parcel. They do do some horrible things and then they start packing their bags even before you've discovered what they've done because they know you're going to find out. Crack-taking, prostitution, letting boys in, stealing, it can be very worrying what they get up to.

What surprises me all the time about fostering is how many children are moved about quite often and how impossible it seems to be to help them and sort out all their problems and, especially, their history, which I always feel hasn't been dealt with or talked about. I find it very surprising that children have gone for long periods without counselling or proper support. Things get lost, things that were supposed to have been done and dealt with don't happen because placements break down and they get moved on and have to start all over again. I think that might be changing gradually. I've had training in using a new much more detailed form to be filled out in reviews and placements, which might help. It's hard when you find out that a child has had ongoing problems for years and years and they never seem to have been dealt with, like at the last review I had when the social worker said 'I've never heard the child talking about these issues before' and suddenly she's talking about them with me and it just feels like maybe they've never given her the time she's needed. The saddest thing is seeing children whose parents have totally rejected them.

The most enjoyable thing about fostering is being a big family and sticking together, getting to know the child and getting to the stage where you feel they belong, and when other children leave, like when we get an emergency for a few days, and the longer-term foster child says 'It's nice to be just us again'.

'A Special Mother's Day Card'
Elizabeth and Mary's Story

Elizabeth and Mary are two white lesbians who have been together for ten years. They are in their forties and both continue with their demanding full-time work. They have provided respite care for Peter for seven years and were approved for a permanent full-time placement of a child of primary school age in 1994. A year later, Daniel came to live with them, followed by a cat, a guinea-pig and several fish but not (yet) the dog he craves. They were interviewed by another lesbian couple.

It seems a long time ago that we made the decision that we wanted to adopt. We had talked about wanting children from the time we got together. Our first thoughts were to 'grow our own' rather than to get one 'off the peg'. We did put some energy into thinking of inseminating and joined a self-help insemination group. We found the whole process of meeting donors very strange and stressful. Only one of us could try inseminating and we were both pretty freaked out by the whole thing and, especially, the uncertainty and stress of waiting for a period and for fertile times. We just didn't have the stamina to go on for more than a few months.

We first approached social services as a general enquiry. One of us rang the advertised fostering number. She'd been feeling fed-up with work and wanted to get on with other parts of life, like being with children. We were sent a pack of information. We'd also seen a piece in the first *Out on Tuesday* series on television about respite care and this seemed the right thing for us at that time. When we rang back to tell them we were interested, a social worker came to see us the following week.

We didn't 'come out' straight away, although we were clear that we were both interested and were committed to living together and we owned the house together. One of us applied as a single carer with the other also involved. The social worker set up meetings with us, with specific topics to discuss at the meetings. These included: discipline, food, money and other issues. She also asked us to write down our life stories for her. That's when we came out. The social worker knew that the council had an equal opportunities policy which covered sexuality and thought it would be all right. She said she would check with the boss what was involved because she was new. She came back the next week and asked us about our attitude to men and variations around that question.

We didn't know any other lesbians who had been through the assessment process openly as lesbians. We did know one carer who is a lesbian but had not been out when she was assessed. She knew others and one woman set up a support group. She was very active in the Foster Care Association locally so she was able to get their support. There were about five single lesbian carers or couples involved in that early support group but none of the others had been out when they were first assessed. Some of them did an enormous amount of difficult work with many children.

We were questioned about our attitudes towards men during our assessment. There weren't many men in our circle at that time. We emphasised that we weren't antagonistic to men and that we weren't separatists, but the social worker didn't know what that meant! We said things like 'we get on well with male colleagues at work', 'we get on well with our brothers'. We had both lived in women's houses before moving in together.

Our social worker didn't offer any apologies for asking these questions and we laughed about it in between the sessions, wondering what she would come back and ask next. The rest was so positive that we just took it in our stride. We asked her to assess us as two individual carers (who were each out lesbians and in a couple) because we didn't trust the confidentiality throughout the department. We didn't want to be 'Miss A and Miss B' on all the files, making it really obvious, although we were happy to be out in the small print inside the files. She colluded with this.

We don't remember her asking about 'role models' but she did ask about the way we divided household tasks. Sometimes, we were not sure what was going to go in the report and what was the social worker's personal interest in comparing our life with her married life!

We were each approved. We began respite care in the name of one of us. We didn't come out to the child's family, although we didn't hide our close relationship and they accepted that we were both equally involved. With hindsight, it might have been easier to be out from the start but we had decided not to as we usually only expect to tell friends once they know us and understand our lives. In fact, the family has been very supportive and we are still caring for Peter seven years later. The original arrangement was for one weekend a month and one week of the summer holidays and we have maintained that level of involvement.

One of the difficulties of being assessed separately was that they had one of us on the books with no child placed. They approached us to take another. After some time we had another child on a different weekend in the month. This was an older girl with very different needs. We found it difficult that we had not been out to the family and doubted that they would have accepted the placement if they had known. This was a tension. We found this second placement too much and had to withdraw. Again, the social worker was very supportive and helpful about the way we felt in letting the child down. After that, we asked them to more formally recognise us as a couple caring for Peter.

Later, we joined a support group concerned about the issues for lesbian and gay foster and adoptive parents. Through the group we learnt a lot more about what was involved in fostering full-time and the extent to which lesbians and gay men were being accepted. We were already providing respite care to Peter and we finally decided that we were ready to apply for full-time fostering. At the first interview we thought the social worker was really trying to put us off. We accepted that it was not because we were lesbians, it was because she wanted to be sure we knew that taking on 'damaged' children would be challenging and that they had very few young children. We still said that we were interested.

We waited several months and were then given only one week's notice of a course over six weekday evenings, which was the next stage. We felt that other carers there had, perhaps, had more preparation for the course than we had. There were about sixteen people in the group – two single carers, six heterosexual couples and us. We had not met the social workers leading the course but we were pretty sure they knew about us. Our sexuality was not concealed but it was also not openly discussed in the group as a whole. Sometimes, it was not clear which group we should join when we split into smaller groups. Did we both go with the women (which we did) or would it have worked better if we had split up as a couple?

The classes were not part of the assessment but you have to attend the classes before they will start your interviews for the Form F. We enjoyed the sessions on child development, including a graphic illustration of the long-term damage that missing a stage in development can cause. There were also discussions about sexual abuse and what it is like for the birth parents and foster children moving to a new home.

We waited some more months before our assessment interviews started. Our social worker was very open and willing to learn from us about the way we lived and our relationship and we were open with her from the start.

We had a tricky time discussing the gender of the child we would want. It had not been an issue when we first decided to do respite care. It turned out that one of us (who had brothers and had provided care for a friend's boy) had a preference for a boy and the other (who had sisters and nieces and had cared for a girl) preferred a girl. Our social worker thought it might be more difficult to get approval if we specified a girl because of our sexuality but was willing to talk it through. In the end we said 'one or two children of either sex'. It was also a factor that the authority had far more boys than girls to place.

We were shown the full write-up of our interviews before it went to panel and were told straight away after the panel meeting that we had been approved. It had taken a year from our enquiry to approval. We had not told many people, except close friends, about our application until we were approved. It was good to tell people that we were planning to adopt and our families were supportive, although concerned about what we were taking on.

It took another year before we had a child placed. After we were approved we were in line to take a girl and, although we had not met her, we had moved her in in our heads. Then her circumstances changed and she was no longer available to be placed. That was a blow and we needed to grieve.

We considered other children suggested by our placement worker and also looked at the adverts in the NFCA (National Foster Care Association) and BAAF (British Agencies for Adoption and Fostering) papers. We rang up about one young boy from another authority. We came out to the placement worker on the telephone and she was enthusiastic. Later, another social worker left an answerphone message to say that the child needed a father. We now know that he was placed with a single woman. That experience put us off dealing with other authorities. Even within our authority we had the impression that some social workers dragged their heels in providing information to us about possible children. It didn't feel like we could do anything about that.

We did consider several other children and talked to their social workers. When we decided that they were not the right child for us, usually because they sounded too challenging, we were not put under any pressure to agree. We were also, sometimes, disappointed when a child we had been asked about was not available. At least once this was because a family from 'Catholic Rescue' had come forward. We didn't try and compete! Each time we were thinking about a child it was very stressful. All we knew about the children was a summary of their situation passed on by our placement worker or their social worker. We were never shown photos but we still felt very involved.

We did feel that the social workers pushed our limits. We had said 'primary school age'. The children that were suggested were in the last year of primary and we realised that we wanted a younger one, so we told them to adjust our age range to eight and under. (The child placed with us was seven years and eleven months!)

With regard to telling others about our sexuality, we have just told school and other authorities that we are both his parents without any further discussion of what that means. Informal situations can be difficult as there are so many complications. The simple question on the beach 'are you here with your mum and dad?' has so many complications for Daniel that the enquirer gets a confused picture, of which the two female parents is only a small part!

Daniel's social worker was interested in the respite placement we already had because he knew Daniel needed two actively involved parents. He accepted that was more likely to come from us than many heterosexual couples and felt it was demonstrated in our care of Peter. Other factors he was looking at included how we (and he) would explain that Daniel had two mums, how Daniel would adjust to a non-traditional family (he thought, better than many children) and the male role model issue. He seemed to be really trying to work out what type of placement would suit the child and whether we fitted the bill. On the other hand, he had not had any other offers!

Daniel has had mixed reactions to having two mothers. He doesn't call either of us Mum, we use our first names. His school has been supportive. When he did his first 'Mother's Day' card at school, it was a teapot. His had two tea-bags in while everybody else's only had one! In our circles he probably gets more hurtful teasing from children about being fostered than he does about having lesbian parents. That may change as he gets older.

'No Regrets'
Shula's Story

Shula is a 34-year-old black lesbian who has a nine-year-old black girl, Yasmin, placed with her for adoption. She was out when approved as a single adopter and she and Yasmin now live with her new partner, Teresa, who is white. Teresa is currently being assessed by the adoption agency.

I've always toyed with the idea of adoption, just as I've toyed with the idea of having my own birth children, but I finally decided on adoption because of a combination of age and finance. Finance because I work full-time and I felt I couldn't afford to have a baby and pay for full-time childcare, and age because I don't want to be starting with a baby now. I first planned to have children in my twenties in a previous relationship. When we decided to have children, my partner had our first child, Tanya, and the idea was that I was going to have our second baby. But the relationship finished. I still have links with Tanya despite a very difficult period in between. So I didn't have birth children at the time I had thought and that, coupled with the fact that initial enquiries into finding a black donor proved very difficult, started me on the path of thinking seriously about adoption.

I think I'm not so hung up on blood ties as a lot of people. Part of that is probably being brought up in an African country. Although blood ties were important, there's also the extended family system and kids aren't necessarily brought up by their biological parents. The issue of having to have your own birth mother to look after you is not strong in me. Also, when I was thirteen, my family fostered an eighteen-month-old little girl. I was hooked from day one! Over the summer holidays I was her primary carer and this, more than anything, taught me that you can bond without blood ties.

When I finally decided to apply to adopt I didn't tell a lot of people at first. My family and close friends knew. My mum was ambivalent, partly because she would have liked me to have had a birth child and also because she had already lost a grandchild through the break-up of my previous relationship and she could see similar insecurities in adoption. For my younger brother, my whole lifestyle is an enigma and he accepts it all as fine. My older brother doesn't agree with anything I do so I'm not bothered about him. My friends generally said: 'it's a tough decision, but good luck'. Some people said that they could never do it, they would shy away from the assessment procedure or from the potential problems in placement. The reaction I hated the most was "Oh, you're so wonderful and heroic, imagine doing that!"

I started the process about two-and-a-half years ago when I went on a preparation course. I was lucky that there was another single black woman in the group and the course was very good. I didn't come out on the preparation course but I was out to my social worker from day one as I had no intention of doing it any other way. I found her very supportive, almost too enthusiastic in the sense that she sometimes had to be reminded by her colleagues that the panel might see things differently.

In the assessment she asked a lot about my cultural background and was particularly interested in the fact that I had been brought up in an African country and my 'culture' was in-built rather than learnt from a book, if you know what I mean. She asked how I would deal with the racial background of my child as I would almost certainly have a child who was either of African-Caribbean heritage or from a different part of Africa. I talked about how I would try to find out more about the child's background as well as giving him or her what I could from my own culture. I felt we covered a lot of ground in depth and I don't recall feeling upset at any point or that there were any gaps. The only thing I would say, and I imagine this goes for most black people interviewed by white interviewers, is that there's an in-built assumption that if you're black you know how to deal with it all and I suppose that because I wanted to pass the assessment, I didn't dissuade her of that idea!

In terms of how she handled the issue of me being a lesbian, she was careful to stress that she and I had to present my case to a panel of people who might have prejudices and therefore it was important to anticipate any areas of concern and have answers to them. It felt like a collaborative effort to me. I didn't get the impression that she was treating me any differently because of my sexuality, except, perhaps, that I had to show that I had adequate male role models in my support network. You see, when I first wrote down people in my support network, I put my female friends, many of whom have male partners. I was told it might be assumed that they were all lesbians, which would have been incorrect, so I said 'fine, I'll put down all their partners as well', thus presenting a picture that would satisfy the panel.

At the time of the assessment I wasn't too bothered about gender, in relation to which children I would take, except that I wanted a girl first because of a biological tradition in my mum's family that has run girl, boy, girl, boy – a pattern I didn't want to upset (as I tried to explain to an incredulous social worker!). I was quite happy to take a sibling group of a girl and a boy. I didn't want any larger group because I was single at the time and knew my limits. I have since felt I might find it far more difficult than I envisaged coping with a teenage lad so I have revised my ideas about having a boy if I had another placement.

Going to panel was delayed because the social worker decided that it was better to wait until a clear year had passed since the break-up of my previous relationship in order to ensure the panel would not be able to say I was emotionally unstable. It went through panel without any hitches as far as I know and I was approved for up to two children aged between four and eight.

Then started the rollercoaster. The first child I looked at was the most heartbreaking. She was, actually, the same racial mix as me. By the time my social worker finally got to talk to the child's social worker after a three-week delay, I'd already settled in my mind that she was mine! But by then she had already been placed with another family. I was really upset. After that it was one child after another, some got as far as exchanging forms, but there was always something wrong that stopped it, like one child was completely allergic to animals, which we have, another had been abused by her mother and it was felt an all-female house wasn't suitable and some were very disturbed and my social worker said that it was my decision but I had to be aware that if this was what they were admitting to in the advert, the reality would be much worse. Also, there was always the underlying fear that even if initial responses were good, the panel of that county or city would turn me down due to my sexuality.

I left all these contacts up to my social worker. Almost the first question I would ask if she came back with a positive response was 'Have you told them yet?' and the answer was always 'yes'. It was her policy to tell them about my sexuality straight away so that if they were going to be 'iffy' she wouldn't have to waste everyone's time. There was one contact with a London borough where she was fairly sure my application would be turned down because of the social worker's attitude on the phone.

I had been approved in January and Yasmin came into the picture in June, so it wasn't actually too long, although it seemed like a lifetime! When I was approved she was already placed for adoption in another authority but the placement broke down and she was returned to emergency foster care in this authority. It's difficult not to feel desperate and when she was suggested to me, I was acutely aware of the advantages of having a child from our own authority. I couldn't help thinking, if I pass her up will I get anyone else? I was aware that there were issues about why the placement had broken down. They were implying that this was to do with the carer but they hinted at issues of attachment, which, at the time, meant nothing to me!

At this point I was still living apart from my current partner and my social worker suggested that for the purpose of the panel, and also to ensure the success of the placement, it would be wiser for us not to live together before matching and, preferrably, not before adoption, which I agreed to. It was a scary decision because then it started to become real.

The linking panel was in July and Yasmin was placed with me at the beginning of August. The introductions were much faster than anticipated and she settled very quickly. One thing that was really good was being able to have time off work, it really made a difference. I had adoption leave, which, with my employer, was one week on full pay and the rest on half pay. It gave us time to get to know each other and even after she went back to school it gave us time after school and I know she misses that. After I went back to work it took her ages to understand that after I picked her up from the after-school club there wasn't the same time we'd had before to do all those things before bedtime.

Since the placement I have, in fact, moved in with Teresa. My mum is seriously ill and I just couldn't handle the stress of juggling two households on top of everything else. But I see my social worker's point as well because the upheaval has been an issue for Yasmin, even though she gets on very well with Teresa and has taken her on as another mum. Teresa went into the report for the linking panel as a significant other and she's now undergoing a proper assessment.

The social workers did mention the fact that I was a lesbian to Yasmin before she was placed. In the first week of her placement we went through all the 'major' issues from periods through condoms to transgender and lesbianism! I still don't know if she was trying to shock me. I answered everything Yasmin asked about on the level she was asking the questions. She seems to be quite okay about me being a lesbian but I'm not sure she knows what it's about. But then, how many kids of her age understand their parents' sexuality, whatever its orientation? Recently, she brought a new friend to tea and the friend asked Teresa 'is it true you're a lesbian?' and Teresa said 'yes', so Yasmin is obviously talking about it all over the place. I have no illusions about being in the closet with her around! She's probably talked about it at school but it doesn't seem to have caused her any difficulties yet. She's more bothered about being called for her appearance than about me.

Yasmin is quite confused about all the placements she's had. She separates out her birth mother and can be quite protective about her. She understands that she wasn't well and couldn't look after Yasmin and that's why she had to leave. Mind you, one time when Yasmin was angry she said she was angry with her birth mother 'because if it wasn't for her I wouldn't be in this state'. I feel that it's quite healthy that she can be angry with her birth mother's behaviour as well as having feelings of love and concern. Because she's moved about so much from being so young, she seems to have all these 'mummy' figures lined up in her head. For example, she talks about having five mums and then wonders why her classmates are confused! I mentioned this to my social worker, who says she will talk to Yasmin's social worker about doing some life story work with her to help her place things more in the past. I don't think much work has been done with her because everything has been so topsy turvy. Her two previous adoption placements were short and broke down quickly, whereas her so-called short-term foster placements were long, so it's no wonder she's confused.

When Yasmin was placed with me it was a long-term foster placement with a view to adoption because she was considered to be very anti-adoption after her previous experiences. Then, shortly after she came, a stand-in social worker mentioned adoption by mistake and then tried to backtrack, but Yasmin picked up on it and insisted that although she had not wanted to be adopted by the previous carer, she did want to be adopted by me. The idea of adoption appeals to her but I wonder if she knows what it means. I don't know if it has a fairy-tale meaning for her or if she realises that it's just regular family life, warts and all. I think it will take quite some time for her to work through some of the stuff she's gone through. She can be very affectionate but sometimes I wonder how much she's doing it because she's been taught that's how it ought to be. She has had to adapt to so many different situations that I feel she adapts on a very surface level. For example, I still find it frightening how readily she will go to strangers.

Currently, we are coming to the end of the 'honeymoon period'. We've had this wonderfully 'ordinary' child who did what she was told generally and had the odd spat. But now (possibly because of a number of things: the house move, the worry about my mum's health, Yasmin's social worker informing her of arrangements for her to meet her birth mother, who she hasn't seen for about eighteen months, etc.) we've had some bouts of extreme defiance, or being herself but ten times bouncier. It's been quite stressful keeping up with it all. It's good that she has actually talked about being angry about things, like being moved about so much. When she said this we had a bit of a chat about it and that seemed to help. Mostly, it's just the day-to-day battle of coping with what's thrown up. Sometimes it's difficult to remember that all kids can be hellish sometimes (weren't we, after all?) and not everything Yasmin does is a reaction to her past. All I can say is that I have no regrets at all and that the hugs and the cards that say 'I love you, mum' and all the other 'ups' far outweigh the 'downs'!

Editorial Essay

Introduction

Lesbians and gay men have always been involved in having and raising children. Throughout history, in societies and cultures across the world, this has been in a wide variety of ways, including participation in extended family networks, involvement in formal and informal childcare and through their participation in heterosexual partnerships while maintaining a secret gay identity. In this century, lesbians and gay men in Britain have become more visible and able to live a slightly more open lifestyle (Jivani 1997). There is greater acceptance and tolerance and the recognition, in policy terms, of a right to protection against discrimination in certain limited spheres such as some local authority employment. More lesbians and gay men are now open about their identity or relationships and some are living openly with their partners. There is a real possibility now for some gay people, particularly those living in major cities with substantial and visible gay communities, to live as members of the community, being themselves and being open about their sexuality and relationships.

A fundamental component for some lesbians and gay men of being able to lead an ordinary life in the community is being able to have children. Increasingly, lesbians and gay men who have not had children prior to coming out as gay are able to consider a range of options for having children in their lives. The possibilities are much greater for lesbians than for gay men and developments in fertility treatment have enabled significant numbers of lesbians to have children through self-insemination, using known or anonymous donors (Saffron 1994).

For both lesbians and gay men, fostering and adoption offer key ways in which they are able to care for children as members of their own family. As such, fostering and adoption rank infinitely higher on the agenda for lesbians and gay men than they do for prospective heterosexual parents. Their greater likelihood to consider fostering or adoption as a first choice would appear to make prospective lesbian and gay parents a primary pool for recruitment by fostering and adoption agencies, but there is a prevailing social consensus which continues to see gay people as unsuitable parents. The personal accounts gathered here demonstrate how, in many instances, prospective lesbian and gay foster and adoptive parents have either been actively discouraged by agencies or discouraged through institutional inertia and have only prevailed through their own determination and resilience.

Themes from the Stories

Reasons for Choosing to Foster or Adopt

In exploring the themes emerging from these stories, the most obvious starting point is the decision to pursue fostering or adoption and the reasons behind the decision. There are differences between those who made this as a first choice in deciding how to have children and those who came to it later, and between those opting for long-term placements through adoption or long-term foster care and those choosing short-term care. Many of the contributors describe always having wanted children and having to take a long-term view of how to bring this about in their lives.

For some, the idea of fostering or adopting came out of their work with children and families in the caring professions and their consequent acquaintance with the processes involved in fostering and adoption. It is interesting to note the employment profile of the contributors, which has a heavy bias towards the public and voluntary sectors and the caring professions. This conforms with general employment trends for lesbians and gay men, which show a disproportionately high number employed in the public sector, as with other minority groups (Badgett and King 1997). Several contributors cited their careers in social work as a primary factor in raising their awareness of fostering and adoption and influencing their own decisions. For Paul and Richard, this was linked to their experiences in the gay rights movement and their belief in their ability and right to have the opportunity to care for children. Several contributors highlight the fact that lesbian and gay community activism has played a key role both in increasing the willingness of agencies to consider lesbian and gay applicants and in affirming for lesbians and gay men a belief in themselves as potential carers.

Simon, Mike and Brian, Olivette, and Nita and Clare were motivated to apply by seeing adverts put out by local authority agencies claiming their openness to considering a wide range of different people to be foster and adoptive parents. The existence of equal opportunities statements specifically mentioning 'sexual orientation' was also a positive factor. Kate was prompted to act after seeing an article about a neighbouring authority that was actively recruiting lesbian and gay foster parents. Elizabeth and Mary saw the *Out On*

Tuesday programme (Parmar 1989) featuring a respite carer called Marion and were persuaded that this was the right thing for them.

For more than half the contributors, fostering or adoption was their first choice in considering ways of having children, which had nothing to do with issues of 'childlessness' and the failure to conceive a child biologically. For Kate, respite care was something she chose to do before having made any decisions about whether or not she wanted to have her own children, and Olivette talks about adoption being her first option. This is an important point since some social workers seem to regard adoption as a 'second-best' option for applicants, most of whom have been biologically unable to have birth children. This may well be the case for many heterosexual couples (Triseliotis, Shireman and Hundleby 1997) but it does not always apply and it is far less so with lesbians or gay men.

Nita and Clare, and Shula, link choosing adoption with a lack of interest in blood ties. Shula describes experiences of living with a foster child in her own childhood and she and Dfiza both describe the African cultures they grew up in, where informal foster and adoptive arrangements were widespread and routine. They see these experiences as positively influencing them in favour of fostering and adoption. Nita and Shula also identify the difficulties for black women in trying to find known black donors or in positively affirming their children's heritage where a donor is unknown. It is interesting to note that all the black lesbians included in this book saw adoption as a first choice, though for Shula this is not straightforward as she describes an earlier point in her life when she planned to have a birth child by self-insemination.

Some of the lesbians who have contributed to this book did try self-insemination first without success, but they do not regard their foster children as a poor alternative. Elizabeth and Mary made initial investigations about insemination but were put off. Emma and Louise attempted it for a while but were unsuccessful. Shula and Jean had both been in relationships where their partner had had a child by self-insemination and, for Jean, the child has remained part of her family alongside her foster child. Olivette was approved to adopt but, following an experience where a placement was withdrawn at the last minute, she reluctantly decided to pursue self-insemination.

For many contributors, the decision to foster or adopt came out of a process of settling down in their lives, relationships becoming established, work and home lives feeling secure and the question of 'starting a family' arising as it does for some people when they reach a settled plateau in their twenties or thirties. Mike and Brian talk about reaching a stage of wanting something else in their lives to work on together:

We were both coming up to forty at the time that we discussed fostering and decided that either we could grow old, fat and boring or could do a bit more with our lives… you can let the years pass and you look back asking what you have done with your lives and what you have added to the world. One of our strengths as a couple has been that there have been things we have wanted to work on together.

Shula identifies the timing in her life as influencing her decision to adopt rather than explore having her own child. Kath, Barbara, and Nita and Clare all talk about knowing they have a lot to offer to young people and wanting to make a contribution that will help children already alive in the world as well as being personally rewarding and life-changing. The idea of offering a home and a family to children already needing that love and care is valued against the option of bringing more children into the world:

> I feel there's something about the state the world's in that means that if there's a child there who's got a life already who I can offer something to, I would rather do that than go through the whole process of having a baby. (Kath)

There are many reasons why the contributors chose either adoption or fostering, but some carers have ended up doing both. Barbara, for example, registered as a foster carer but eventually adopted three of her foster sons. Others, such as Nita and Clare, chose adoption over fostering because they wanted to provide a permanent home for a child from an early age. Some chose fostering over adoption, often with the view that they wanted to achieve certain tasks with children who need specific short-term help rather than wanting to offer a long-term home. Kate chose to do respite care because it suited her lifestyle; she and her partner, Poppy, have full-time jobs and busy lives and Kate saw respite care as a way of being involved with a child and still being quite free to continue with the other things in their lives. Sandra wanted to offer a family environment to teenage young women for whom adoption was not an option. Simon initially did emergency fostering but later changed to do longer-term care. Barbara describes how she initially went into fostering with the view to working with children to reunite them with siblings or birth parents if they were to return home. These are specific, short-term tasks often performed by 'emergency' or 'community' or 'task-centred' foster carers.

Issues for Gay Men

For gay men, the issues are slightly different. Unless they have either had birth children from a previous heterosexual relationship or have entered into a co-parenting arrangement with women for whom they have been the donor for insemination, the options for having children are more limited. Surrogacy is an ethically and practically complex arrangement open only to a few (though there are examples, such as the recent case of Bill Zachs and Martin Adam in Edinburgh – see *Gay Times*, 1997) but, for many gay men who want to become the carers of children, fostering or adoption may be their only option. This is not to say that the gay men who do apply, and, indeed, those who have contributed to this book, do so as a 'poor alternative' to the real thing. The gay men in this book describe their commitment to providing foster or adoptive care and their commitment to the children in their charge. Nevertheless, there are specific barriers facing gay men, not least notions that men *per se* are not the 'natural' carers of children, often seen as 'women's work', and that gay men pose a 'sexual risk' to children. Simon highlights these attitudes, saying:

> Some people also still have the attitude that all gay men are child abusers or they think that I haven't got the 'correct lifestyle' to bring up young heterosexual men. But they don't think it works the other way around! Also, there's this idea that men don't care for children anyway or, if they do, they're 'odd'. I only know one other gay man who is fostering.

Simon, and Richard and Paul talk of the resistance to seeing men as main or sole carers and describe how, even within the gay community, they encountered some mistrust and hostility towards what they were trying to do. Mike and Brian point out that for some children, particularly young men who have had difficult experiences with mothers or female carers, it can be helpful to have a placement with solely male carers. They point out that, given the diversity of children needing foster homes, a corresponding diversity of placements is necessary to meet their needs. Mark and Paul also talk of wanting to offer a non-traditional foster placement:

> We felt that we wanted to offer our services as a foster placement that wasn't seen as a traditional family unit since many young people or children in care have difficulties with traditional family units and often want a break from these.

When it comes to adoption, as opposed to fostering, it is rare to find openly gay men who have been approved to adopt. All the gay men in this book applied to foster but it is likely that Paul and Richard will go on to adopt their foster child, Patrick. There does seem to be a general tendency to place young people (often young men) for shorter-term forms of care with gay men. Having said this, all the gay men contributing to this book currently have, or have had, children or young adults on long-term placements with them. It also seems to be the case that many of the gay men who have been approved have had some previous knowledge of the care system behind them to help them deal with the resistance they encountered, as Paul and Richard point out:

> There must be any number of potential gay male foster carers going to waste because they don't have the 'know how' to challenge the system or all the necessary time and energy to devote to the struggle. More importantly, there are a lot of kids in care who are missing out as a result.

It is also less common to find gay men caring for children, in comparison to lesbians. Certainly, in fostering and adoption networks gay men are in the minority and it is partly for this reason that there are more lesbian contributors to this book than gay men. We do not see this as a problem however. It would have been pointless for us to attempt to get an even gender divide of contributors when that would not have reflected the fact that gay men are less likely to be carers than lesbians. Nevertheless, a third of our contributors are gay men. The stories of both Simon, and Paul and Richard note that other gay men themselves are sometimes uninterested or even disapproving of those gay men who care for children. Paul and Richard note that some gay men may have inherited and accepted the view that they cannot, or should not, care for children.

Issues for Black Lesbians and Gay Men

Issues of race and ethnicity are also a feature of some of these stories, particularly where black children are requiring placements. Many social services departments have policies of placing black children with black carers wherever possible and all of the black carers in this volume are caring for black children, sometimes with partners and sometimes without. These cases are made more complex by the issues of language, culture and religion, which also have to be considered but are sometimes seen as applying to black children only.

We are pleased that we have been able to include a number of black lesbians, and one gay man, in this book as previous research (Skeates and Jabri 1988) and the *Out On Tuesday* film (Parmar 1989) found that black lesbian or gay foster or adoptive carers were rare. This was due to a combination of factors, including racism within social work and the dilemmas for black lesbians and gay men in coming out in their own communities. We think that this is changing and that black lesbians and gay men recognise themselves as a vital resource for the care of black children and are also now more prepared to come out to social work agencies. Nita, Shula, Dfiza and Olivette all recognise the need for more black people to foster or adopt and all talk of a commitment to providing homes for black children. However, black lesbian and gay applicants still face racism as well as homophobia from social work agencies and the black contributors highlight some of these difficulties.

Figures of actual numbers of black children in care are hard to come by but, of existing research studies, what is clear is that black and, especially, mixed-race children are disproportionately represented in the care system (Barn 1993; Bebbington and Miles 1989; Cheetham 1986; Rhodes 1992; Triseliotis, Shireman and Hundleby 1997). They are also more likely to be 'children who wait' (Rowe and Lambert 1973) – that is, waiting in residential establishments for foster or adoptive homes. In her story, Olivette refers to the larger numbers of younger black children needing placements.

Ravinder Barn (1993), for example, found that of all the children looked after by one inner-city local authority social services department, 27 per cent were African-Caribbean, 5 per cent West African, 1 per cent Asian, 1 per cent Turkish Cypriot and 18 per cent were of mixed origin, but such figures partly depend upon the racial make-up of local communities. In the Bebbington and Miles study (1989), more than half of the children admitted into care in one authority were black, but this percentage was in line with the racial make-up of the local population. Children of mixed ethnicity, however, were two-and-a-half times more likely to enter care as their white peers. The reasons for this are complex, but are certainly to do with racist social work practices in which black children are more likely to be removed into care but then are also likely to wait longer for permanent placements due to social work agencies failing to recruit enough black families to meet such children's needs. Contrary to popular belief, black children are regularly placed trans-racially, particularly in emergency or short-term foster homes, while they wait for appropriate permanent placements.

Black lesbian and gay applicants are, therefore, assessed according to their 'race' as much as sexuality and it is interesting to note Shula's comment that black carers may be expected to have 'all the answers' to the needs of black children by white social workers just because of their racial heritage:

> The only thing I would say, and I imagine this goes for most black people interviewed by white interviewers, is that there's an in-built assumption that if you're black you know how to deal with it all and I suppose that because I wanted to pass the assessment, I didn't dissuade her of that idea!

It is also interesting that both Dfiza and Shula comment on the fact that substitute care is more commonly accepted within some African cultures, so, for both of them, it was something they had already experienced within extended family systems. We recognise and experience the fact that black lesbians and gay men are faced with institutional racism as much as homophobia when applying to foster or adopt but this does not prevent black lesbians and gay men from applying and, as the examples in this book show, being approved to care for children. Black children need foster and adoptive homes and this is an important part of the motivations of the black contributors to this book.

Another issue that black carers are often aware of in having black children placed with them is that some black children have been placed with white carers for a long time and may not identify as black or feel positive about being with black carers. Considerable work may have to be done to help them feel positive about being black.

Nita and Clare describe how they were turned down at the stage of a linking panel for a sibling group of Asian girls on the grounds that their being lesbians was 'against the children's religion', Hinduism. The children were described as having experienced various religions and as not being brought up in any particular faith. They were split up in several different white foster homes and there were no other families being considered for them, yet Nita and Clare were rejected. The implication of this decision seems to be that the expressed need for the children to be placed together, and in a permanent placement, was superseded by the purported unacceptability of lesbian relationships in the Asian community. Yet, when they lodged a complaint, the investigating officer concluded that there was no consensus within the Hindu faith on the legitimacy of lesbian relationships. Indeed, Nita and Clare subsequently had a child of Hindu heritage placed with them.

There is a danger here of the white social work establishment adopting rigid and stereotypical definitions of communities, cultures and religions that are actually diverse and continually changing. There is as wide a range of opinions of gay relationships in Hinduism as there is in the Church of England and a much greater tradition of celebrating lesbian and gay relationships in religious texts, art and sculpture (Thadani 1996). In the hostile environment of a racist society it is true that defensive and reactionary elements have a stronghold in some black communities, but these communities are much more diverse than their community or religious leaders suggest and social workers should not use narrow and racist definitions of what is acceptable in order to discriminate against black lesbian and gay carers. Surely, black carers themselves know as well as anyone what is acceptable in their own communities and what support black children in lesbian and gay households need? There are accommodations of lesbian and gay relationships in all cultures, however expressed or mediated, and many societies outside the West have been much more liberal and tolerant of difference than the Christian world has been.

Single Carers and Those in Relationships

Lesbians and gay men may foster or adopt as single people or as couples and both are reflected in the range of our contributors. Although single carers have been regarded as inferior or inadequate in policy terms by government sources, most agencies consider applications from single carers and many value the unique commitment of a single carer as being particularly appropriate for certain children and, indeed, superior to care by a couple, particularly a heterosexual couple. Simon was told by his agency that, as a single man, he had 'the same chance as anyone else' and Kath received positive feedback from her social worker about her strengths as a single woman adopter, but in neither case was the social worker aware of their sexuality at the time. Being single enabled Shula to go through the preparation group as a single adopter without revealing that she was a lesbian, but she made the choice to come out to the social worker assessing her.

For single people, lack of support is a very real issue, as Kath highlights:

> The biggest thing for me is having someone to share the pains your child goes through... You can end up taking on so much and at least if there's someone else who's done that you've got someone to share it with and you don't have to go over old ground or explain yourself. I'm lucky that I know some other people who have adopted and I've got a lot of support from friends and family, but the load is spread a bit and it's having one place to go that would make a lot of difference.

Whilst a couple may be able to support each other with the day-to-day problems and dilemmas involved, single carers have to look for support elsewhere, from friends, family or formal groups. Lesbian and gay carers are very adept at developing their own support networks amongst their friends, many of whom they regard as 'family', but there is also the need for carers to be able to off-load their own problems. Most lesbians and gay men do not feel comfortable amongst largely heterosexual adoptive or foster carer support groups and they may feel isolated or their experiences denied. LAGFAPN, and other groups, provide an important lesbian and gay-specific source of support for such carers.

Some of the contributors applied as single people but later formed relationships with a partner, while others have been through the break-up of a former relationship and gone on to form others. These are important dynamics which have to be negotiated within households or within relationships between children and their carers, sometimes not without difficulty. Another important issue is that, for those who were not out at the point of approval, the arrival of a new same-sex partner may result in their having to come out to social workers for the first time. Jean and Trixie describe the process of informing social services of their new relationship as daunting. Nevertheless, they were keen that it should be done properly and pushed for a full re-assessment of them both as a couple rather than adding Trixie onto Jean's initial assessment as 'just a friend in the same house'. Of the process of informing social services of their new relationship, they say:

> It felt worse than coming out to our parents, in that a professional assessment would have to be undertaken and police checks made. Our relationship, and Trixie's past, would have to be discussed and our children interviewed. At least with our parents we could adopt the 'it's our lives and if you can't cope with it, it's your problem' approach!

Sandra describes her dilemmas over deciding when is the appropriate moment to inform social services of a new relationship, knowing that means subjecting her new partner to a whole process of assessment and police checks that can be stressful and intrusive. This is not an easy thing to ask a new partner to do but it is important. Simon describes the extreme care he took to inform social services at an early stage of his new relationship, even though his own link-worker thought he was being 'over-cautious'.

Simon and Sandra also point to the fact that, as a lesbian or gay man with foster children, the forming of a new relationship can be difficult. Some lesbians and gay men are not interested in children and when they hear that you are a foster or adoptive parent, they might 'run a mile,' as Simon notes. The lesbian and gay club scene does not cater to the needs of lesbian or gay parents and rarely, if ever, acknowledges their existence, and some are still shocked to discover that lesbians and gay men do have children.

Range of Care Options

The accounts given show contributors involved in a wide range of care situations from straightforward adoption of a single child (not so straight-forward for lesbian and gay adopters) to adoption of sibling groups, respite care, care for adults with learning difficulties and a whole range of foster care situations variously described by different agencies as short-term, long-term, permanent, emergency, task-centred and community fostering. Some contributors have been involved in informal personal arrangements which may or may not have been formalised legally.

Many contributors have been involved in offering more than one kind of care, either at the same time or at different times, and some had changed the kind of care they were approved for. For instance, Barbara was involved in taking large numbers of emergency and short-term foster children but ended up adopting three of the boys she fostered; Sandra was approved to foster short-term but found some of her placements became long-term; Simon began doing emergency foster care and changed to long-term care; Paul and Richard were approved for a permanent placement but did teenage fostering and respite care until, almost by default, they got the sort of placement they were seeking.

The basic differences are between respite care, short-term or emergency foster care, long-term fostering and adoption. All of these require the lengthy assessment of carers before they can be taken on. Foster carers (including respite) receive remuneration for their services whilst adopters may receive discretionary adoption allowances, especially for children over five and children who are considered 'hard to place'.

Respite care involves caring for disabled children for short periods, such as weekends or school holidays, to give their families a break. Kate and Poppy have cared for Joshua on this basis for eleven years:

> We find part-time parenting really suits us. It meets all our nurturing needs, although the garden meets the rest of Poppy's, and also we get on and enjoy the rest of our lives as total free spirits.

Simon describes being involved in a private respite care arrangement for Andrew that involved an unusually high time commitment after school as well as at weekends. He maintains this commitment today, while also having children placed with him for emergency fostering and, now, long-term fostering. Elizabeth and Mary's respite care arrangement lasted for some years before they decided to apply to do permanent foster care and has similarly been maintained after they had a child placed with them with a view to adoption. Both these were arrangements chosen by the carers.

Paul and Richard were forced to 'prove themselves', it seemed, by being respite carers and then 'social uncles' to a child in care before they could have that child placed with them. They had been approved for long-term or 'permanent' care but received no placements for some years after approval. Fostering agencies appear to have exhibited extreme nervousness around making a placement with them.

Short-term fostering involves looking after a child temporarily who has had to be removed from the family for a short period while his or her needs are assessed. The word 'short' in this context is infinitely flexible as the process of assessing a child's needs and making a decision on his or her long-term future can be extremely protracted. Nita and Clare refer to their adopted daughter having been in a 'short-term' foster placement which ended up lasting for four years and Barbara eventually adopted three boys she originally took as short-term foster placements. Sandra provides short-term foster placements to teenagers but points out that both the long-term children she had came initially for one night only as emergency placements but ended up staying for two years.

Usually, the reasons a child is taken into care are not problems that can be quickly resolved. The initial aim of short-term care is to support and maintain the relationship between the child and the birth family with a view to returning the child to the family, but, often, the work to achieve this fails and a decision is made in favour of adoption.

The foster carer is often involved in a number of contact arrangements with birth parents, siblings who may be in other placements, grandparents and, eventually, in introductions to adopters or long-term foster carers. Barbara describes this work:

> We did a lot of work to reunite children with their families, bringing sibling groups back together again, preparing children to be adopted and taking children from placement breakdowns. We were a bit like a rescue service! I remember one Christmas we had nine children! I think the hardest thing we used to do was introducing children to their new adoptive parents when they had to move on. We did a lot of this but I always found it hard to see them go and I always worried that no one could look after them like I could!

There is a heavy stress in this work on not becoming too attached to children you are ultimately working to move on and being clear with the children about the temporary nature of your role in their lives. Simon describes how rewarding it was to work with two boys whom he returned to their birth family in a much more positive state, with the result that the family no longer needed social work involvement. Current thinking on good practice in social work discourages people who really want to adopt from fostering and discourages foster parents from applying to adopt children in their temporary care but, sometimes, social workers and carers decide that short-term placements should become permanent. Nita and Clare were encouraged to consider fostering after they had been waiting 18 months for an adoptive placement.

Simon, Barbara, Mike and Brian, and Mark and Paul were all approved to take short-term placements and describe being very heavily used, particularly Barbara and Simon who are single carers. Barbara has had more than fifty placements, Simon refers to having fifteen placements over two years and Mike and Brian have had eleven placements. They all describe situations in which their social workers appeared to have a great deal of confidence in them and used them to the extent of completely overloading them, yet, when complaints were made, it was hard for them to get any support. Short-term carers are particularly vulnerable to allegations of abuse from young people in states of emotional disruption and trauma in their lives since, sometimes, carers are an obvious target to hit out at and both child and carer need considerable support. After his experience of a complaint investigation, Simon changed from short-term care to long-term fostering to give himself more security.

Long-term fostering is designed to accommodate children away from their birth families on a long-term or permanent basis where there are reasons why adoption has not been chosen. It is often the option chosen for older children and may involve looking after them until they are eighteen. Parental responsibility for the child remains with the local authority and the birth parent(s) in legal terms and so birth parents continue to attend statutory reviews and to have a say in decisions made about their children. For disabled children, or those with particular needs, there may be more support services available to the child and the carers than for adopted children and the foster carer will receive a fostering allowance for caring for the child. The foster carers will have an ongoing relationship with social services and will be involved in regular reviews of the child's needs and development. They may also be involved in facilitating regular contact between the child and birth family, as specified in the placement agreement.

Adoption is probably best understood by the wider society and involves taking on legal parental responsibility for the child and becoming his or her parent for life. Once the adoption has been completed in court there is no requirement for continuing contact between the new family and the adoption agency, except in relation to any contact with the birth family that has been agreed as part of the adoption order. Adoption law and practice has changed considerably in the last decade, particularly in relation to the issue of continuing contact with birth families (Triseliotis, Shireman and Hundleby 1997), sometimes called 'open adoption' or 'adoption with contact'. It has been acknowledged that previous practice, which severed all links between an adopted child and the birth family and made accessing information extremely difficult for both parties, has had detrimental effects on many adopted children. The current trend is towards some form of contact being maintained and an awareness of birth parents being an ordinary part of the child's life rather than a mysterious taboo subject. This was one of the recommendations of the adoption White Paper (DoH 1993). It is quite usual these days for contact to be maintained with a birth parent through exchange of cards, photos and letters via the adoption agency. Face-to-face contact between the child and birth parent or parents is sometimes written into adoption orders but is much less common, although in some instances a final contact visit may be arranged before the adoption order is obtained through the court.

All the contributors who applied to adopt at the outset were lesbians and all are now in the position of having adoptive placements. Three families have been to court and received their adoption orders. Kath, who was not out during the process, was granted an adoption order as a single adopter. This was also the case with Barbara's adoption of her boys. Nita and Clare, who were out, were granted an adoption order to Nita as a single adopter and a joint residence order to both of them, giving equal parental responsibility to both partners. For Kath, the process was relatively straightforward and completed within a year of the placement. For Nita and Clare, it was more complicated and took eighteen months. As their story reveals, there was uncertainty about the outcome until the very end. However, the recent court judgement *Re W* (*The Times* 1997) has removed the lack of any reported legal precedent that hung over Nita and Clare and we hope this decision will be used in future cases. Several other families are going to court soon and this is mentioned by Paul and Richard, as well as Sarah and Christine, who note that only one of the partnership will be the named adopter in law and so joint residence orders will be sought.

Some of the placements, although intended in the long term as adoption placements, were initially presented as long-term foster placements. For Shula, this was to manage what were perceived as very negative feelings from Yasmin about adoption due to previous placement breakdowns. For Dfiza and Anne, it was for financial reasons to secure a fostering allowance during a period when Anne had no income due to finishing a full-time course. Children are regularly placed in long-term foster care with the explicit view to their being eventually adopted by the carers. This is often because the legal process of adoption is a long and drawn out one and children need to be placed with their carers in the meantime in order to prepare them for adoption and to give them some sense of security. It is rare these days for older children being adopted to wait until the adoption has been agreed in the court before they are placed with their adoptive parents and this is reflected in the stories told by Nita and Clare, Sarah and Christine, Shula, and Dfiza and Anne, all of whom cared for, or are caring for, their children in advance of the adoption being heard in the court. Some agencies prefer that lesbians and gay men continue as foster carers for a number of years prior to approaching a court for an adoption order. The reasons vary, from wanting the court to see how well the children have settled to trying to avoid facing a confrontation with the possibly homophobic views of courts or birth parents. For instance, Olivette mentions delays in taking the adoption to court because of debates about the birth mother's 'need to know' her sexuality.

Adoption is also legally complicated for lesbian or gay couples since the law allows for only one person to be named as the legal adopter. Only married heterosexual couples can adopt jointly. In the case of black children placed with couples, one of whom is black and the other white, it is the black carer who is generally named as the adopter in law due to the policies of placing authorities. For all couples, this means that one person is not legally recognised as the adoptive parent and this has implications for both child and carers, not least regarding inheritance, parental responsibility and agreeing contact should the couple split. This means that lesbian or gay adopters often go for a joint residence order under the Children Act 1989, granting both carers parental responsibility, and this may be done at the time of the adoption, as Nita and Clare have described (and see Beresford 1994; Mulholland 1997). A joint residence order, granting both partners equal parental responsibility, ensures that the partner who is not the named adopter will retain parental responsibility if the other partner dies, can take all decisions on an equal basis (e.g. in the event of emergency medical care, schools, etc.) and ensures that if they split up, the couple can go back to court to determine who the child is to live with.

Choices About Children

People who foster or adopt have important choices to make about the kinds of children for whom they would like to care. Boys, girls or both? What age ranges? Single children, brothers and sisters or larger sibling groups? Disabled children or children with other particular needs? Can they cope with a child who has been sexually abused? Black children, particularly, need black adopters and foster carers to come forward and, for prospective black foster and adoptive carers, there are sometimes complex issues around religion, culture and identity when considering what children they would be most appropriately matched with. All of these questions are important, and the contributors to this book represent a range of differing responses. There are lesbians here who care for boys whilst others want to care for girls only. Similarly gay men usually care for boys but, occasionally, girls also. The black contributors to this book all recognise the need for positive resources for black children who may have received particularly negative images about themselves in their past or within the care system. Many contributors have offered themselves to care for disabled children specifically, especially in respite care schemes, whilst others are caring for children with difficult histories of abuse. The ages of the children and young people cared for by the contributors cover a wide range, from babies through to teenagers and sibling groups.

Some contributors discuss the dilemmas and difficulties they had in communicating to social workers the sort of placements they envisaged for themselves. At the initial point of assessment it is not always easy to consider in the abstract what kind of children you feel you can take and what you say may be governed as much by what the social worker seems to suggest is appropriate to say as by what you actually want. There are also differences between what people were approved for and the placements they subsequently took. For instance, Nita and Clare, and Elizabeth and Mary ended up taking children who were slightly older than the upper limit they had chosen themselves. Several contributors also spoke of the pressures put on them by social workers to accept children who did not fit the profile they had originally specified.

Some lesbian adopters felt under pressure from social workers to take boys. Nita and Clare recall conversations with their social worker around their voicing a preference for taking girls. This was also an issue for Emma and Louise and they stress the importance of being honest about what you want:

> It's very important at this stage that you be honest about what type of children and behaviours you are willing to deal with as you are the ones who will live with the children. No matter how prepared you think you might be, there will always be things that crop up that you feel ill-equipped to cope with.

Most of the gay men contributing have only ever taken boys and the assumption in their agencies seems to have been to place boys with them. Simon identifies the decision to specify boys in his application as the social workers' decision but says that he would not have felt it appropriate for him to care for young women. John and Rob were turned down in their application to foster Nazan, the sister of their current foster child, even though she was subsequently placed in a hostel because no other family placement could be found for her. It is interesting to note that while agencies tended to assume that it was appropriate for gay men to care only for boys, it did not appear to be advisable for lesbians to express a desire to care only for girls. This may be to do with different perceptions particular social workers had about gender choices of lesbian and gay carers or it may be to do with the greater number of boys needing placements.

The gender issue is a particularly interesting one here and one in which the responses of social workers are especially inconsistent. All foster and adoptive applicants are asked whether they have a gender preference and this is seen as acceptable (Triseliotis, Shireman and Hundleby 1997). However, lesbians and gay men who express a preference may face some strange responses from social workers or panels. On the one hand there may be suspicions about why lesbians wish to care for girls or gay men for boys – Barbara faced such suspicion and Nita and Clare were advised not to state such a strong preference for girls. On the other hand, Sandra reports being advised to take only teenage girls as a single parent of young children and all the gay male contributors have had only boys placed with them. Caring for a child of the opposite sex is more acceptable for lesbian carers but less so for gay men.

The black contributors identify some confusion and lack of understanding among social workers in dealing with black carers' choices about children, particularly for black carers in relationships with a white partner. While black people from all communities share a common experience of racism in this country, there are, quite obviously, specific cultural differences between communities originating from different continents, countries and regions and different experiences and traditions. Shula is positive about how her social worker explored the issues for her in taking a child who was African-Caribbean, or from a part of Africa other than the area where she had grown up, but she also describes feeling that it was assumed that she knew how to deal with all the issues for any black child simply because she was black. Dfiza and Anne describe being uncertain as to whether they would be considered for a black child who wasn't mixed race because they were a mixed couple themselves, and being rejected in one case because they were a mixed couple and the agency felt the child was 'quite dark', although her heritage was unclear. They also describe being offered a placement they felt was totally inappropriate immediately after approval:

> ...they rang up and said that they knew we wanted black children but would we take these four white boys? It felt a bit insensitive. They make out there's this desperate need for black carers, and Dfiza being black, and Elliot and Ella are here for more than three months of the year, and they're asking us to take four white children.

Nita and Clare also describe being offered placements they felt were not appropriate matches for the needs of the children and their account reflects a tendency among social workers to perceive Asian children solely in terms of religion.

Sandra's birth children are black and she expresses regret that she is not normally considered for the placement of black foster children because she is white, although she did once have a placement of a mixed-race child. She describes dealing with the racism of some of the white children placed with her as an issue for her and her children and notes that there are many black children in all white homes, or waiting for placement, that she feels she could help. This is echoed in the examples given by black contributors of children they enquired about who were being cared for in white foster homes.

More than half the contributors were approved for more than one child, though some of these subsequently took a placement of a single child, such as Nita and Clare, and Shula. Those who took sibling groups took groups where at least the youngest child was five or under and, in all cases, they were children with substantial experiences of abuse, as reported by Sarah and Christine. Across all the contributors, a significant proportion of children placed have experienced physical and sexual abuse.

Considering Disabled Children

The issue of caring for disabled children is one that remains significant to lesbian and gay foster or adoptive parents. In the *Out On Tuesday* film (Parmar 1989), Judith Weeks noted that there has been a long tradition of placing disabled children with lesbians and gay men, an unacknowledged 'policy'. She describes this as a discriminatory practice which reinforces the ideas that 'second-class children' should go to 'second-class' carers. This is raised by Olivette:

> I have to ask the question that no doubt many other lesbians and gay men have asked: 'If there are such anxieties around our sexuality and we are considered to be inferior or second-class citizens, why place children who need extra special care and attention with us?' I would like to believe it is because social workers feel we may empathise more because of our own experiences of being treated differently. However, I wonder if that is really the case or are we seen as the last resort?

This point seems to be confirmed by existing research (Hicks 1996; Skeates and Jabri 1988) and many of the carers in this book have looked after such children, sometimes having to deal with child or adult deaths arising from terminal illness, as reported by Jean and Trixie, and Mark and Paul. This is not to say that lesbian and gay carers regard disabled children as second class, far from it! The contributors to this book are all committed to the care of disabled children and some of them chose this over other options, like Kate or Mark and Paul. But the point to be made here is that many find the placement of disabled children with lesbians and gay men somehow more acceptable, and this was reinforced in the adoption law review comments (DoH/Welsh Office 1992).

This seems to be partly to do with the notion that disabled children are either far less likely to understand that they are living with lesbian or gay carers or that their own sexuality is far less likely to be influenced by having lesbian or gay parents. We find these ideas totally objectionable, not least because they do place disabled people, and lesbians and gay men, as 'second-class citizens'. Nor does this logic seem to follow anyway, for if disabled children require particularly skilled carers, which some undoubtedly do, then why place them with people who are seen as a 'last resort'? (Hicks 1996).

Some carers identify an assumption they felt was around the fact that they could only expect to be offered children with 'special needs'[1] because they were lesbian or gay. Simon describes how he feels he has been 'bracketed' as a gay carer of special needs children and Emma and Louise thought when they set out that they would only be considered for children with special needs. When Olivette's two-year-old daughter was placed with her, Olivette had to ask for her to be assessed and it was only then that her moderate learning difficulties were identified. Other carers intended to offer placements to children with special needs, such as Paul and Richard, Barbara, and Jean and Trixie. The majority of contributors have children placed with them who have some level of special need, particularly emotional and behavioural difficulties and learning difficulties. Some have multiple special needs requiring high levels of care. This reflects the fact that the majority of children in care have some emotional and behavioural difficulties due to their previous experiences and many suffer from developmental delay and some level of learning difficulty. However, Nita and Clare have adopted a child who is a high achiever at school and their social worker was adamant they should not be pigeon-holed into having children with special needs if they didn't want this. Dfiza and Anne, Shula and Kath have all had children placed with them who have no identified special need.

Coming Out, and Coming Out, and Coming Out...

The issue of 'coming out' as lesbian or gay, and being out, is central to most of the stories in this volume. For all of us who are lesbian or gay, coming out is never a one-off event after which we simply inhabit a publicly lesbian or gay identity free of oppression, it is, instead, a constant process of negotiation and decision making depending on particular contexts. We come out thousands of times, to work colleagues, to family, to friends, to students, to children, to social workers, to schools, to other parents/carers, etc., but the choice to do so may sometimes depend upon context – that is, how safe we feel at that time to do so. All of the contributors to this book are out in some sense or another, not least to themselves and to the children that they care for. But one of the key issues for

---

1   When we use the term 'special needs' here, we refer to needs arising from children's delayed development, educational ability, behaviour, histories of abuse and neglect or emotional factors, rather than issues of disability.

lesbians and gay men who apply to foster or adopt is whether to come out to the social workers and agency that will assess them.

There have always been, and will continue to be, lesbians and gay men who apply to foster or adopt who do not feel able to come out to social workers. This is usually because they have a very justifiable fear that if they do so, their sexuality will be taken as a reason to reject them. For some, the desire to care for a child so outweighs other aspects that they are prepared to hide their sexuality in the short term so that they will have more chance of getting through the social work assessment. We understand the reasons for this but we do think that this approach is likely to cause problems at some later point. Honesty with children being fostered or adopted is key, not least about sexuality, and the carer will be 'found out' at some stage.

There are a range of ways of coming out represented in this book. Some people chose to be up-front about their sexuality from the start, as Kate explains:

> I came out to the social workers almost at the very start of the assessment process, probably in the first meeting. Partly, this is because I can never remember that being a lesbian is something you are not supposed to just tell everyone!... but also I thought that if there was going to be any hassle, I'd get it out the way now and then if the social workers said they didn't want any 'dykes', that would be the end of it.

Some contributors came out during the assessment process while others did not come out during the assessment but did much later on. John, for example, although he felt that social workers knew about his sexuality, came out when his new partner Rob moved into the household some time after he had been caring for Ismail. Simon was out to social workers, though this was not explicit at the start, but had to come out to the young people for whom he was caring later as they had not been told he was gay. Olivette went through the assessment process twice, the first time without declaring her sexuality, the second time being out.

One of the reasons that lesbians and gay men who are contemplating fostering or adoption are wary of coming out to social services departments is their scepticism about professional practice on confidentiality. Elizabeth and Mary asked for their initial application to be handled separately as two individual applications as they did not want to be on file as a lesbian couple. Lesbian and gay foster and adoptive carers are likely to be concerned about confidentiality not only amongst fostering and adoption social workers but also with children's social workers in area teams, former foster carers, birth parents, schools and other support services involved with their children.

All contributors involved in long-term fostering or adoption speak about being out to their children. For some, this was something made clear to the child before placement, for others it was something that happened after placement. For all, it was central to their relationship with the children in their family that the children should know who they are and see that they are proud of their gay identity. Some of the children and young people knew about lesbians or gay men via characters in television 'soaps' and this is raised in some of the stories. Simon talks about how this can be used to explain the carer's sexuality to children or young people.

For short-term carers, there are different issues with safety and privacy becoming paramount issues, particularly in situations where gay men are caring for older boys for short periods who may move on from their care to live in the same area and take with them considerable information about the carers. Contributors involved in short-term care talk about the ways in which they make their relationship apparent to children and young people placed with them and seek to have an open relationship with the children while coping with birth parents, social workers and previous foster carers' reactions.

Coming out to social workers and agencies is never easy, however. Paul and Richard, for example, were rejected by many authorities out of hand once they learnt that they were gay men and Sarah and Christine also report negative reactions to their being lesbians by some agencies. Nita and Clare chose carefully who first to tell that they were lesbians as they were the first openly lesbian couple to be approved for adoption by their authority. Nevertheless, when applying to be considered for some children after having been approved, they felt they were sometimes turned down by placing agencies because of their sexuality.

Kath, a single carer, chose not to be out to the agency at all but was out to the child she adopted. She describes the stress caused by maintaining the concealment and the ambivalent responses of various social workers who may or may not have suspected:

> I was in the position of playing a game because Rosie's social worker was certainly wondering about my sexuality and, possibly, the foster carer... There were suspicions and there seemed to be a message that it was all right, but for me to have actually come out would have been quite difficult. I found that whole experience of not being able to be open and suspecting that everybody was colluding didn't sit very well and I wish I could have felt able to be out in the first place.

She suggests that, in some instances, the social workers knew but colluded with her decision not to be out as it was easier for them. This has often been the practice of social workers assessing single women adopters they suspect to be lesbians. No contributors were outed to their agencies or social workers by children placed with them, or by outside people, but this is always a possibility for those who decide not to be out themselves. For couples living together, not being out is a possible but severely problematic option and not one that was chosen by any of the couples contributing to the book, though Nita and Clare speak of knowing another lesbian couple who did choose not to be out and highlight some of the difficulties around following this path. Most couples came out very early in the process, either to the agency they contacted or to the social worker allocated to assess them.

Mark and Paul describe an experience of having an adult placed with them who had not been told they were gay and who, when he discovered this, was so afraid he decided to leave. They felt social workers should have told him. Barbara and Simon both report experiences of caring for children short term and, in Barbara's case, sometimes, children under two, where it was felt to be inappropriate or unnecessary to come out, but both also, interestingly, later came out to children placed longer term.

For some contributors, decisions about how and when to come out were affected by what they knew of what other lesbian and gay people had done. Several describe the difficulty and loneliness of not knowing any other gay person or couple that had applied to foster or adopt, or only knowing people who had been unsuccessful or had done it without declaring that they were gay. Several contributors referred to the support they get now from knowing other lesbian and gay foster and adoptive carers and being in a support group. The value of this experience also extends to their children, who are positively affirmed by being with children of other lesbian and gay carers.

Some people were encouraged to apply to foster or adopt openly as lesbians or gay men by advertising from the local authority or the progressive stance they perceived their local authority to take on lesbian and gay issues generally. Even those who did not have any particular expectations of their local authority still perceived the local authority as the agency most likely to consider them and no contributors approached any of the non-statutory adoption agencies, such as The Children's Society (which actually has a policy barring any applications to be carers by lesbians or gay men), Barnardos or the church-based adoption agencies. Some contributors made an anonymous enquiry first to ascertain the attitude of the agency to prospective lesbian and gay carers and, if they received a positive response, made an initial contact, which might be by one person in a couple until they had established who they would be dealing with on a regular basis. Contributors tended to feel it was quite important not to be out until you were sure who you were dealing with and were quite sceptical of confidentiality procedures regarding prospective adopters.

Certainly, all the contributors have tales of coming out to children and we feel that this is not only because they do not want to deny a part of themselves which is their sexuality and identity as a lesbian or gay man but also because they want to be honest with the children for whom they are caring. Shula, Mark and Paul, Barbara, Paul and Richard, Simon, and Kath all speak about coming out and being out to children. Shula, for example, says:

> ...the social workers did mention the fact that I was a lesbian to Yasmin before she was placed...She seems to be quite okay about me being lesbian, but I'm not sure she really knows what it's about...Recently, she brought a new friend to tea and the friend asked Teresa 'Is it true you're a lesbian?' and Teresa said 'yes'. So Yasmin's obviously talking about it all over the place. I have no illusions about being in the closet with her around!

This kind of 'outing' to others by children may also be inevitable and is echoed in Emma and Louise's account of preparations for their son's parents' evening:

> The teacher asked around the classroom whose parents were coming and he announced to everyone: 'my two mums are coming, they're lesbians'.

Other stories show how children and young people are able to cope with having lesbian or gay carers and how they handle this information with their peers or families of birth.

In that sense, having children who know you are lesbian or gay is likely to involve being out, of necessity, to their friends, schools, clubs or other parents. Children may quite innocently 'out' their carers. Barbara, for example, talks about how there had been some teasing of her boys at school about her lesbianism and how this prompted her to come out to her children in order to discuss this and protect them. She reports that one of her sons had not told her about the teasing because he did not want to upset his mum, he was trying to protect her! She also came out to her children's schools with the hope of working constructively with teachers and in one school a supportive relationship evolved but not in the other. Sandra also refers to coming out to the school because of the openness of her own birth children about their home life.

Helping children to understand and explain their families and histories is an important part of fostering and adoption and a considerable challenge, as many contributors identify:

> The simple question on the beach, 'are you here with your Mum and Dad?', has so many complications for Daniel that the enquirer gets a confused

picture, of which the two female parents is only a small part! (Elizabeth and Mary)

Several contributors talk of the work they have done to help their children feel positive about the families they are living in. Jean and Trixie talk of their complex family and how each child is clear about their own background and how they came to be part of the family. Others talk of how positive their children are about having gay and lesbian parents. Several contributors talk about being 'outed' by proud and unconcerned children in school and social situations. Jean and Trixie see being out and visible in the community as an inevitable part of fostering and highlight the effect of this for a teenager, who tends to find her parents excruciatingly embarrassing anyway. In Mark and Paul's case, a school which found out about what it obviously regarded as their illicit relationship actually reported them to social services, only to discover that the fact that they were gay was already known and accepted.

Some contributors are very much out in their local communities, others, such as Dfiza and Anne, speak of being quite isolated in their neighbourhood. Sandra expresses surprise at the absence of any hostility or disapproval from neighbours and is positive about the area she has moved to because there are more black people. Mike and Brian describe their neighbours as being very supportive of their relationship and their fostering and feel very strongly about being out in their local community, this despite the fact that they have suffered considerable harassment from the media. Mark and Paul also speak of having understanding and supportive neighbours and of being supported in the gay community. However, Paul and Richard encountered some hostility in the gay community and discuss the prejudice against gay men as parents that they feel has been internalised by some gay men. This is also noted by Simon. Jean and Trixie, on the other hand, talk of the support they have found in the lesbian and gay community and Jean describes the incredible groundswell of support she received from people she hardly knew in the lesbian and gay community who came forward to help when James, her foster son, died.

Most contributors are out to family and friends and talk of having support from them. For some, this was mingled with concern at what they were taking on and the possibilities of rejection and disappointment. Some contributors speak of mixed reactions and some disapproval from particular family members or friends – for instance, Jean and Trixie describe the open hostility of Jean's mother, who refuses to talk to Trixie. For some, this was part of a general disapproval of their lifestyle and relationships while for others it was more specifically to do with fostering and adoption. Olivette, on the other hand, talks of the importance of her mother's support and acceptance in helping her to take on a foster child. Mike and Brian describe how a gay couple they were friendly with stopped seeing them when they started fostering because they were worried about being linked if the media got hold of the story. Paul and Richard point out how direct experience of gay parents can change homophobic attitudes:

> Our experience has been that when faced with the reality of a gay household with children, people are much more ready to accept people on their own terms than the worst tabloids would have you think.

The other major factor about being out or not is in relation to children's families of birth. In respite schemes, for example, most of the carers here have been out to the child's birth family and have seen this as important. As a respite carer, Kate describes how she was introduced to Joshua's mother, Mary, before being 'outed' to her as a lesbian and how they went on to develop a positive working relationship. For children being fostered or adopted, however, the issues are slightly different. Shorter-term fostering arrangements often involve frequent contact with birth parents and siblings and, therefore, it may be important to share information about the carer's sexuality. There is a duty to promote such contact under the Children Act 1989 and lesbian and gay foster carers often have little choice about being out to birth families. Most lesbian and gay carers want to be out about their sexuality but, sometimes, this is made difficult by the objections of some birth parents to lesbians and gay men. Contributors providing short-term, emergency and even long-term fostering sometimes had to deal with anger and hostility from birth parents angry with social workers and critical of placements. Sandra describes having to deal with birth parents' complaints about her and allegations being made, which she felt were inspired by birth parents attempting to sabotage placements:

> When a parent finds out that their child has been placed with a lesbian, they tend to start to complain about other issues. The latest have been that I had no carpet because my floorboards are stripped and varnished, that I was a single parent. Parents have also complained that they think their children will be abused by me. You have to be quite strong and not listen too much because it feels like you've got to prove to that parent that you're an okay person.

All foster carers have to deal with difficult reactions from birth parents looking for reasons to object to the placement of their child. Lesbian and gay foster carers are particularly vulnerable to such objections because of their marginal and contested position in relation to childcare and it is important that agencies which use lesbian and gay carers are prepared to demonstrate full confidence in their carers and support them against homophobic reactions. This is noted by Simon, who describes the negative reactions of some birth parents to his being a single male carer and to his being gay.

In adoption situations the current trend for adoption with contact, or open adoption, may also necessitate adoptive carers coming out to birth families as lesbian or gay. Birth families, particularly in contested fostering or adoption arrangements, often object to their children being placed with substitute carers, whoever they are, and the grounds of sexuality may present an ideal opportunity to oppose such decisions. This book does not contain any examples of the sexuality of carers being used to contest an adoption in the Court and, indeed, the recent ruling in *Re W* (*The Times* 1997) suggested that sexuality alone is not an acceptable ground upon which to deny an adoption. The very fact that the *Re W* ruling exists, however, indicates that arguments against adoptions being granted on the grounds of a lesbian or gay sexuality are made in court and we know of examples where local authorities have not been prepared to take lesbian or gay prospective adopters on because of this. However, other birth parents are supportive of the adoption of their children by lesbian or gay people and this is noted by Sarah and Christine:

> The birth family knows we're lesbians too. Their mum wanted to meet us before the girls came to live with us to see if we had horns or something. She had a look, saw we were okay, and said: 'You'll give them a good education, won't you'. It was really good that we met her. The kids have even got a letter from their birth mother saying 'Be good for your two mums' It makes such a difference for them to know that their mum knows and is in favour.

Social Work Support

There are both negative and positive experiences of social work support reported in this book. For instance, Olivette describes the homophobia of a social worker who made clear his abhorrence of lesbian and gay relationships. On the other hand, Elizabeth and Mary's social worker acknowledged the particular skills and commitment they offered as lesbian carers. Social workers are operating in a general climate in society that is homophobic and is particularly hostile to the involvement of lesbians and gay men in the care of children. Not all individual social workers are homophobic; some are lesbian or gay themselves, and some work actively to promote anti-oppressive values in working with lesbian or gay carers. However, social workers with positive or supportive attitudes are scattered randomly across agencies and the accounts given here suggest that the response lesbian and gay applicants can expect is extremely varied and unpredictable.

One of the major problems for supportive social work staff is a lack of policy or management back-up, so that 'sticking your neck out' to approve and work with lesbian or gay carers can sometimes feel like just that, which it should not. Lesbian and gay applicants are assessed like anyone else and approved by a formal panel on the basis of their abilities to meet the needs of children. Yet these accounts suggest there are often inconsistencies between agencies, or even within agencies, in how they respond to lesbian and gay applicants. Most agencies have no policies or procedures regarding lesbian and gay carers at present, and we are aware that many social workers feel unsupported in their attempts to develop good practice with lesbians and gay men. It is important therefore that agencies develop and clarify their policies and procedures in relation to lesbian and gay carers to avoid some of the confusions and delays experienced by some of our contributors. Nita and Clare refer to the delay in taking their application to panel while the panel received awareness-raising training to counter homophobic attitudes, and Olivette describes similar delays in processing the placement of a child with her.

It is also important that individual social workers are prepared for the issues that will come up for them in working with lesbian and gay carers. They need to be aware of homophobic assumptions and stereotypes that they may be carrying and whether these will interfere with their assessment of potential carers. Examining their own attitudes on this issue should be part of their training, yet we know that it rarely is. Social workers need to be careful not to assume automatic parenting skills in heterosexual applicants, just as they need to be careful not to assume unsuitability for parenting in lesbian and gay applicants. The sexuality of a potential carer does not of itself indicate anything about his or her interests, lifestyle, relationships, values, or ability to care for children who have had difficult experiences. Social workers need to explore openly with each individual their experiences, skills and values in relation to caring for children.

Some contributors note that social workers showed an intrusive and unecessary interest in their lifestyle, focusing on their sexuality above all else in the assessment. Others describe a process in which their lesbian or gay identity seemed to be of minimal importance; for instance, Nita and Clare's social worker told them they had their same chance as anyone else of getting a 'normal healthy child, a baby even' and underestimated the difficulties they would face in getting a placement. Being lesbian or gay is both a significant part of our identity and a key factor in assessing how to work with and support lesbian and gay carers in the context of a homophobic society. But it is not all that defines us; we are also defined by gender, race, class, religion, community, ability, interests, and so on. Lesbian and gay carers are asking to be treated 'like everyone else' in the sense that each carer is acknowledged as an individual with particular issues and circumstances that need to be addressed in the course of assessment and placement. Part of this process is acknowledging specific issues that arise for lesbian and gay carers and dealing with them appropriately; for instance, around confidentiality, contact with birth families, legal issues around care orders, adoption and residence orders, and strategies for dealing with hostile attitudes. 'Don't ask, don't tell' responses by social workers are not helpful to lesbians and gay men, and our sexuality needs consideration as a part of the assessment as a whole.

One of the reasons that social work agencies remain cautious about the issue of lesbian and gay carers is the constant threat of media exposure involved, and social workers may be just as likely as carers to 'get it in the neck' from the press for the sake of a good story: 'Children handed over to gays', 'My boy went to homosexual couple' and all the rest. Indeed, we were very sorry that one gay couple, whom we shall call Frank and Steve, felt that they had to withdraw their own very interesting story from this book because of fears about past and current media attention, despite the fact that it would have been anonymised. Unwanted media attention also features in Mike and Brian's story, and in Olivette's, where her placement was delayed due to the local authority's fears of press exposure following tabloid headlines about a neighbouring borough's approval of gay men.

Being rejected outright by social work agencies, at the point of first applying to be assessed, just because of sexuality is reported by many of the contributors. For instance, Sarah and Christine describe the kind of response they often received:

> The tone was generally unpleasant and very negative. On one occasion we were even told that unless we were married there was nothing they could do for us, which seemed a rather bizarre suggestion to make to two lesbians.

Emma and Louise describe having been rejected four times in a long struggle to find an agency that would assess them and the bigotry and blatant homophobia that they encountered. Dfiza and Anne were told they would only be considered for teenagers by one agency. Such an *a priori* rejection is the 'unofficial policy' of many statutory social work agencies, despite the fact that it contravenes their own guidelines on equality of opportunity.

Many contributors also record experiences of being rejected from consideration for a child by a child's social worker as soon as the fact that they were lesbian or gay was disclosed. Nita and Clare document a phone enquiry which ends abruptly when their sexuality becomes apparent. This also features in Sarah and Christine's account. Barbara reports that some social workers in her authority refuse to place children with her.

It is clear from the stories both that the contributors share a wealth of experience and skill in parenting difficult and damaged children and that social workers have confidence in their abilities from the placements they are prepared to make with them, whether or not they will say it openly. The issue of acknowledgement is an important one and one that some contributors feel strongly about. Barbara, Simon, and Mark and Paul all talk about being used and, indeed, overloaded but never being acknowledged as some of the most competent carers their agencies have. They complain about having to educate their agencies without receiving any support or acknowledgement. Sometimes, carers have felt that they were left 'high and dry' by social workers when allegations were made against them, but Simon, and Mark and Paul did feel supported. There are also examples of positive acknowledgement of the contribution of lesbian and gay carers. For instance, Mike and Brian report that:

> Our fostering officer has said to us, particularly when the going has been tough, what a great asset we are to the department.

Jean and Trixie talk about the difficulties of not feeling able to admit weakness because of always feeling they had to prove themselves:

> I think that we exerted pressure on ourselves and I think that this is true of any foster carer who is attempting, inevitably, to be a better parent than the child's birth parent. I believe, however, that the pressures become more for lesbian carers due to the questions that always arise during discussions on the issue. For example, people say 'I'm sure you'd be wonderful parents, but our concern lies with the children....they need ordinary families so that they have as many chances as possible of reversing the damage'.

Sandra highlights how, as an emergency foster carer of difficult teenagers, she feels she receives little support and is handling very challenging behaviour with little training. She is particularly critical of the lack of support offered to the children themselves and the bureaucratic constraints she feels she and the children are subject to while the really serious issues in their lives are neglected or not dealt with over long periods of time. She is also critical of how social workers deal with complaints against her when birth parents find out that she's a lesbian. Homophobic reactions within social work departments are also reported by John and Rob, Sarah and Christine, and Mark and Paul. Others report positive and helpful working relationships with social workers. Kate, for example, describes the help she received from Janet in the early stages of Joshua's placement.

Being Assessed

For those lesbians and gay men who do get through the door, the assessment process is a key factor in whether they will be accepted as the potential carers of children (Hicks 1996). After initial enquiries, most applicants are interviewed and then asked to attend a preparation or training group, in advance of the home study (Form F – see British Agencies for Adoption and Fostering 1991). Following the lengthy home study, a report is written and presented to the formal fostering or adoption panel for approval or not (see Triseliotis, Shireman and Hundleby 1995; Triseliotis, Sellick and Short 1997). All of the contributors to this book have been through this process, but not without some struggles. Nevertheless, this is an important point that we would like to make here. This book presents the stories of lesbians and gay men who are caring for children and who, therefore, have been approved by social work agencies. The book does not include the many stories of lesbians and gay men who have been rejected or, indeed, approved but who never had children placed with them. Certainly, LAGFAPN has had such members and has seen its role to support them through such difficult times.

For most contributors, their initial approach to an agency was fraught with anxiety, dilemmas about if, how and when to be out and the expectation of rejection. For some, this was confirmed by their first attempts. Others met with initial encouragement but faced obstacles and rejection further down the road.

Many of our contributors talk about preparation or training groups and these are used by social workers both to train applicants about the kinds of issues they will have to deal with as carers (sexual abuse, difficult behaviour, child development, working with social workers as a team, children moving on, for example) and to assess applicants' attitudes and skills in advance of the home study. Sandra was assessed entirely on a one-to-one basis and is critical of this as she feels she would have benefited from participation in a group.

Contributors had varied experiences of these training/preparation courses. Some found themselves in quite large groups, mainly or exclusively with heterosexual couples, while some were on courses for single adopters only. Many lesbian or gay applicants report being 'stuck in with' a mainly heterosexual group and sometimes feeling out of place or like the 'token queers'. Dfiza and Anne are particularly positive about their course, which was very mixed, including single people, couples, black and white adopters, disabled adopters and themselves, still the only out gay couple in the group. They praise the social workers running the course who did everything to make everyone feel safe. Emma and Louise, on the other hand, describe a situation in which, having been out to the group, they were used by the tutors to educate the other participants.

Shula, Elizabeth and Mary, and Nita and Clare decided not to be out on their preparation courses. Elizabeth and Mary were assessed separately as single carers when they originally applied to do respite care. When they later applied for permanent fostering, they attended the preparation course again as single carers and came out to the social worker as a lesbian couple when she began interviewing them to complete the forms. Nita went on a small preparation course put on specifically for black single carers and came out to the social worker on her first visit to start the assessment, which was then delayed to the next visit so that the social worker could meet Clare.

After attending a course, prospective adopters and foster parents are asked to contact the agency if they still want to go ahead with the assessment. A social worker is allocated and begins visiting the prospective carers at home to interview them and complete the statutory assessment required for all foster and adoptive parents. Sometimes, the assessment will be carried out at the same time as carers are attending a preparation course.

Some of the contributors describe the assessment process as a positive experience and appear to have had good relationships with their social workers. Others felt the level of questioning about their lifestyle went beyond what was required for the Form F and showed a lack of knowledge and understanding on the part of the social worker. Simon, and Mark and Paul were allocated lesbian and gay social workers, which, they state, was not necessarily helpful. Others have different opinions about this and feel a lesbian or gay social worker may have a better grasp of some of the issues. Emma and Louise highlight how stressful the process can be, especially when it is extremely protracted, as their assessment was:

> If you get pregnant, even if it has taken some time to come to that decision and for it to happen, once its done there's not much you can do apart from wait for it to be born. But when going through a lengthy process of other people questioning your lifestyle, relationship, personality, etc, it can really make you begin to doubt that you have anything to offer.

Some couples found the social workers confused and uncertain about how to deal with their applications, particularly in agencies that had not approved an out lesbian or gay couple before. They were uncertain whether to process them as a single carer with a significant other, two single carers or as a couple. Most carers were eventually assessed as couples but Elizabeth and Mary were assessed as two single individuals at their own request to preserve their confidentiality in the agency's files and protect them from being identified as a lesbian couple.

Some social workers were very positive about what distinguished lesbian and gay carers from most heterosexual carers. Elizabeth and Mary, and Dfiza and Anne describe how their social workers recognised that a couple with two women had a lot more to offer, in terms of quality of care and equal sharing of responsibility for care, than most heterosexual couples applying to foster or adopt:

> The girls' social worker said....when she read our form she knew we would be perfect for them. Because the girls had such strong personalities, they needed two strong people who would take equal responsibility for them. (Dfiza and Anne)

Several contributors were told that their Form Fs were much more detailed and of a much higher standard than any others the social workers had ever done and, for some, there was praise at panel as well for the combinations of skills and qualities offered by the carers.

The issue of concern about gender role models comes up frequently in the assessments of lesbian and gay carers (Hicks 1997). Social workers are often at pains to prove, either to themselves or to panels, that lesbians and gay men can provide opposite-sex role models and balanced gender roles and that lesbians are not 'anti-men' and gay men not 'anti-women'. Lesbian contributors, particularly, report questions about their attitudes towards men and we think that some of this stems from stereotypical views of all lesbians as 'man-haters'. We think that children actually 'see gender' in a far wider range of contexts than just at home, some of the most stereotypical images of which are to be found at school, on television or in films, in public institutions, at the workplace and amongst peers. Good practice in social work also discourages carers from reinforcing stereotypical views of gender in their children, yet lesbians and gay men seem to be asked by social workers to do just that: 'what opposite sex role models can you provide?', 'how many men are your friends and how many visit the house?'.

The issue of support networks is broader than the issue of whether applicants have sufficient role models of the opposite sex in their networks. Jean and Trixie highlight the importance of friendships and support networks within the lesbian and gay community which function as alternative extended families. Such networks are not always understood or valued by social workers.

For new partners joining a family where a fostering arrangement was already in place, the stress of entering an already established household and taking on a possibly unexpected parenting role was combined with the stress of a fostering assessment by social services. Jean and Trixie describe the difficulties of this process and so do John and Rob, and Simon. In Shula's case, she was advised not to live with her new partner before the adoption had gone to court as she was going to court as a single adopter.

When the assessment is complete, the application goes to an adoption or fostering panel (some agencies have one panel for both) and all contributors who refer to this part of the process describe it as unproblematic. This is because if there are potential problems with an application, it is unlikely to be taken to panel until they have been resolved, though panels do have the powers to refer an assessment for further work or to reject applicants. Barbara was advised by social workers not to be out in her assessment because of the composition of her local panel. Nita and Clare experienced delays in going to panel while the agency put its panel through equal opportunities training on sexuality issues and waited for a particularly homophobic member to leave. Most contributors describe realising that being approved was only the first step and it was still a long and uncertain road to having a child placed to live with them. Some had been warned that this might never happen, that it was easy to be approved because it made the agencies look good in terms of equal opportunities, but that afterwards they would always find somewhere else to place a child that was less effort and less controversial.

Delays Following Approval

Of course, getting through the assessment process and being approved is not the end of the story. Many of the contributors describe the lengthy process of delay following approval that they faced before actually having any child placed with them. Emma and Louise's story, for example, is, in many ways, a portrayal of the great strength and determination needed by some lesbian or gay applicants not to be put off by the whole process. They describe the great strain put on their relationship by the process of assessment and constant dead-ends they faced, covering a period of eight years in all, from when they first made enquiries about adoption to eventually being approved by a panel. Sarah and Christine's story similarly describes a long process of five years in all from their first inquiries to the eventual placement of the four girls, three years of which represented delay following their approval as adopters.

For others, the greatest frustrations came after having been approved as carers. Nita and Clare describe how it was eighteen disheartening months after being approved as adopters that they finally saw the details about their now adopted daughter Lubna in a magazine, another six before she eventually came to live with them and a further eighteen months before the adoption was heard in the High Court. Of course, this kind of delay is a feature of much adoption and fostering these days, but for lesbian or gay carers delay can also be caused by the unwillingness of some social workers to consider them for certain children and, sometimes, by the objections of children, young people or birth parents themselves. Lengthy delay in getting a placement is reported by Elizabeth and Mary, Sarah and Christine, Shula, Paul and Richard, Dfiza and Anne, and Simon. Paul and Richard eventually entered into a respite care arrangement with their now fostered son, Patrick, and they felt that social workers wanted them to prove themselves adequate carers before they would be considered as potential fosterers. It took six years for them to finally achieve their goal of having a child placed with them on a permanent basis. John was forced to take his case to the ombudsman and was successful in vindicating his suitability as a carer for Ismail.

Once assessed, contributors have had very different experiences of getting placements. Most foster carers have placements suggested to them by social workers from within their own agency. The contributors approved for short-term and emergency fostering seem to have been used very regularly and heavily by their agencies, but Paul and Richard, who were approved for long-term placements, experienced serious delays. Prospective adopters can also wait for their social workers to find a possible placement or they can look for possible children themselves by getting the national fostering and adoption magazines and ringing children's social workers direct. Some prospective adopters were approached with a placement within a few months of approval, others had to wait longer or were approached with possible children where they felt the match was not appropriate.

Nita and Clare describe approaching other agencies direct and being put off on the phone once the social worker realised they were a lesbian couple, as do Sarah and Christine, and others have similar stories. Paul and Richard remember approaching as many as 25 agencies. Shula describes how her social worker made it clear to children's social workers that her adopter was a lesbian in order not to have to waste time with social workers who would not be comfortable with this. This social worker was also reluctant to seek placement of a child from outside the agency, despite this being standard procedure with black adopters, because she did not want her adopter to have to deal with homophobic responses and she felt there would be more accountability within her own agency.

Dfiza and Anne, and Nita and Clare relate instances where their enquiries about sibling groups were rejected by the agency and, later, they saw the same children advertised again, obviously still not placed or, worse still, advertised separately, when the contributors would have taken them as a sibling group. Mark and Paul describe how a child was placed in a residential unit rather than in their family and John and Rob recount that Nazan, their foster son's sister, was placed in a hostel rather than with her brother in their family. Elizabeth and Mary, Nita and Clare, Kath, and Dfiza and Anne all describe experiences of pursuing a particular child or sibling group a long way down the road to linking and having the placement fall apart or collapse at a late stage, which was painful and stressful.

Some black contributors identify particular issues for them in the kinds of placements that were suggested to them by social workers. Dfiza and Anne describe being asked to take a sibling group of white boys directly after they were approved, which they found puzzling and disturbing. They felt they were clearly a valuable prospective family for black children and were also already caring for two black children as part of their family, so they were surprised and angry to find that anyone should think it would be appropriate to place a larger group of white children with them. It seemed to them a disservice to the children they were currently caring for and a disservice to all the black children in care for whom there are not enough black families available. Nita and Clare encountered some difficulty in being taken seriously as potential carers for Asian or Asian mixed-race children because they follow no particular religion and Nita is not fluent in an Asian language. They describe instances where children they enquired about had been with white carers for some years and were not receiving any positive reinforcement of their Asian identity, yet social workers refused to consider them on the grounds that they did not offer a close enough match to the children, although there were no other prospective adopters being considered.

Two of the white contributors discuss the issue of having black children placed with them. Sandra's own birth children are black and she expresses her desire to foster other black children as she feels her household is a positive environment for black children. John describes how it was suggested to him that he needed to address issues of race in taking on a black foster child but there was no advice on this from social services. The social work department was prepared to place Ismail trans-racially and pointed out that John might need extra input on this issue, yet did nothing to follow this up.

Placements

How placements are prepared for, and handled by social workers and previous carers, is a big issue for all foster and adoptive carers but is particularly acute for lesbian and gay carers where there is a greater possibility of hostility from former carers. For some foster carers, particularly short-term foster carers, there is often little or no preparation before a child arrives, which can cause difficulties. Sandra describes taking children for emergency care having received no information about their situations or histories. With long-term and adoptive placements, the stories reveal very different experiences at the point of placement. Several contributors stress the importance of being assertive about what you feel should happen and John and Rob, Kath, and Mark and Paul describe having to complain formally when they were not happy with the way things were being handled:

> There have been many occasions where I've had to take risks and push for Rosie's needs to be met and, sometimes, my own. I think you have to be prepared to do that if you're clear about what you want and what you think is right. You've got to be prepared to push, to write letters of complaint, challenge social workers, write to the court about their inadequate new building, request financial help, whatever it takes. (Kath)

Paul and Richard encountered huge resistance and had to struggle for some years to break this down. Nita and Clare describe having to argue strongly for their introductions to Lubna to happen in the time scale they felt was appropriate. They talk of the commitment of Lubna's foster parent in supporting the placement. Dfiza and Anne, on the other hand, describe a situation where the previous foster carer and her whole family were deeply opposed to the placement and attempted to sabotage it. The serious lack of support from the social workers in dealing with this situation jeopardised the placement in its first few weeks.

Some adoptive carers were able to negotiate adoption leave when their children were first placed with them. There is no statutory provision for such leave but many local authorities and some voluntary organisations include some provision for adoption leave in their conditions of service. The lengths of time on full pay, half pay and unpaid vary. Nita was able to get adoption leave from the voluntary organisation she worked for and there may be other employers who have some kind of provision. Although Sarah was able to get adoption leave, she wanted to keep this quiet from her work colleagues, despite being out.

Many contributors faced very challenging behaviour from children placed with them, particularly in the first few months of the placement. Many describe being tested by children who had experienced repeated rejection in their lives and found it hard to believe they had reached somewhere safe and secure. Difficult behaviour arose from initial survival strategies children employed to protect themselves from being hurt again. Sandra describes how she was tested to the limit by children convinced she would reject them and how she had to stick with them to prove her commitment:

> One important thing is that a foster child will test you to the limit to see if you'll say 'right, that's it, you've got to go'. They're treated like a parcel. One

child told me that she felt like a pass the parcel. They do do some horrible things and then they start packing their bags even before you've discovered what they've done...

Dfiza and Anne had to deal with deep hostility and resistance from Carla and Tanya when they were first placed and describe their behaviour as out of control and dangerous to themselves and each other, but, six months later, a firm, committed and consistent response had given the children security and boundaries within which they were blossoming.

Mike and Brian describe experiences of taking teenage boys who were extremely angry and violent, and, of Shane, they say:

> He was very wound up and, eventually, we sat him down and asked him what was wrong. 'When are you going to have an argument?' was the response. He had been so used to living in the midst of conflict that he couldn't cope with the uncertainty of waiting for it to erupt again.

Simon identifies the 'sometimes horrendous' behaviour of children he has cared for, including physical violence, smashing up the house, self-harm or 'kicking off' in the middle of the street, as the most difficult aspect of fostering and he describes how utterly draining it can be at times:

> Fostering can feel like it's taken over your whole life at times and you can feel like you've given so much of yourself that there's nothing left.....I don't really know why I do it and, sometimes, I really do wonder why...but when Peter asks for a hug, that makes a huge difference because he's never hugged anyone before....You have to be so many things – mother, father, saint, sinner, counsellor, cleaner, cook....and I wouldn't have it any other way!

Such challenging behaviour was referred to by Simon's social worker as that of 'heavy-duty kids' and can include children's physical violence, sexualised behaviour, destructiveness and children showing attachment disorder. For many contributors, difficult and, sometimes, violent behaviour is an ongoing issue resulting from the long-term hurt and damage their children have suffered. This is evident in the account given by Sarah and Christine. Feelings of anger and self-hate manifest themselves in a whole range of destructive and self-destructive behaviours which are very difficult to deal with. Some contributors found lack of support from their agency a big issue while others talk of receiving valuable support from social workers. For some, more difficult behaviour emerged in adolescence, which parallels the experiences of most families, however they are constituted.

Jean and Trixie talk of how Claire's difficult and anti-social behaviour, including physical violence, sexualised behaviour and self-harm, profoundly affected the whole family. Her sexualised behaviour required Trixie to rethink her response to things like requests for hugs and necessitated considerable work with all the children on protecting themselves. Sarah and Christine, Kate and Sandra also talk of being forced to approach nudity in the house differently from how they had done before they fostered in order to take account of the needs and experiences of their children. Sandra has fostered teenage girls who have mostly been sexually active and talking to them about sex and helping them to keep safe has been an important part of the work she has done with them.

Kate describes the challenges and rewards of caring for a child with learning difficulties over a period of ten years:

> Perhaps the hardest thing is just how slow change is. Just until recently, when he had a bit of a spurt, you know his development has been painfully slow....On the other hand, he is a total joy....He is just so good natured. He has been coming for ten years and I think just once he was in a slightly bad mood!

She had good social work support at the beginning when she needed it and, later, had very little contact. She talks of being very involved with the special school Joshua attends, first through a long battle to get his statement of educational needs changed and, later, as a governor. Mark and Paul have cared for a child with a complex syndrome of disability. They found his behaviour challenging at first but feel they have achieved a lot by listening to him and giving him attention.

Those contributors with other children in the family talk of the effects of placements on their other children. Sandra describes how positive her birth children are about having foster children in the family. Jean and Trixie, on the other hand, describe the difficulties of introducing Trixie's birth children to Jean's foster child. Dfiza and Anne also talk of the care they had to take to introduce their children placed for adoption to two other children they had fostered previously for a long time and who remained part of the family. Some contributors describe arguments and resentments that can arise between birth children and fostered or adopted children, or between a child newly arrived in the family home and those already in placement.

Mike and Brian talk of the effects of fostering on their own relationship, describing how more aware and careful they have to be of how they show affection when fostering boys and young men on a short-term basis, but also how they appreciate the time they have together more. Jean and Trixie describe the strain for them in moving from a situation where they had both been financially independent working women to one where childcare needs required one of them to stay at home full time and how difficult that loss of financial independence was. Trixie also talks of the process of learning to love foster children whose lives and histories can only ever be partially known and the difference in role from being a birth parent.

The awareness, described by Mike and Brian, of the need to consider what is appropriate behaviour in front of children, including affection between partners, is also raised by Kate, Paul and Richard, Sandra, and Sarah and Christine. This is an important issue, especially where carers are dealing with children who have survived sexual abuse, but also, not least, because of the fact that some carers have faced allegations being made against them by children. Even when such allegations are unfounded, lesbian and gay carers are particularly vulnerable to such suspicions since these simply confirm, in the minds of some, our unsuitability to care for children.

Class difference is raised as an issue by contributors who identify as middle-class but took working-class children. Kate describes how she and Poppy tried to restrict their spending on Joshua because they knew that his mother, Mary, had a limited income. The shock of moving from one class to another for children is raised in Sarah and Christine's account and these issues are also implicit in Mike and Brian's story. Sandra recounts the objections of some birth parents to her 'alternative lifestyle' – the way she dresses, her interior decoration, attending pop festivals. This is not to say, however, that all lesbians and gay men who foster or adopt are middle-class. Certainly, they are not and some of the contributors to this book are working-class. Kath lives in a working-class area alongside many Asian families, which some children's social workers saw in a negative light, the traditional view being that white children should be adopted into 'nice', white middle-class areas. Nor are all children in care from working-class families. Some of those taken on board by our contributors come from middle-class backgrounds.

Not all placements are always 'successful'. There are reports of placement breakdown in this book. In Sarah and Christine's story, Wendy's violence was a precursor to her eventually leaving the placement:

We all went away for the weekend and Wendy was dreadful the whole time. She sat in the middle of the road, she was violent, she pulled our hair, kicked, bit and 'snotted' at us. Eventually, we got back home and hoped she would then calm down, but she didn't. A horrendous scene in the library shortly afterwards, where she kicked and screamed at Sarah, was the last straw. Wendy herself was phoning her social worker saying that she didn't want to live with us anymore. Sarah already believed that Wendy shouldn't live with us any longer. But Christine continued to agonise about it. She was having great difficulty saying 'Wendy has to go'. Although she gradually accepted it, it was still a very difficult conflict between us. Eventually, we were both thankful that it was Wendy who made the decision to leave herself.

In Jean and Trixie's case, Claire moved on into residential care. It is, sometimes, all too easy to view such situations as 'failures', but, in Jean's case, for example, she had cared for Claire for ten years before the placement eventually ended. Puberty is often a significant factor in such situations and it may be that the kinds of histories of abuse that such children have to deal with become far harder for them to manage in teenage years. They may then choose to actively reject their carers, siblings or both and their behaviour may become unmanageable. In other cases, it may be that children only feel able to truly exhibit the extent of their disturbance once they are firmly established within a placement or they may have great difficulty being able to trust any adult enough to form any kind of secure attachment, as reported by Sarah and Christine. As children develop and grow into young adults, placements change as they have to adapt to the demands of puberty, sexual awareness and a growing independence from adults. Kate describes how the sudden awareness that a child has developed into a young person, and a sexual being, can be quite a shock!

Support Groups

The importance of support systems, including support groups such as LAGFAPN, for foster and adoptive carers is noted by Elizabeth and Mary, Nita and Clare, Emma and Louise, Dfiza and Anne, Olivette and Simon. Lesbians and gay men draw their personal support systems from a wide range of sources, which include friends as much as family, the lesbian and gay community, other parents/carers and more formal support groups. This is noted in Jean and Trixie's story, where Jean talks about the genuine support she received from other lesbians and gay men when her foster son died. Olivette also mentions the extended lesbian and gay 'family' as being important to her as well as her biological family.

One of the prime reasons for the existence of LAGFAPN is to act as a source of personal support for lesbians and gay men either applying to foster or adopt or currently caring for children. It also gives the children a chance to mix in the crèche with others who have gay dads or lesbian mums. Barbara describes the benefits for her:

When I found out about the northern support group it was great. I read about it in the gay press and I really enjoy going. It's nice to meet other gay carers and some of us have been away on holiday together with all the kids, which was good fun. Also, it's nice to get out of my local area and meet up with others and talk about the problems and the good times.

It is necessary for such groups to exist, and to be supported, for two main reasons. First, more general carer support groups are usually heterosexually dominated and lesbians and gay men feel very marginalised in such settings. This is commented upon by Barbara, who also describes her experience of being involved in training foster carers. When she highlighted the homophobia of many existing foster carers, she was removed as a trainer and the issues she raised were never addressed. Second, the lesbian and gay community is not particularly child-friendly, with most events and spaces catering to younger people out to have a good time! All of the contributors to this book like to go out and have a good time too, but only if they can either get a child-minder or can take children with them! Hence the need for LAGFAPN and other groups.

Some of the contributors talk about how the support group helped them directly in making the decision to apply, as hearing about other lesbians' and gay men's experiences, and seeing others with children, can act as a great source of inspiration as well as support. LAGFAPN has organised two national conferences/get-togethers for lesbian and gay foster/adoptive carers and their children in the past, one in London in March 1992 and another jointly organised by one of the editors in Manchester in April 1994. Many of the contributors to this book attended such events and they are a great way of meeting other carers.

Issues of Research and Policy

In considering how lesbian and gay fostering and adoption has changed in recent years, a good starting point is to look back upon *Fostering and Adoption by Lesbians and Gay Men*, the pioneering study carried out by Jane Skeates and Dorian Jabri in 1988. This was the first such study in Britain to tackle the topic in any depth, as previous work had focused on lesbian mothers and custody (Hanscombe and Forster 1981; Rights of Women Lesbian Custody Group 1986). It is interesting, therefore, to see how things have changed with regard to the policy and practice of lesbian and gay fostering and adoption since its publication.

There have been a few notable publications since 1988 dealing with lesbian and gay parenting (Ali 1996; Benkov 1994; Griffin and Mulholl 1997; Groocock 1995; Martin 1993; Saffron 1996; Wakeling and Bradstock 1995) but none has been specifically devoted to fostering and adoption. This is one of the main reasons that the Lesbian and Gay Foster and Adoptive Parents Network wanted to produce this book. We wanted to record the contributions that lesbians and gay men have made to fostering and adoption in this country. We wanted to tell our stories and we wanted to show how being a foster or adoptive carer is different from other forms of parenting.

Researching Lesbian and Gay Fostering and Adoption

The Skeates and Jabri (1988) study was something of a 'landmark' of its time. It was the first British publication to deal with lesbian and gay fostering and adoption and was widely discussed by lesbians and gay men, including a featured slot on the first ever Channel 4 series *Out On Tuesday* in 1989 (Parmar 1989). The study firmly argued for a right of entitlement – that is, that lesbians and gay men should be considered for fostering and adoption and that we should not be rejected on the basis of our sexuality alone.

Skeates and Jabri (1988) talked to thirteen lesbians and gay men who had been through the assessment process and also profiled the policies on lesbian and gay carers of six inner-London boroughs. Most of the lesbians and gay men they interviewed had been out to social services but they reported a less favourable response because of this. In particular, the study found that black and disabled lesbians and gay men who applied to be carers faced a process of 'double discrimination'. White social workers, who were suspicious, confused or simply racist in their handling of black carers generally, were even more suspicious and uncomfortable when faced with the challenge of assessing black carers who were gay or lesbian.

In general, the study found that lesbians and gay men felt that their sexuality was poorly handled as an issue in social work assessment and there was an emphasis on concerns that they would be unable to provide acceptable male and female gender roles for children. Lesbian and gay applicants were placed under greater scrutiny than their heterosexual counterparts (or, perhaps, we should say those people who did not declare their sexuality).

In terms of placement outcomes, lesbian and gay carers were far more likely to be caring for disabled children, children with 'special needs' and those considered 'hard to place'. The study was published just as Section 28 of the Local Government Act 1988 was enacted and the authors themselves noted that a 'backlash' in the commitment of local authorities to lesbians and gay men was a distinct possibility. We certainly believe that this was the case by the late 1980s and many authorities continue to this day to shun specific commitments to services for lesbians and gay men. The outright rejection by many authorities of lesbian and gay applicants seeking to provide foster and adoptive care is a continuing example of this backlash.

Skeates and Jabri (1988) therefore noted that more research on lesbian and gay fostering and adoption would be needed in this country post-Section 28. Whilst there has been very little such research (see Brown 1991, 1992; Hicks 1996, 1997), we hope that this book contributes an important insight into the positive care that many lesbians and gay men are providing for children and also communicates the message that lesbian and gay fostering and adoption is on the increase, if very slowly.

One of the problems with the Skeates and Jabri study was that it concentrated solely upon London boroughs. We recognise that this was bound to be one of the limitations of small-scale and, presumably, inadequately funded research. This book, therefore, does not present the picture from London alone but covers significant parts of the North of England as well. In fact, nine of the seventeen stories are from contributors who live in the North. Unfortunately, the book does not address the experience in either Wales or Scotland.

It is our view that there are probably far more lesbians and gay men caring for fostered or adopted children in the late 1990s than there were at the time that the Skeates and Jabri study was carried out, and this is also reflected in this book. All of the contributors to this book are caring for children, often after long and difficult 'battles' to do so, but, nevertheless, they are stories of success, care and triumph. Partly, this may be to do with the fact that there are some local authorities who have been prepared to develop good practice with lesbian and gay carers and have been prepared to place children in their care. Nationally-known examples (such as Birmingham, Manchester, Hampshire, some London boroughs) have appeared in the press in recent years.

Existing research points to the assessment process as especially crucial to lesbian and gay applicants (Hicks 1996). It is in being assessed as a potential carer that the attitudes and values of social workers, and social work agencies, come into play. The decision by the Children's Society to reject any applications to care for children by lesbians and gay men (Gregory and Saxton 1994; Pilkington 1994) is a disheartening example of the kinds of discriminatory values still employed by some social work agencies. Nevertheless, there are local authorities prepared to assess lesbian or gay applicants and all of the contributors to this book have been through such a process, difficult as it sometimes is. Ricketts (1991) has noted that '...when open lesbians and gay men have succeeded in becoming foster parents, they have done so only after being thoroughly and rigorously evaluated...even more extensively than other applicants.' (p.10). Don Smart (1991), for example, describes how he and his partner, John, were interviewed by a psychiatrist when they applied to adopt, something that heterosexual applicants did not have to go through.

Much of the assessment process, as it is experienced by lesbians and gay men, depends upon the attitudes and values of social workers and this is highlighted in the work of Helen Cosis Brown (1991, 1992). She suggests that social workers doing assessments of lesbian or gay applicants need to first ask themselves what skills, knowledge and values they have regarding such a piece of work. She argues that the 'false dichotomy' of 'gay rights *versus* children need normal families' should be replaced by assessment practices which focus on the child's right to a good placement (1991, pp.11–13). This means that no adult, whatever their sexuality, has an automatic 'right' to be a foster or adoptive carer but that they should be assessed according to whether they have adequate childcare skills. Brown suggests that social workers need to acquaint themselves with existing research knowledge on children who live with lesbians and gay men since such studies do not support commonly held concerns about 'risks' to such children (see Hicks 1997). Brown argues that assessments of lesbians and gay men ought to focus on their sexuality, but as a part of the whole, rather than being exclusive of all else.

Research being carried out by Stephen Hicks (1996, 1997) has focused on the assessment of lesbians and gay men, initially considering applicants themselves and currently looking at the role of social workers in fostering and adoption units. The assessment is a key point of gatekeeping in the process used to weed out unsuitable applicants, but many lesbians and gay men are still rejected outright by agencies. For those who do get through to being assessed, many feel that they have to educate their social worker about lesbian and gay issues or raise issues of sexuality themselves. Lesbian and gay applicants commonly report that their assessments either focus exclusively on their sexuality, or, at the opposite extreme, ignore it. Such assessments may also construct lesbians and gay men as potential 'risks' to children, suggesting that they will become gay or be abused, have distorted gender role models or suffer undue stigma due to the sexuality of their carers, none of which is supported by existing research.

We think that one of the major changes since the Skeates and Jabri study is that now, more than ever, lesbians and gay men are *coming out* to social work agencies when asking to be considered as the potential carers of children. Of course, there are still those who feel unable to come out. In the past this was more likely to be the case, but now there are significant numbers of fosterers and adopters who are open about their sexuality (Ricketts and Achtenberg 1987, 1990). This has led to what we might term the 'rights' issue – that is, the question that is now often asked is 'do lesbians and gay men have the right to care for children?'

Some commentators have suggested that we have no such 'rights' and that we should be prevented from caring for children (Whitfield 1991). Whitfield, for example, sees this as the 'lesbian and gay rights' agenda – that is, an adult agenda – rather than being about the needs of children. We don't agree with this, of course, and, like Brown (1991), we feel this is a false dichotomy. Indeed, in a BBC *Heart of the Matter* programme (1993), young people accommodated in a children's home talked about how they felt that the most important things about carers were the love and security that they could offer, rather than their sexuality. Kelly commented:

> There weren't foster parents for me because, they were saying, foster parents don't want teenage children now, they want young children...If you ask me, if there were more gay and lesbian foster parents they might take on teenagers and there'd be a lot more foster parents for teenagers, not just young kids.

We believe that lesbians and gay men should have the 'right' to be considered and assessed as potential carers in the same way as any other adult and our rejection on the grounds of our sexuality alone by some agencies is, therefore, a 'rights' issue. Where lesbian or gay applicants are assessed as being able to meet the needs of children, they should be able to do just that and this does not take away from the 'rights' of children and young people to good childcare. We take issue with the suggestion that any adult, whatever their sexuality, has a 'right' to a child. Children are not our property, they are not objects and they have their own particular needs, which must be met by their carers.

Another point that is often raised, linked to the 'rights' issue, is the view that lesbians and gay men only apply to foster or adopt either to 'prove a point' or to 'ape heterosexuals' in some way. We feel that neither is true. You will see from this book that all the contributors have been through fairly long and arduous processes of assessment in order to become approved as carers and that the children for whom they care present particularly challenging dilemmas. Many of the children placed with lesbians and gay men have very difficult personal histories of abuse, violence and rejection or they have particular special needs, and none of their carers is doing so just to 'prove a point'. Nor do these 'families' simply mirror heterosexual lifestyles. In fact, far from it!

Looking back at the *Out On Tuesday* feature (Parmar 1989) now, we were struck not only by how little some things have changed but also by how much others have. In the film, Dorian Jabri spoke about the fact that lesbian and gay carers have been used for years by local authorities but that their sexuality was never acknowledged, what he called 'tacit acknowledgement'. We think that this has changed because there are now more lesbian and gay applicants who are not prepared to hide their sexuality. This is true of most, though not all, of the contributors to this book. Helen Cosis Brown talked in the film about how many do not get past the assessment stage of the process. We think that the assessment still plays a key role in whether lesbians and gay men are accepted as the carers of children. You will find that many of the stories in this book point to discriminatory practices around assessment, including some outright rejections.

Judith Weeks and Pat Romans, who are well known for their fostering of many children since 1971 and have also adopted, talked about the 'unofficial policy' of placing disabled children with lesbians and gay men. Judith said that this reflected discriminatory values in which 'second-class children' are placed with 'second-class carers'. We think that, in some ways, this remains the case. Whilst there are lesbians and gay men who wish to care for disabled children, many others are also asked to care for children who are 'hard to place', having needs arising either from a disability, educational difficulties or histories of abuse and neglect. We recognise that this is now the case for many children 'looked after' by local authorities but we also think there is an expectation that lesbians and gay men will cope with the most difficult of children. Lesbians and gay men may also be less likely to turn down a disabled child because of their own experiences of discrimination. For other lesbian and gay applicants, the feeling that there will be less competition for 'harder to place' children may affect their decision to take such children on.

The *Out On Tuesday* film also pointed out that few black lesbians and gay men applied to care for children and that this was to do with racism within fostering and adoption services as much as heterosexism. This too has changed as there are now more black lesbians and gay men fostering or adopting children and this is partly reflected in the varied heritages of the different contributors to this book. The professional orthodoxy of trans-racial placements has become largely discredited and has been supplanted in many agencies by a 'same race' placement policy. The consequent drives to recruit more black carers for black children have raised the profile of adoption and fostering in black communities generally. The change has been not so much in the direction of decreased racism in agencies as in a greater practical need for many more black carers to meet both the needs of the disproportionately high numbers of black children in their care and the requirements of same-race policy decisions.

Alongside this, the numbers of black lesbians and gay men coming out in the gay community is increasing slowly and, as it does, perceptions of the gay community as an exclusively white place are changing. The black communities are also changing and black lesbians and gay men feel more able to make relationship, lifestyle and identity choices outside community traditions, as do their heterosexual counterparts. The choice of a gay identity implies finding new ways to have and care for children and so fostering and adoption are increasingly on the agenda for those of us black lesbians and gay men who want to be involved in bringing up children.

Children Who Live with Lesbians and Gay Men

One of the chief concerns raised about all forms of lesbian and gay parenting, including fostering and adoption, is to do with the supposed 'effects' that this will have upon children as they grow up. These concerns are commonly couched in the form of potential 'risks' to children, these being that such children will be 'at risk' of sexual abuse, impaired social development or relations with peers, distorted psychological and gender role development, and dysfunctional sexuality (Hicks 1997). In particular, it is assumed that children living with lesbians and gay men will themselves 'become gay' or that they will be exposed to dangerous and corrupting sexual practices, that they will not properly understand the differences between 'men' and 'women' and that their lives will be dominated by merciless teasing at school (Hicks 1997).

There is, at present, little research evidence on children who are fostered or adopted by lesbians and gay men but there are studies of children who have come to have lesbian or gay parents by other means – from previous heterosexual partnerships, from self-insemination arrangements and by co-parenting (Bailey *et al.* 1995; Barret and Robinson 1990; Green and Bozett 1991; King 1995; Patterson 1992; Saffron 1996; Tasker and Golombok 1997). None of this existing research points to any problems in the psychological, social or sexual development of the children, all of whom develop in very similar ways indeed to the children of heterosexual parents. Further, none of the studies has found any evidence of the sexual abuse, or any greater likelihood of such abuse, of children by lesbians or gay men. Indeed, what we do know about sexual abuse indicates that children are at far greater risk from heterosexual men than anyone else (Barret and Robinson 1990; Patterson 1992). In fact, the 'concerns' raised about the children of lesbians and gay men betray far more about the consensus that enforces heterosexuality and traditional gender roles than they do about genuine issues in our understanding of child development (Hicks 1997).

Of the existing studies, Fiona Tasker and Susan Golombok's *Growing Up in a Lesbian Family* (1997) is the most extensive to date, being based upon longitudinal research with the children of lesbian mothers. The study began in

1976, when the children were around ten years old, and compared them with a control group of the children of single heterosexual mothers. Follow-up research was completed in 1991, when the children were adults of around twenty-five years. In summary, the study found that the adult children of lesbian mothers had good mental health, good peer relationships and were functioning healthily. Whilst the young adults were more likely to *remember* name-calling in school relating to sexuality, they were *no more likely* to report having been picked on by classmates. Similarly, though they were more likely *to have considered* a lesbian or gay sexuality for themselves, they were *no more likely* to grow up to be gay or lesbian than children of heterosexual parents.

Interestingly, the study did find that the young adults reported more positive relationships with their mothers' lesbian partners than did those whose heterosexual mothers had formed new relationships with a male partner, and they enjoyed good relationships with their nonresident fathers. Tasker and Golombok conclude that their findings 'show that young people brought up by a lesbian mother do well in adulthood and have good relationships with their family, friends, and partners. In policy decisions about who should and should not be allowed to raise children, negative outcomes for children should not be assumed on the basis of a mother's sexual orientation' (p.155).

Research on the children of gay fathers is more limited but the study by Bailey *et al.* (1995) found that, of the sons of gay fathers whose sexual orientation they could rate with confidence, 9 per cent were non-heterosexual and 91 per cent heterosexual (p. 126). They concluded that 'sexual orientation was not positively correlated with the amount of time that sons lived with their [gay] fathers' (p.128).

All existing research, therefore, highlights that sexuality is in no way an indicator of the ability to parent or care for children. Indeed, Charlotte Patterson's (1992) review of existing research on the children of lesbians and gay men concluded that 'not a single study has found children of gay or lesbian parents to be disadvantaged in any significant respect relative to children of heterosexual parents' (p.1036). This important research evidence is, therefore, directly applicable to lesbian and gay fostering or adoption and ought to be considered by social work agencies when conducting assessments, presenting these to panels and in going to court.

Legislation and Policy Issues

As well as being the year that Skeates and Jabri published *Fostering and Adoption by Lesbians and Gay Men*, 1988 will also be remembered as the year of Section 28 of the Local Government Act 1988 and the 'pretended family relationship'

(Gooding 1992). In a sense, then, this book is a collection of 'pretending families' since, to a large extent, we are still regarded as outside of the norm, especially within law and policy. Section 28, whilst it has never been tested in law, still has the potential to be very damaging to the children of lesbians and gay men since it attempts to prevent any acknowledgement within schools that some children have gay parents. It is this kind of denial of the realities of some children's lives that is damaging to all children's understanding of their social context, and particularly damaging to the self-image and self-esteem of the children of lesbian and gay parents.

It was with specific consultation regarding family placement issues under the Children Act 1989 that the issue of lesbian and gay fostering became the subject of national debate once again (DoH 1990, 1991). Paragraph 16 of the consultation paper on foster placement stated that '…it would be wrong arbitrarily to exclude any particular groups of people from consideration. But the chosen way of life of some adults may mean that they would not be able to provide a suitable environment for the care and nurture of a child. No one has a "right" to be a foster parent. "Equal rights" and "gay rights" policies have no place in fostering services.' (DoH 1990, para.16). Apart from the fact that this reduces the complexity of lesbian and gay experience, identity and politics to a 'lifestyle choice', this paragraph offered social work agencies *carte blanche* to reject any lesbian or gay applicants outright.

There was much debate and protest against paragraph 16 within the lesbian and gay community and representations were made to the Department of Health, not only by lesbian and gay groups but also by professional bodies concerned with childcare. As a result, the reference to 'gay rights' was removed from the final document (DoH 1991). The Positive Parenting Campaign was formed in Manchester specifically to challenge paragraph 16 and the group continues to be active around lesbian and gay parenting issues today, recently organising a national conference on lesbian and gay fostering for social work practitioners, educators and students.

Nevertheless, the 'chosen way of life' reference remains and is open to discriminatory interpretation with regard to sexuality. The Children Act guidance remains contradictory in this respect since paragraph 9.53 states that 'gay young men and women may require very sympathetic carers to enable them to accept their sexuality and to develop their own self esteem.' (DoH 1991, para.98). In their story, Nita and Clare describe how the 'chosen way of life' wording in the guidance was used to justify refusing to match them with a sibling group on the grounds of their sexuality, even when the agency acknowledged that Nita and Clare could meet all the children's needs.

In England and Wales the fostering process does not require court approval and local authorities responsible for the placement of children are free to consider any applicants they choose, including lesbian and gay applicants (Gooding 1992). They are also free to formulate their own policies on whom they exclude from consideration. So, for instance, some authorities will not consider applicants who smoke. Some of these agreed criteria are expressed in written policies whilst others operate as an informal consensus within the department and have the same effect as a written policy in screening potential applicants. However, we are not aware of any local authorities that specifically preclude lesbian and gay applicants from consideration for fostering. The situation in Scotland, however, is different since point 12(4) of the Fostering Regulations states that any couples who apply should be a man and a woman who are married.

Adoption is slightly more complicated because, in addition to the requirement that applicants be approved by a recognised adoption agency, it also involves a legal process in which an adoption order must be made by a court. However, Bromley Council, for example, made a recent public statement that they would not consider applications to adopt from lesbians, gay men and single people (Waugh 1997). We are not aware of any other local authorities making such policy decisions. Current adoption law in England and Wales rules out applications by couples unless they are married and, therefore, heterosexual. However, single people can apply to adopt and lesbian and gay applicants are treated as such for legal purposes. Again, there has been much debate about lesbian and gay adoptions, partly due to the recent adoption law review which expressly addressed this issue: '…we do not propose any changes to the law relating to single applicants, including lesbians and gay men. There are examples of extremely successful adoptions, particularly of older children and children with disabilities, by single adopters.' (DoH/Welsh Office 1992, para.50).

Following publication of the review, ministers, in particular the then junior health minister Tim Yeo, went to great lengths to insist that '…the vast majority of children benefit from having two loving parents of opposite sexes, and adoption agencies should make strenuous efforts to find such couples.' (reported in Marchant 1992, p.1). He suggested that single people, and lesbians and gay men, should be used only as a 'last resort' for adoption (Hicks 1996), backing up his arguments with the assertion that 'babies' are best placed with 'married couples'. This backlash against the recognition by the review, albeit in rather negative terms, that lesbians and gay men had indeed been providing good adoptive care was further emphasised in the eventual publication of the adoption White Paper (DoH 1993).

Whilst the adoption White Paper did have many positive contributions to make to the recognition of the changing nature of modern adoptions, it also sets up *a priori* qualities for who make good parents and a hierarchy of most acceptable 'family structures'. It suggested that 'common sense', whatever that is, should prevail in decisions about assessing prospective adopters and promotes married couples as always providing the best of placements for children. This positions lesbians and gay men, once again, at a point of being used only as a 'last resort' (Hicks 1996). Once more, there is tacit acceptance that lesbians and gay men can make good adopters, but only in exceptional circumstances. This is likely to confirm the 'unofficial policy' of placing disabled, or particularly 'hard to place', children with lesbians and gay men.

As yet, the Adoption Bill has not been fully debated by Parliament, although a failed attempt was made in 1996 (Triseliotis, Shireman and Hundleby 1997, p.248). The Bill did receive some initial hearings but was then dropped from debates with the coming of the 1997 general election. A recent court judgement, *Re W (a Minor) (Adoption: Homosexual adopter)*, found nothing in current adoption law to preclude a single person applying to adopt, even if he or she was living in a gay or lesbian relationship at the time, and that any other decision to prevent this on the grounds of sexual orientation would be 'illogical, arbitrary and inappropriately discriminatory' (*The Times* 1997).

In 1994 a further development in case law, *Re C*, was the granting of a joint residence order to a lesbian who had had a child by artificial insemination and her partner, giving both partners equal parental responsibility for the child in law (Beresford 1994). One of the couples contributing to this book has followed this example and successfully obtained a joint residence order alongside the adoption order, which has to be in a single name, thus securing the equal rights and responsibility of the partner who is not the legal adopter. In another case in 1996, a gay man in Scotland was given an adoption order in the court of appeal (Powell 1997).

Finally, the *Out On Tuesday* film featured a woman called Marion who spoke about being open as a lesbian providing respite care for a seven-year-old boy with special needs. She also talked about the launch of the Lesbian and Gay Foster and Adoptive Parents Network (LAGFAPN) in London in July 1988, saying that the group had been set up to support lesbians and gay men at various stages of the fostering or adoption process, to raise the profile of lesbian and gay carers so that they would be taken more seriously and to encourage social work agencies to regard us as a resource for the care of children. Her feature inspired one of our contributing couples to apply to do respite care and we are delighted that, ten years on, LAGFAPN continues to exist with a

Northern group having been established since June 1994. A success story indeed!

Conclusion

The lesbians and gay men who have contributed to this book speak of the great rewards involved in fostering or adopting children. Many of them have taken on children or young people who are particularly demanding, yet, despite the fact that this has meant placement breakdowns in some cases, there are a great number of success stories in the book. This is often the case only because lesbian and gay carers have persevered in their determination to offer a loving home to children. Many lesbians and gay men feel that they are a neglected resource with regard to fostering and adoption, and this is often simply because of prejudice against them:

> Many gay carers do not have children of their own and anyone we choose to foster is like our 'own'. We – gay and lesbian carers – are a valuable, under-represented resource that could and should be tapped into. Local authorities need to 'wake up' and use us as potential placements. No child need be without a loving home. (John and Rob)

The struggles of some of the contributors over the last ten years or so have paved the way for other lesbians and gay men to come forward, and we hope they have had an impact on the policies and practice of fostering and adoption agencies. Certainly, the number of openly lesbian and gay applicants being approved, and having children placed with them, has increased steadily and more agencies have experience of working with lesbian and gay carers.

We hope that this book has shown the opportunities that lesbians and gay men offer to fostering and adoption agencies for increasing their pool of skilled, loving, committed and tenacious carers. It is to the credit of the lesbians and gay men in this book that they have persevered in their aspirations to care for children in the face of discrimination and resistance. All the contributors attest to the tremendous rewards which have made their persistence worthwhile and we hope that this book will act as an inspiration to those other lesbians and gay men who might be considering fostering or adoption. The struggles documented in these stories represent great staying power and, above all, a commitment to children:

> I think that what I provide Rosie with more than anything is total commitment. Children's needs do differ but, in this case, as someone once said to me, 'what children who have been in care really need is someone to stick to them like glue.' (Kath)

Appendix: Useful Organisations

Albert Kennedy Trust
23, New Mount Street
Manchester M4 4DE
tel: 0161 953 4059
email: info@akt.org.uk
web-site: http://www.akt.org.uk
and
Unit 305a 16/16a
Baldwin Gardens
London EC1N 7RJ
tel: 0171 831 6562

Happy Families
P.O. Box 1060
Askern
Doncaster DN6 9QE
tel: 0130 270 2601

Lesbian and Gay Foster & Adoptive Parents Network (LAGFAPN)
London group to be contacted via the Stonewall Parenting Group (see below).
Northern group can be contacted at: Dept. 7,
1, Newton Street
Manchester M1 1HW

Positive Parenting Campaign
Dept. 7
1, Newton Street
Manchester M1 1HW

Rights of Women Lesbian Custody Project
52-54, Featherstone Street
London EC1Y 8RT
fax: 0171 608 0928
Lesbian parenting line, tel: 0171 251 6576

Stonewall Parenting Group
Stonewall
16, Clerkenwell Close
London EC1R 0AA
tel: 0171 336 8860
fax: 0171 336 8864
Email: info@stonewall.org.uk
web-site: http://www.stonewall.org.uk/parenting

BIBLIOGRAPHY

Ali, T. (1996) *We Are Family: Testimonies of Lesbian and Gay Parents*. London: Cassell.

Badgett, M.V.L. and King, M.C. (1997) 'Lesbian and Gay Occupational Strategies.' In A. Gluckman and B. Reed (eds) *Homo Economics: Capitalism, Community, and Lesbian & Gay Life*. New York: Routledge.

Bailey, J. M., Bobrow, D., Wolfe, M. and Mikach, S. (1995) 'Sexual Orientation of Adult Sons of Gay Fathers.' *Developmental Psychology*, 31,1, 124–129.

Barn, R. (1993) *Black Children in the Public Care System*. London: B.T. Batsford Ltd.

Barret, R.L. and Robinson, B.E. (1990) *Gay Fathers*. Lexington: Lexington Books.

BBC (1993) 'Fostering Prejudice.' *Heart of the Matter*, BBC 1, 14/2/93.

Bebbington, A. and Miles, J. (1989) 'The Background of Children Who Enter Local Authority Care.' *British Journal of Social Work*, 19, 349–368.

Benkov, L. (1994) *Reinventing the Family: The Emerging Story of Lesbian and Gay Parents*. New York: Crown Publishers.

Beresford, S. (1994) 'Lesbians in Residence and Parental Responsibility Cases.' *Family Law*, November, 643–645.

British Agencies for Adoption and Fostering (BAAF) (1991) *Form F: Information on Prospective Substitute Parent(s)*. London: BAAF.

Brown, H.C. (1991) 'Competent Child-Focused Practice: Working with Lesbian and Gay Carers.' *Adoption & Fostering*, 15, 2, 11–17.

Brown, H.C. (1992) 'Gender, Sex and Sexuality in the Assessment of Prospective Carers.' *Adoption & Fostering*, 16, 2, 30–34.

Brown, H.C. (1998) *Social Work and Sexuality: Working with Lesbians and Gay Men*. Houndmills: Macmillan.

Cheetham, J. (1986) Introduction. In S. Ahmed, J. Cheetham and J. Small (eds) *Social Work with Black Children and their Families*. London: B.T. Batsford Ltd.

Department of Health (1990) *Foster Placement (Guidance and Regulations) Consultation Paper No. 16*. London: HMSO.

Department of Health (1991) *The Children Act 1989 Guidance and Regulations: Volume 3, Family Placements.* London: HMSO.

Department of Health/Welsh Office (1992) *Review of Adoption Law: Report to Ministers of an Interdepartmental Working Group: A Consultation Document.* London: HMSO.

Department of Health/Welsh Office/Home Office/Lord Chancellor's Department (1993) *Adoption: The Future.* London: HMSO.

Evans, B. (director) (1995) 'My Mother is an Alien.' *Film for Channel 4 series 'Out'.*

Gay Times (1997) Special Issue: 'Gay Men and Children', Issue 225 (June).

Gooding, C. (1992) *Trouble with the Law? A Legal Handbook for Lesbians and Gay Men.* London: The Gay Men's Press.

Green, G.D. and Bozett, F.W. (1991) 'Lesbian Mothers and Gay Fathers.' In J.C. Gonsiorek & J.D. Weinrich (eds) *Homosexuality: Research Implications for Public Policy.* London: Sage.

Gregory, A. and Saxton, A. (1994) 'Top Children's Charity Battles Over Gay Ban.' *The Pink Paper*, October 28, No. 351, 1.

Griffin, K. and Mulholland, L.A. (eds) (1997) *Lesbian Motherhood in Europe.* London: Cassell.

Groocock, V. (1995) *Changing Our Lives: Lesbian Passions, Politics, Priorities.* London: Cassell.

Hanscombe, G.E. and Forster, J. (1981) *Rocking the Cradle: Lesbian Mothers, A Challenge in Family Living.* London: Peter Owen Ltd..

Harne, L. and Rights of Women (1997) *Valued Families: The Lesbian Mothers' Legal Handbook* (revised and updated edition). London: The Women's Press.

Hicks, S. (1996) 'The "Last Resort"?: Lesbian and Gay Experiences of the Social Work Assessment Process in Fostering and Adoption.' *Practice*, 8, 2, 15–24.

Hicks, S. (1997) 'Taking the Risk? Assessing Lesbian and Gay Carers.' In H. Kemshall and J. Pritchard (eds) *Good Practice in Risk Assessment and Risk Management 2: Protection, Rights and Responsibilities.* London: Jessica Kingsley Publishers.

Jivani, A. (1997) *It's Not Unusual: A History of Lesbian and Gay Britain in the Twentieth Century.* London: Michael O'Mara Books/B.B.C.

King, M.B. (1995) 'Parents Who Are Gay or Lesbian.' In P. Reder and C. Lucey (eds) *Assessment of Parenting: Psychiatric and Psychological Contributions.* London: Routledge.

Marchant, C. (1992) 'Adoption Shake-Up Avoids Blanket Ban.' *Community Care*, 22/10/92, 1.

Martin, A. (1993) *The Lesbian and Gay Parenting Handbook: Creating and Raising Our Families*. New York: Harper Perennial.

Mulholland, L.A. (1997) 'Getting Kids.' In K. Griffin and L.A. Mulholland (eds) *Lesbian Motherhood in Europe*. London: Cassell.

Parmar, P. (director) (1989) 'Fostering and Adoption by Lesbians and Gay Men.' *Film for 'Out On Tuesday', Channel 4, March 1989*.

Patterson, C.J. (1992) 'Children of Lesbian and Gay Parents.' *Child Development*, 63, 1025–1042.

Pilkington, E. (1994) 'Anger at Gay Foster Ban.' *The Guardian*, October 28.

Powell, V. (1997) 'Fighting Fathers' Corner.' *Gay Times*, 225 (June), 12–14.

Rafkin, L. (ed) (1990) *Different Mothers: Sons and Daughters of Lesbians Talk about their Lives*. Pittsburgh: Cleis Press.

Rhodes, P. (1992) *'Racial Matching' in Fostering: The Challenge to Social Work Practice*. Aldershot: Avebury.

Ricketts, W. (1991) *Lesbians and Gay Men as Foster Parents*. Portland: University of Southern Maine, National Child Welfare Resource Center for Management and Administration.

Ricketts, W. and Achtenberg, R. (1987) 'The Adoptive and Foster Gay and Lesbian Parent.' F.W. Bozett (ed) *Gay and Lesbian Parents*. New York: Praeger.

Ricketts, W. and Achtenberg, R. (1990) 'Adoption and Foster Parenting for Lesbians and Gay Men: Creating New Traditions in Family.' *Marriage & Family Review*, 14, 3/4, 83–118.

Rights of Women Lesbian Custody Group (1986) *Lesbian Mothers' Legal Handbook*. London: The Women's Press.

Rowe, J. and Lambert, L. (1973) *Children Who Wait*. London: Association of British Adoption Agencies.

Saffron, L. (1994) *Challenging Conceptions: Pregnancy and Parenting Beyond the Traditional Family: Planning a Family by Self-Insemination*. London: Cassell.

Saffron, L. (1996) *'What About the Children?' Sons and Daughters of Lesbian and Gay Parents Talk About Their Lives*. London: Cassell.

Skeates, J. and Jabri, D. (eds) (1988) *Fostering and Adoption by Lesbians and Gay Men*. London: London Strategic Policy Unit.

Smart, D. (1991) 'A Chance for Gay People.' *Community Care*, 24 January, 17.

Tasker, F.L. and Golombok, S. (1997) *Growing Up in a Lesbian Family: Effects on Child Development*. New York: Guilford Press.

Thadani, G. (1996) *Sakhiyani: Lesbian Desire in Ancient and Modern India*. London: Cassell.

The Times (1997) 'Lesbian Couple Can Adopt Child', 21 May.

Triseliotis, J., Sellick, C. and Short, R. (1995) *Foster Care: Theory and Practice.* London: B.T. Batsford Ltd..

Triseliotis, J., Shireman, J. and Hundleby, M. (1997) *Adoption: Theory, Policy and Practice.* London: Cassell.

Wakeling, L. and Bradstock, M. (eds) (1995) *Beyond Blood: Writings on the Lesbian and Gay Family.* Sydney: BlackWattle Press.

Waugh, P. (1997) 'Adoption Ban on Gay Couples.' *London Evening Standard,* 29 October.

Weston, K. (1991) *Families We Choose: Lesbians, Gays, Kinship.* New York: Columbia University Press.

Whitfield, R. (1991) 'Don't Give In to Pressure.' *Community Care,* 24 January, 16.

About the Editors

Stephen Hicks is a founder member of the Northern section of the Lesbian and Gay Foster and Adoptive Parents Network (LAGFAPN). He has been involved in campaigning and research about lesbians and gay men who foster or adopt for some years and is currently doing postgraduate work on this at Lancaster University. He was previously a social worker for children but now works in the Department of Applied Community Studies at Manchester Metropolitan University. His article, 'Taking the Risk? Assessing Lesbian and Gay Carers', appeared in *Good Practice in Risk Assessment and Risk Management 2: Protection, Rights and Responsibilities* edited by Hazel Kemshall and Jacki Pritchard (1997, Jessica Kingsley Publishers).

Janet McDermott is an Asian woman writer who works part-time in a voluntary training project for Asian women in Sheffield. She is a member of the Northern section of LAGFAPN. Her first novel, *Yasmin*, was published in 1992 (Mantra), and a short story was published in *Flaming Spirit: Stories from the Asian Women Writers' Collective* edited by Rukhsana Ahmad and Rahila Gupta (1994, Virago). She is currently working on a second novel.

Printed in the United States
24385LVS00002B/1-60